Unearthed

A History Nerd Abroad in Europe

Scott Edwin Williams

Sydney, Australia

First published by Unearthed Abroad Books, 2025
admin@unearthedabroad.com
www.unearthedabroad.com

Text copyright: Scott Edwin Williams 2025

ISBN: 978-1-7640672-0-1
978-1-7640672-1-8 (ebook)

 A catalogue record for this book is available from the National Library of Australia

All rights reserved. Except for brief quotations in critical articles or reviews, no part of this book may be reproduced in any manner without prior written permission from the publishers. The rights of Scott Edwin Williams as author have been asserted in accordance with the Copyright, Designs and Patents Act 1988.

The cover and all images have been created by Scott Edwin Williams for Unearthed Abroad Books using a combination of hand drawing, Procreate, Adobe Photoshop, and AI.

Mandarin translation by Lisa Li

Unearthed

A History Nerd Abroad in Europe

Scott Edwin Williams

Also by Scott Edwin Williams:

Lightbulb Moments Series:

Lightbulb Moments in Human History: From Cave to Colosseum
Lightbulb Moments in Human History: From Priests to Polymaths

Unearthed Series:

Unearthed: A History Nerd Abroad in Europe

Peaby's Civilization Series:

We Invented Civilization?: Twisted Ancient History
We Rescued Civilization?: Twisted Medieval History
We Renaissanced Civilization?: Twisted Renaissance History (forthcoming)

For Lisa

有你相伴，
岁月静好，
与爱同行，
不枉此生。

With you by my side,
the years are peaceful;
to walk with love
is to live without regret.

Contents

The Unlock Code to My Tourette's 1

Is No Problem. We Are Family 7

With Comforting Thoughts of Human Sacrifice 21

No Shitting in the Onboard Toilet 40

That's Some Erection! 57

Is Anything Alright? 80

I Slept Through George Carlin 98

Dante's Leather Emporium 119

The Professor of Pompeian Graffiti 142

Vatican Airways: Join Our Kids Club! 158

Flayed Saxophonists Won't Teach Me
Anything About Life 177

Let's Just Say, I Had an Epiphany 192

Churchill's Chamber Pot 211

A Demented Gerbil on Speed 231

Keep Your Hands Off Our Barmaids 242

I Raise a Glass 248

Because Apparently, Facts Matter 251

The Unlock Code to My Tourette's

I could already picture the headline:
Author Arrested in Mona Lisa Mayhem
But I hadn't set out to cause an international incident.
All I'd done was stop for a selfie.
Was that too much to ask?
Apparently yes.
But what had I done?
Had I wandered too close?
Maybe I'd crossed an invisible boundary and set off a silent alarm.
Whatever the reason, a Louvre guard came storming toward me out of nowhere—face contorted with rage, arms flailing, fingers grabbing.
Time slowed...
Over the guard's shoulder, the Mona Lisa's enigmatic smile mocked me, her gaze unflinching as the crowd's hum faded to an echoing silence.
I saw all possibilities at once.
Arrest.
Infamy.
Headlines.
Would I go viral and sell more books?
They say any publicity is good publicity.
Right?
Right?!

But in that frozen moment, I began to question everything.

Why was the guard so aggressive?

Had I derailed my too-long-awaited European adventure in less than a week?

Maybe he thought I was a protester.

The Mona Lisa had been the target of a number of attacks in recent years: cake, paint, and soup.

But the bulletproof glass encasing da Vinci's masterpiece had deflected it all with ease.

As the guard flew toward me in slow motion, I wondered: Was I about to become part of its story?

I had come to Europe to see history up close…

Just… not this close.

How did I get in this position?

A few minutes earlier, I'd lost sight of CJ in the flood of humanity heading toward the Mona Lisa. The crowd swept me toward the tiny—and, if I'm being honest, slightly overrated—painting. I dodged elbows, body odor, and the occasional sharp "excusez-moi!" and "merde!"

When the moment presented itself, I took it.

Snap. My first selfie wasn't great—me grinning like an idiot in the foreground, Mona Lisa looking unimpressed in the middle distance—but it would have to do. I'd seen enough. I pushed sideways through the crush of people, and into the clear.

Relieved, I began to skirt around the display.

I needed to be somewhere less mobbed by tourists.

But just then I was swept into another current of humanity—those bypassing the Mona Lisa crowd. This flow carried me past the exit to the original queue, where, for one shining, inexplicable moment, I found myself closer to da Vinci's masterpiece than I'd been before.

A second chance for a Mona Lisa selfie.

It wasn't the perfect shot. An acute angle, sure, but one that captured everything. I raised my phone, ready to seize the moment.

And just like that, time restarted.

The guard was on me, fingers grabbing for my phone. I jerked it away without thinking.

"Fuck off!" I spat, the words bursting out before I could stop them. Normally, the strongest language I'd use is a polite "Sorry."

Turns out, overzealous Louvre guards are the unlock code to my Tourette's.

I don't know what would have happened if the surge of humanity hadn't spirited me away from the clutches of my new nemesis and into the stream of people leaving La Gioconda.

CJ was suddenly back at my side, shoving me deeper into the throng, laughing, but his eyes wide with disbelief. "What just happened? Did you try to steal the Mona Lisa?"

"I honestly can't tell you," I replied, still catching my breath. "But at least it won't make tomorrow's Sydney Morning Herald."

It was a chaotic way to kick off a trip I'd waited half a lifetime to take. Then again, chaotic would become something of a recurring theme.

Less than a week in and I'd already pissed off Louvre security and spewed obscenities in front of a national treasure. I had no idea if French museums could press charges—and I didn't want to find out.

And honestly? "Tell the Louvre's angriest hall monitor to fuck off and get deported" hadn't been on my bucket list.

Let's get one thing straight.

I'm not critical of the guard's zeal for his job. Sure, he could use a little anger management, but his desire to protect one of the world's historical treasures was something I understood. After all, I'd spent years championing humanity's cultural heritage—though, admittedly, with less flailing and fury than my Parisian friend.

Like the guard, I knew what it meant to feel deeply about preserving history. But here's the difference: his passion was visceral—he'd put his body on the line. Mine, for all its depth, had always been secondhand—learned from books, filtered through lectures, and confined to the safety of my study.

This moment crystallized my reasons for embarking on this journey in the first place. The facts I'd gathered were just fragments, like shards of pottery. The real treasures—the context, the atmosphere, the human connection—were still buried, waiting to be unearthed in the places themselves.

I wanted to stand where they stood, see what they saw.

I didn't just want to read history; I wanted to feel it.

And yet, here I was, in the Louvre, caught between the weight of history and the mayhem of modern tourism. The Mona Lisa's enigmatic smile seemed to mock me again, as if to say:

Good luck finding your connection here.

It wasn't going to be easy.

But then again, history rarely is.

Until recently, though, I'd never been to most of the places I'd written about—not even the most obvious ones.

I'd been to the UK twice as a teenager, but I remembered very little. I was too young, too distracted, and, frankly, too much of an adolescent asshole to take anything in.

Then came marriage, family life, divorce. And then for variety: remarriage, more family life... and—surprise—divorce again. Throw in a long stint as a single parent, and my wings stayed pretty thoroughly clipped for well over two decades.

Just as things began to ease—financially, emotionally, and logistically—COVID hit and grounded me again.

When I turned 60, I couldn't escape the truth: I'd lost so much time.

I'd never visited Europe's most iconic historical destinations—the places I'd spent years reading, writing, and dreaming about.

Worse, I'd watched my younger colleagues bounce around the world while I stayed rooted to the spot.

It was time.

Deciding where to begin was easy.

England would be my first stop—to visit my sister Maggie, reacquaint myself with London, and explore historical sites that had fascinated me for years.

With the U.K. as my home base, I could cross the Channel and dive into Europe's greatest hits: the Eiffel Tower and Louvre in Paris, Venice's canals, the beauty of Florence, Rome's ancient glory, Pompeii's haunting ruins, and even check out Amsterdam's Red Light District.

This wouldn't be a leisurely year-long sabbatical. With just five weeks at my disposal, I needed a meticulous plan—at least for some of it. Navigating Europe on my own—with its apps, e-tickets, and unfamiliar landscapes—felt intimidating.

So I reluctantly booked a mid-range coach tour for part of the trip.

While I considered organized tours 'lowbrow', I'd done a few over the years.

Still, signing up for this one felt like admitting defeat.

When I casually mentioned my plans to CJ—my best friend since 1983, when we met on a South Pacific cruise—I heard words I never expected:

"Do you want company?"

"Yes!"

"Do we have to do the tour though?" CJ asked. "Can't we plan it ourselves?"

"But we did that Contiki tour," I pointed out.

"That was forty years ago," he said.

"But I've already booked it."

"You're allowed to *un*book it."

I had my reasons, but after some back-and-forth, we struck a compromise. We'd bookend the tour with self-guided segments in London and extend our stay afterward with time in Rome, Amsterdam, and back to London.

I'd arrive in London three days before CJ to explore sites he wasn't interested in—like Stonehenge and Hampton Court—and catch up with my sister. Then we'd link up for three weeks before CJ returned to Australia and I finished the rest of the trip.

Deal done.

After all those years on hold, actually booking the tickets—through an old-school travel agent, of course—hardly felt real.

This was happening.

And it wasn't about chasing bucket-list sights or racking up selfies for Instagram.

I was after something deeper—connection, meaning, and figuring out what, exactly, I'd been chasing all these years with my history obsession.

This wasn't just a long-delayed holiday.

This was a reckoning.

What followed was a patchwork of sharp memories, near misses, overdue dreams, and the odd miracle—strung together by history, mayhem, and the people who helped me survive it all.

There'd be laughter, awe, near-catastrophes, and beer.

Inordinate amounts of beer...

But for the first time in decades, I wouldn't just be writing about the past.

I'd be digging deep into its messiness.

And what I unearthed doesn't appear in any guidebook.

***

Is No Problem. We Are Family

I watched the roofs of London drift by outside the window of the Asiana Airlines A350.

This wasn't the postcard-perfect London of Big Ben or Tower Bridge—just factories, rows of houses, and traffic-clogged roads. Still, the view of the ground, mundane as it was, felt like a welcome sight, softened by the golden light of the setting sun.

I was just one of over eighty million passengers who fly into Heathrow every year, and like them, I was here for a reason.

Not the same reason, of course, but we'd all come with a purpose. My goals were varied and deeply personal. I wanted to connect the history I'd read to a sense of place, to challenge my assumptions, and to learn—not just about the world, but maybe a bit about myself.

This trip was also about reconnection: catching up with family after years apart, and finally upgrading my banter with CJ from virtual nonsense to the real-life kind.

But before I could do any of that, I had to survive the landing.

I'll let you in on a little secret: I'm a nervous flyer. My YouTube algorithm is a testament to this, warped by an embarrassing obsession with crash investigation videos. One tidbit I'd latched onto during my late-night rabbit holes was that over 50% of airline accidents happen during landing.

Worse, one crash I'd replayed far too many times was Asiana Airlines Flight 214, which struck a seawall on final approach to San Francisco in 2013. The footage shows the Boeing 777 cartwheeling down the runway in flames.

The fact that I was flying with Asiana Airlines now was not lost on me.

Sure, only three people died in that crash, and that should've been comforting. But it wasn't. I white-knuckled my way through our descent, my heart pounding as the ground grew larger in the window. And yet, despite my worst fears, we touched down smoothly. An incident-free landing.

Up yours, YouTube.

From the plane, I entered the maze that is Heathrow Airport. My fellow passengers and I wandered zombielike through corridors lined with gigantic wall art of Englishmen (and women) welcoming me to their country. Famous sportspeople, vaguely familiar celebrities, beefeaters, and even King Charles III all leering down at me in a way that was unsettling.

To my surprise, I had my bags and had cleared immigration in record time. So far, so good. The next step was to catch the Underground to meet my sister Maggie at Stratford Station. This would be the first real test of my travel skills. Of course, it wasn't exactly a grueling test—I just had to hop on the Underground's shiny new Elizabeth Line, and thirteen stops later I'd be there.

But first, I needed to find the Heathrow Underground station. It wasn't a difficult assignment, but my confidence was still shaky from two days earlier during my stopover in South Korea. Navigating Seoul's Airport Railroad Express, or AREX, from Incheon Airport had been more challenging than I'd expected. Despite the signage being in both Korean and English, the whole experience had left me feeling unsteady.

Two days earlier, in Seoul...
Oh, I found the AREX station easily enough.

It was what came next that threw me. I should have caught a train to a stop near my hotel, but I couldn't figure out how, and in the end, I gave up—I'd take a taxi instead. The problem? Uber was practically nonexistent, and Korea's Kakao T rideshare app refused to accept foreign credit cards.

I walked back out of the AREX station, probably looking as bewildered as I felt.

And that's when I made a rookie mistake.

"Hello. Need a lift?"

"Sure," I said, assuming this well-dressed and polite Korean gentleman was a taxi driver.

"Follow me, please," he said, grabbing my bags and walking away with me in tow. Already, my brain was beginning to clock that this was a bad idea.

We passed through doors, down escalators, and finally, into an elevator that descended into a quiet parking lot. My spidey senses, dulled by the ten-hour flight, were now fully tingling. This was no taxi rank.

How could I have been so stupid?

My driver directed me to a very large, black Kia eight-seater with dark tinted windows. As he hefted my bags into the back, I noted the distinct lack of any taxi signage on his big, black, murder-mobile.

"Er—how much is this going to cost?" I asked.

My life?

"₩40,000," he said.

Luckily, I'd boned up on the exchange rate: ₩10,000 is roughly $7 USD, so ₩40,000 seemed reasonable.

"Okay," I heard myself say.

What the hell was I doing?

During the twenty-minute trip, my driver tried out his very limited English on me. He seemed like a nice guy. But for all I knew, I'd been taken by a North Korean sleeper agent.

Luckily for me, he wasn't.

True to his word, my new Korean friend delivered me safely to the Hotel Ibis in Incheon. I was nervous, exhausted, starving, and ready to collapse into bed. He effortlessly lifted my heavy bags out of the car, and I paid him in cash I'd exchanged back in Sydney.

I thanked him and was on my way.

After checking in, I dragged my bags into an elevator where I was met with a wall of cologne—and two men who looked like extras from a Russian mafia movie. Both were well over six feet tall, with angular faces, close-cropped hair, and enough muscle to fill the elevator.

"Hello, my friend!" boomed one of them in a thick Russian accent. A beefy hand clapped me on the shoulder, almost sending me sprawling.

"G-G'day."

"Where are you from?"

"Australia," I squeaked.

"Australia! Ah, good! Very good!" Ivan—as I immediately dubbed him—still had his massive paw clamped on my arm like we were long-lost comrades.

"Australia is nice. Very far, though," said the other one—who, in my head, was now Boris.

"You guys visiting Korea?"

"Yes, on business." Ivan threw a meaty arm around Boris' shoulders. "We are friends. I am from Russia, he is from Ukraine."

"Wait." I looked from one to the other, "You're Russian and you're Ukrainian?"

"Is no problem. We are family," Probably-not-Boris assured me.

"Then..." I ventured hesitantly, "we can all be family!"

Hearty fake laughter ensued, punctuated with even more hearty not-so-fake back-slaps. Thankfully, before things could get any more awkward, the elevator reached their floor, and they departed—never to be seen again.

When I finally found my room, I discovered two things.

First, the view out of the window was of Incheon Airport—so close to the taxiway I could practically count the rivets on the planes. So why the hell had it taken my driver so long to get here?

Second, and far more critically, I had left the power cord for my

CPAP machine back in Sydney.

Now, this might not seem like a big deal—unless you know what a CPAP machine does. It's a device that treats sleep apnea, a condition that basically turns me into Darth Vader after fifty beers when I sleep. I snore loud enough to frighten small animals and, worse, stop breathing multiple times an hour. Untreated, it puts a strain on the heart and prevents REM sleep.

The CPAP machine basically keeps me alive and sleeping, by pumping air into my face like a tiny, personal leaf blower. But with the power cord over eight thousand kilometers away, my leaves were not going to get blown that night.

Instead, I flopped around gasping like a fish out of water, waking up regularly, and trying to convince myself that sleep was optional.

Usually, this misery is mine alone to bear—I sleep solo, after all. But in less than a week, I'd have to share a room with CJ, and I didn't fancy hearing his complaints about my snoring.

After zero sleep and a decent buffet breakfast, I finally got on the AREX to meet the first of many bus tours I would take in the next five weeks. This one was to the DMZ, which is much, much closer to Seoul than I'd realized.

The tour leader was a dynamic young woman named Chaeyoung, whose English was excellent, if slightly eccentric. At the first stop in the DMZ, she gathered us around a couple of statues.

"Who you think South Koreans like more, North Koreans or Japanese?" Chaeyoung asked.

Most of the westerners on-board the tour voted for Japanese.

"No, no, no! The North Koreans are family, okay?" she said. "All we want is reunification. Who knows what these statues are for?"

Blank stares all around.

"They are memorial to the Korean women used as sex-slaves by Japanese troops in World War II."

On that very heavy note, the tour continued, taking us down into the invasion tunnels North Korea had dug beneath the border. As we descended into the deep tunnels, the temperature dropped markedly. They were carved directly into hard, unforgiving stone—there was no need for wooden bracing like in a mineshaft.

"We have found four, but they think there are twenty, okay?" Chaeyoung said. "They think that North Korea could bring thirty thousand troops through these tunnels every hour, okay?"

Later, I stood near a South Korean guard post, looking out over North Korea. From a distance, it didn't look nearly as bleak as I'd expected. I could see a pleasant pastoral scene with small farm houses in the distance. Of course, this was all behind razor wire.

Could this be the rogue nation that's causing all the trouble?

Sure it could.

But Chaeyoung's perspective on the North's kinship with the South shifted something in me. I had always thought of North Korea as a looming, faceless villain. Now, for the first time, I saw it not just as a rogue state, but as a fractured piece of something whole. It wasn't just geopolitics—it was family.

After the tour, I spent a couple of hours at Craft Hans, a cool craft beer pub buzzing with locals and expats, sipping Hans' Mango Pale Ale—which was absolutely delicious. Then, I joined my second tour of the day: Changgyeonggung Palace and the night markets.

Once a royal retreat for queens and concubines, Changgyeonggung Palace has seen it all—fires, invasions, and even a stint as a zoo during Japanese occupation. Today, it's back to being a beautiful, peaceful slice of Seoul.

I briefly made two friends on this tour—Angie, an American working remotely from Seoul, and Rowan, a Canadian who had clearly been to Asia many times before and wasn't afraid to remind everyone of the fact.

"I've been living and working in Seoul for six months," said Angie. "But I'm technically 'working from home,' so I work Seattle office hours."

"Do your colleagues know where you are?" I asked.

"Only the ones that need to," she said.

"I did that for a while when I lived in Japan," Rowan said.

"Ever been to China?" I asked.

"Not yet, but I've done Vietnam, Cambodia, Thailand, and Malaysia," he said, with the air of a seasoned explorer. Then, as if he'd almost forgotten, he added, "Oh, and the Philippines, of course."

The Changgyeonggung Palace was stunning—but it had been destroyed in a Japanese invasion in 1592 and rebuilt in 1616. Given that history, it's no wonder South Koreans feel closer to North Koreans—even if reunification still feels like a distant dream.

After the palace tour, we went to dinner at the night markets, which was incredible—except for one local 'delicacy' sannakji, a plate of glossy, writhing gray octopus tentacles.

"Oh, that's a hard no from me," I pushed the plate of chopped, twitching octopus toward Angie.

"That's the stuff of nightmares," Angie said, looking pale.

Even Rowan, the seasoned Asian traveler, shook his head, describing sannakji as "a horror not meant for human consumption."

My time in Seoul was brief but wonderful—the young people on the streets exuded a hip, electric energy, reminiscent of London in the Swinging Sixties. Stylish, K-pop-inspired Koreans effortlessly owned their looks. Oversized woolens, lace, bows, and even diamantes glued to the girls' faces were commonplace, while men sported sharp, modern-cut suits straight out of a fashion magazine.

I'm pretty sure I even spotted the Korean Austin Powers grooving through the streets.

A legitimate but overpriced taxi ride, another sleepless night, and a desperate WhatsApp plea to my sister for a CPAP cord later, I was finally heading back to Incheon Airport.

Next stop, London.

London, Present Day

I'd found Heathrow's Tube station without drama and begun my journey to meet up with Maggie for the first time in seven years—thanks mostly to the tyranny of distance. I scanned my Apple Watch at the turnstiles and boarded the surprisingly modern carriage.

As we pulled out of Heathrow Station, words that would soon become familiar echoed through the carriage: "Mind the gap." They were destined to become my Tube mantra.

By now it was dark, so if I had any illusions of seeing iconic landmarks emerging from Dickensian fogs, my hopes were quickly dashed. And anyway, while the train did emerge briefly from the depths, ninety-nine percent of my journey was to be in a tunnel.

The Tube was much better than I remembered it—modern, clean, quiet, and almost no graffiti. I soon found out this was because I was traveling on the Elizabeth Line.

The Elizabeth Line, opened during Queen Elizabeth II's Platinum Jubilee in 2022, feels almost futuristic compared to the Underground I recalled from 1981.

But even all those years ago, it was more than just a transport system.

As I sat in the carriage, a visitor from a city where the underground is smaller, simpler, and about as reliable as a politician's promise, I couldn't help but marvel at the Tube. It's not just the sheer size of it—though that alone is mind-boggling—it's the fact that it still works.

How does a system that began when steam engines were cutting edge continue to adapt to the demands of a twenty-first-century city?

The answer lies in its dual nature. Sure, it's crowded, messy, and sometimes frustrating, but it's also resilient, adaptable, and essential. Every delay, every signal failure, every rush-hour crush is balanced by the sheer brilliance of its existence. The Tube is a testament to humanity's ability to keep moving forward—even if it's at a crawl and wedged under a stranger's armpit.

"Mind the gap."

The mantra came as a reminder—its meaning stretching beyond the platform edge to something less tangible, something just out of reach, lingering at the edge of my consciousness.

I sat with my knees pressed tightly together, trying to keep my luggage from toppling into the overloaded belongings of the person beside me—who was clearly fighting the same losing battle.

"Mind the gap."

As the train glided on, it struck me: this phrase has guided Londoners for generations, echoing through tunnels that have witnessed nearly two centuries of change.

Opened in 1863, the Metropolitan Railway's three-and-a-half-mile route between Paddington and Farringdon became the world's first underground railway. It was a bold experiment that posed the timeless question: "What if we shove a bunch of people in an underground steam train and dare them not to asphyxiate?"

It seemed that Londoners, faced with the alternative of navigating roads filled with horse-drawn traffic and an ungodly amount of horse shit, decided they'd rather take their chances underground in soot-filled tunnels traveling inside wooden carriages lit with gas. Sure, the air quality was questionable, the carriages were hotter than a blast furnace, and the whole thing probably felt like riding through fiery pits of Hell, but what could possibly go wrong?

Another station. Another "Mind the gap."

It only took a year for the first Tube graffiti to appear, and incredibly, we even know the name of this proto-Banksy: Aquila John Williams. Unfortunately, history doesn't record his message to posterity, as the Victorian press, in a fit of prudishness, refused to print his 'obscene' scrawling. Whatever it was, it was enough to land him in court.

Thankfully for Mr Williams, the judge took an enlightened and lenient view of his artistic endeavors. Instead of sentencing him to transportation to the colonies, he was slapped with a fine of 40 shillings—a sum the judge confidently declared would "be effectual in preventing such conduct in future."

And, as we know, no one ever graffitied the Tube again.

The Underground first proved its value as more than just a transport system during the First World War, when Germany unleashed an armada of zeppelins to bomb London. Roughly 300,000 Londoners descended into the tunnels, turning them into makeshift air raid shelters for the first time. They 'kept calm and carried on' a couple of decades before that was even a thing. Stiff upper lip and all.

"Mind the gap."

I had strict instructions to text my sister as soon as we reached Oxford Circus Station—apparently, this would give them plenty of time to get to Stratford. So, as the train pulled out of the station, I thumbed the message, hoping I wasn't already behind schedule.

"Mind the gap."

The London Underground's visionary leader in the early twentieth century was Frank Pick, whose contributions transformed it from a mere functional transport system into an enduring cultural and design icon. He introduced a cohesive visual identity that still resonates today—in fact, I was surrounded by it, evident in the iconic signage on this very carriage.

Pick commissioned the now-famous Johnston typeface from calligrapher Edward Johnston. At Pick's behest, Johnston also designed the iconic roundel Underground logo, creating a unified branding that was not only modern and timeless, but has become synonymous with London.

"Mind the gap."

However, it's arguable I was staring up at Pick's greatest legacy: the stylized map of the Underground. Pick engaged Harry Beck to create his groundbreaking 1931 Tube map, a simplified, diagrammatic design that revolutionized how people navigated the sprawling system. Even the most geographically challenged could follow it with no problem. Such was its ease of use that the New York Subway, Paris Metro, Madrid Metro, Sydney and Saint Petersburg all plagiarized Beck's design.

And how much did Frank Pick recompense the visionary Mr Beck for his brilliance? Why, I'm glad you asked. He was paid five guineas, which adjusted for inflation is the princely sum of $375.

"Mind the pay gap."

Then in World War II the rail tunnels beneath London once again became the city's unofficial bomb shelters, and the Underground emerged as an unlikely symbol of a nation's resilience. As the Blitz raged overhead, millions huddled in the tunnels, finding camaraderie—and, more often than not, safety.

Unfortunately, safety wasn't always guaranteed. In 1940, more than 60 people died at Balham Station when the street above collapsed under heavy German bombing.

Post-war, the Tube expanded further, adding more lines, more stations, and more opportunities for passengers to complain about delays.

Today, the Underground serves over a billion passengers a year. It's iconic, chaotic, frustrating—and undeniably London. So when you find yourself hurtling along in a train from Heathrow, gripping your luggage to keep it from colliding with the old lady across the aisle, resist the urge to curse. Instead, remember: you're riding through history.

"Mind the gap."

Next stop, Stratford.

After forty-eight sleep-deprived hours in South Korea and a ten-hour flight during which I was too afraid to sleep—convinced my snoring would rival the A350's Rolls-Royce Trent XWB jet engines—I was beyond exhaustion. But salvation was near. Waiting at my sister's place was the unexpected holy grail of this journey: a power cord for my CPAP.

Praise be to Amazon!

As the train approached Stratford, my phone buzzed with a message from Maggie, confirming that she and my brother-in-law Eric were in position, ready to greet me. Her message included detailed instructions on how to find them—helpful, except for the small detail that they were completely incomprehensible to a jet-lagged man who'd never seen Stratford Underground Station in his life.

I checked my bags, phone, and passport for the fifty-fifth time—did I mention I'm slightly OCD when it comes to travel?—reassured myself that all was in order, and prepared to disembark. My smartwatch had slipped into low power mode not long after I boarded, but it didn't matter. I was here, in the UK, after forty-five years.

Sure, I was beyond exhaustion, but life couldn't possibly get better.

I shuffled off the train and followed the mob, vaguely registering small details that might, or might not, have aligned with Maggie's instructions. Every so often, a sign would appear that seemed to confirm I was heading in the right direction, but I'd finally lost all capacity for conscious thought, so I couldn't be sure.

After what felt like an eternity, but was probably less than five minutes, I saw Maggie and Eric, waving at me from the other side of the exit turnstiles. I hadn't seen either of them in years, apart from the occasional Skype call.

Time had inevitably left its mark.

Eric now channeled a retired rock star vibe, courtesy of the hair and beard he'd grown during COVID lockdown—and decided to keep. Maggie, on the other hand, looked just like my big sister from years ago, though she had—as one does—aged an appropriate number of years.

The years hadn't been quite so kind to me. Balder, grayer, and rounder, I was damned close to being the poster boy for middle-aged decline. If they hadn't recognized me, I wouldn't have blamed them. But they did—because family's not about distance. It's about connection—and history.

"Hello, little brother!" Maggie said from behind the barrier.

I managed an exhausted but happy smile as I approached them. Salvation was just a turnstile away.

I pressed the button on my watch to activate my credit card. Nothing. I tried again. Still nothing.

My watch was dead.

That was the moment the weight of it all hit me.

The sleepless nights, the stress, the overwhelming swirl of emotions from seeing Maggie again—and the strange, familiar weight of London itself—all came crashing down at once. I stood there, frozen, as the queue behind me started to build.

Luckily, an Underground employee—clearly a veteran of the stunned mullet traveler look—stepped in and took charge.

"You'll need to swipe off with the same card you swiped on with," he said patiently.

"It's dead," I replied, gesturing to my watch with a helpless shrug. "The physical card is... well..." I pointed vaguely at my suitcase.

He raised an eyebrow. "Do you have your credit card on your phone?"

"No," I said reflexively, panic setting in. Then, as if one last mental cog finally clicked into place, I corrected myself. "I mean... yes. Maybe."

I never used the card on my phone, relying exclusively on the one stored in my watch. But, to my utter relief, when I opened my iPhone, there it was—my Mastercard, nestled safely in the Apple Wallet.

It took a couple of attempts thanks to my trembling, sleep-deprived fingers, but finally, the scanner beeped, and the turnstile swung open.

I was done. Drained, raw, and holding on by a thread, I was finally reunited with my family.

The final leg of the trip was a blur. I vaguely remember talking to Maggie and Eric—though I couldn't tell you what about—then walking to the car, a short drive, and finally arriving at their home.

They showed me to the room where I'd be sleeping, and there, sitting on the bedside table, practically glowing like the Ark of the Covenant in *Raiders of the Lost Ark*, was the new cord for my CPAP.

After a quick shower, I was in bed in no time, the CPAP mask lovingly cradling my face. I pressed the button, and like magic, my personal leaf blower came to life. For the first time in days, I felt the promise of real, restorative sleep.

I snuggled down, anticipating the best night's sleep of my life.

And then the CPAP stopped.

* * *

With Comforting Thoughts of Human Sacrifice

The realization that salvation *wasn't* at hand sent a jolt of adrenaline through me.

I shot upright, ripped the mask from my face, and frantically began reconfiguring the electrical connection. The results were maddeningly consistent: the machine would run for a minute or so, then stop.

Tears of frustration were threatening. After two sleepless nights in Seoul, I knew five weeks without a functioning CPAP would ruin my trip of a lifetime. Could I buy a new machine before the tour started? Probably. Would it cost a fortune? Undoubtedly.

At my lowest point, I was staring at the infuriating contraption when it suddenly sprang to life. Then stopped. Then started again.

My CPAP had turned into the Schrödinger's cat of medical devices: neither fully alive nor fully dead, existing in some binary limbo of functionality. Desperate, I jammed the mask back onto my face. It worked... intermittently.

Good enough. Exhaustion won, and I sank back onto the pillow as everything faded to black.

I awoke to the sound of birdsong and the same on/off rhythm of air blowing in my face. Somehow, I'd survived the night. And, as far as I could tell in those first, groggy moments of waking, I felt refreshed. It seemed a partially functioning CPAP was better than nothing.

As I removed the mask, it hit me: I hadn't just had a refreshing sleep—I was in another country. It felt like waking up in someone else's life.

I got out of bed, and threw open the curtains. The world was illuminated in a weak, early morning light and I could see the surrounding houses. They were subtly different to Australian homes in ways I didn't yet have the wits to articulate.

There was no rush to get going. This was the sole day of rest I'd allowed in my carefully orchestrated tour plan. I sorted through my bags, which—thanks to last night's exhaustion—I'd left in total disarray. I sent a message to CJ to confirm my arrival, checked the news, and then sauntered into the living room, where Maggie was watching television.

"So, what's happening, little brother?"

It was a question that, in retrospect, I'm sure Maggie wished she'd never asked. What followed was a long, wide-ranging discussion about life, family, and, most poignantly, our mother, who had passed away seven years earlier.

With nine years between us and vastly different life experiences, Maggie and I saw things through very different lenses. The conversation was raw and sometimes confronting, stirring up memories we hadn't shared in years. We both learned things we'd never known. After all that deep and meaningful talk, it was clear we'd both had enough. I was mentally drained, and Maggie, by her own admission, had a massive headache.

"Let's not do that again," she said with a rueful smile.

A beat of silence passed. We both needed to shake it off.

Just then, Eric walked in. "Pub for lunch?"

Perfect timing. Who was I to say no?

We went to what, for me, was a quintessentially English pub: the *Victoria Tavern*.

Tucked into a quaint suburban street, the *Victoria Tavern* was small—old by Australian standards, but unremarkable by British ones. It had an outdoor area, what Aussies would call a beer garden, though given the temperature, its existence was optimistic at best. Inside, the wooden bar looked like something out of a British soap opera, complete with an array of hand pumps to 'pull' beers from casks in the cellar.

Behind the bar, a handbell rested on a shelf, ready to signal last drinks, and below it, a brass plaque sternly warned: 'Keep your hands off our barmaids.' Strong aromas of old wood, beer, and pub food wafted from the elevated seating area, where Maggie had already claimed a table.

"What'll it be?" asked the barmaid, who I evidently had to keep my hands off. She seemed nice enough, but that wasn't going to be a problem. She stood behind a bewildering array of beer taps offering unfamiliar brews.

"Er... Eric?" I turned to my brother-in-law, utterly clueless as to what I should order.

"What do you normally drink?" he asked.

"Surprise me," I said, realizing my usual cold lager routine wouldn't cut it here. "I want to get the full experience."

Eric ordered us each a pint of Timothy Taylor's Landlord, a pale ale with a strong hoppy aroma. This was my first taste of real British beer—the kind that, back home, is derided for being 'warm and flat.'

My first surprise? It was neither of those things. Sure, it wasn't as cold as Australian or American beer, and its natural carbonation was subtler than the fizzy lagers I was used to. But the flavor? Rich, balanced—delicious.

The meal arrived: a hefty salt beef and mustard sandwich. Mouth-watering slices of salt beef, generously smeared with hot English mustard, clapped between thick slabs of seeded bread. This masterpiece of 'sandwich art' came with thick-cut chips, which were perfectly seasoned. It was simple, hearty, and unapologetically glorious.

I washed it down with another pint of Timothy Taylor's Landlord.

Our sojourn to the *Victoria Tavern* regretfully over, the three of us returned home satisfied. The rest of the day was spent continuing my recovery and planning the strategy for Day Two. I had to get into London early to meet my first tour. Eric, master tactician of the Tube, set to work determining the best possible route to Victoria Station.

Despite exhaustion creeping back from my extreme sleep deficit over the past seventy-two hours, I couldn't help but feel excited about finally visiting Stonehenge. It wasn't just a pile of rocks to me. Stonehenge was a symbol of humanity's ingenuity and connection to the distant past—a place that had captivated me for decades through its mystery and unanswered questions.

I'd spent years reading and writing about it, but now, I'd finally see those ancient stones. Not only that, I'd splurged on the deluxe tour, which allowed me to walk among the stones rather than view them from afar. For the first time, I'd be able to immerse myself in history—not just observe it from a distance.

It was the first step on a journey I'd been building toward my whole life. Could it live up to my expectations? That uncertainty lingered, but I let it fuel my anticipation rather than diminish it.

And so it was, with comforting thoughts of druids and human sacrifice, I drifted off to sleep that night, lulled by the wheezes of a malfunctioning life support system.

The next morning, I set off to Epping Station. I'd promised myself I wouldn't waste any time and as the tour didn't leave till 10 am, I could fit in a spot of sightseeing beforehand. My first stop: Buckingham Palace.

As per Eric's instructions, I hopped on the Tube to Mile End. It was on the Central line, nowhere near as smooth or modern as the Elizabeth line I'd ridden last night. This was the Underground I remembered, with all the heat, shaking and screeching you could ask for.

I changed trains at Mile End to head toward Victoria. A mix of the Underground and a brisk walk had me standing in front of the

King's primary residence before London was truly awake. I'd come to the UK prepared for the cold, but the morning was mild, and even at that early hour, the sky was a bright blue I didn't associate with merry old England.

I stood alone on the Mall outside the palace. It was completely empty, except for a lone cyclist who whirred past on his way to work, the silence broken only by the soft hum of his bike chain.

It must have been the quietest place in London.

When I visited as a fifteen-year-old in 1979, the Mall had been jam-packed with tourists watching the Changing of the Guard. I remember gray skies and a chill in the air. Back then, I thought the Royal residence was overrated—dirty, not-that-old, and, frankly, unimpressive.

I'm afraid that, despite the brilliant day and my private viewing, my opinion of Buckingham Palace had changed little in forty-five years. Which is surprising. In those years I'd gone from a young monarchist desperate to see the Queen, to a 60-year-old antiroyalist who couldn't have given a shit if King Charles himself had wandered out to greet me in a leather thong and pink feather boa.

It was a lifetime ago. Back then, my parents were alive and younger than I am now. I was still in high school, with almost everything else that makes up a life still ahead of me.

Yet here I was. Standing in the same place, which, apart from the color of the sky and absence of people, was ostensibly unchanged—although the Palace did seem a little cleaner these days. It was a stark reminder that some things remain unchanged even as we grow and evolve.

But Buckingham Palace held no real resonance. To me, it was as empty as the Mall was today—hollow and disconnected, a symbol without substance. Just a convenient tourist stop on the way to somewhere that really meant something: Stonehenge.

Unlike the palace, Stonehenge wasn't tied to pomp or tradition—at least as far as we know. It wasn't about royalty or grandeur either.

It was about something far older and more profound. Its ancient stones stood as a reminder of humanity's ingenuity and enduring curiosity.

For me, Stonehenge represented the timeless pull of history—the wonder and mystery that had ignited my passion all those years ago. It wasn't just another stop on the itinerary; it was a place that connected me to the questions I'd been asking my whole life.

The Platinum Tours 'Private Viewing of Stonehenge Inner Circle and Walking Tour of Bath' didn't come cheap. At over $200, I couldn't help but think: this better be worth it. Still, the start was promising. The bus, built for fifty passengers, carried just fourteen that day. This boded well for the private viewing of Stonehenge later in the day—fewer people meant a more intimate experience.

However, the reduced numbers seemed to come with a trade-off: Nigel, a tour guide who looked like he'd been plucked straight out of the trainee program. Maybe it's just me—I'm 'of a certain age,' after all—but Nigel seemed a little too young and awkward for the job.

The awkwardness became clear before we'd even left the city. Nigel's commentary felt stilted, as if he were scrambling to recall a script he'd skimmed the night before. The low point came during an anecdote about Charles II, when Nigel performed an entire rap from the BBC show *Horrible Histories* with all the confidence of someone who knew they were bombing—and then claimed he and his friends had made it up at school.

I was probably the only one on the bus who recognized the plagiarism, but it made me wary. If Nigel's anecdotes were stolen, what else in his commentary might be suspect?

Thankfully for Nigel—and the rest of us—he had little to do during the three-hour drive to Bath. As we drew closer to our destination, though, his duties ramped up, and to his credit, he handled them as best he could.

"As we approach Bath, remember: you're free to roam the sights for the next five hours. But we must be back on the bus by 6:00 pm."

He delivered this announcement with as much tact as possible. Five hours? I couldn't help but wonder if that was the best use of our time.

A young woman raised her hand and asked, "Bath is where *Bridgerton* is filmed, isn't it?"

The slight clamor of approval from other passengers suggested it was a popular question. Clearly, I was in the minority for not caring about the hit Netflix series. I'd never seen it, but I knew enough to recognize it as a bodice-ripper set in Regency London—an alternate reality where George III had instituted racial equality, accounting for the show's anachronistically diverse cast.

This was where Nigel came into his own, rolling out *Bridgerton*-related facts like an honest-to-god tour-guide:

"When we roll into town, we'll pass the spot where Lady Fanny Clitorbury-Fiddlesnatch had a threesome with the Phallington twins!" Nigel didn't actually say that, but what he did announce sounded equally ridiculous to my ear.

The group gasped—he had eight of the fourteen tourists in the palm of his hand, speculating about which other scenes might have been filmed there.

As the bus zigzagged into Bath, negotiating the winding streets of the beautiful Georgian town, Nigel kept up the *Bridgerton* theme.

"And to your left you'll see the bandstand where Lord Poxworthy seduced Baroness Chlamydia Candidasworth." Nigel was growing in confidence.

For many on the tour, *Bridgerton* was the drawcard. For me, it was just an absurd prelude to the main event: an ancient stone circle on the Salisbury Plain.

Nevertheless, I still had to kill five hours in Bath, where I was interested to see the Roman baths for which it had been named. I'd also done a bit of research and had other plans.

Besides, it was beautiful. I could do five hours here.

What I couldn't do is go five hours without a bathroom. After three hours on the bus and about thirty minutes roaming around Bath, picking up a local map, and passing the Roman Baths twice—dismayed at the long queues, I began looking for a public bathroom in earnest.

If there was one, I couldn't find it. Wandering the streets in ever-increasing desperation, it became clear that the only way to use a toilet was to patronize a local establishment. And so, I ducked into a quaint little pub creatively named the *Ale House* on Terrace Walk.

There, I found relief in the bathroom—and at the bar, where I ordered a pint of Proper Job, a citrusy IPA pulled from a hand pump. From my seat by the window, I sipped my beer, gazed out at the throngs of tourists, and opened Google Maps to plan my assault on Bath.

Inevitably, this beer-centered 'bathroom break' would precipitate another. And another. An endless cycle that would come to define the entire European trip.

I decided to see what I could before braving the Depression-era unemployment line outside the Roman Baths. The Jane Austen Center, 'Celebrating Bath's most famous resident,' seemed as good a place to start as any—especially since it stood right next to Mary Shelley's House of Frankenstein.

Austen and Shelley were two trailblazing British women writers, both intimately connected to Bath and influential in their own ways. Mary, with her invention of the science fiction novel, and Jane, with her sharp wit and snark.

But it nearly hadn't happened.

I first encountered *Pride and Prejudice* when I was seventeen, and to be honest, I wasn't exactly thrilled about it. It had been assigned at school, and like any self-respecting teenager, I had every intention of avoiding it. Then fate stepped in—by which I mean I broke my leg playing soccer and was sentenced to two weeks of bed rest. Keep in mind, this was in the dark ages before the existence of smartphones or gaming systems. With nothing else to do but stare at the ceiling, I grudgingly picked up the book.

What I didn't expect was to get completely sucked in.

By the time Lizzy Bennet had verbally eviscerated Mr. Darcy, I had a new heroine. The wit! The audacity of refusing a man with ten thousand a year! Austen had reached across the centuries, plucked me out of a teenage sulk, and handed me a story that was funny, fresh and alive. By the time I finished, I was a Jane Austen convert.

Now I was in Bath, chasing her down.

I trudged through the streets, moving inexorably toward the Jane Austen Centre. The route took me through areas of Georgian architecture, then modern buildings, and back into Georgian streets again. At every turn, on every corner, it seemed, was a homeless person selling *The Big Issue*—more sellers than I'd ever seen before.

For those unfamiliar, *The Big Issue* is the world's most widely circulated street newspaper, providing homeless or at-risk individuals the chance to earn a legitimate income and reintegrate into society. It's a noble endeavor, but the sheer number of sellers in Bath suggested that something wasn't right.

What would Jane have thought about all the homeless people?

For that matter, what would she have made of the Jane Austen Center?

She'd have had an arch take on it, that's for sure. Her wit was a razor that cut to the heart of absurdity, and she'd have thought a tea house bearing her name was as absurd as it gets.

Jane Austen wasn't just a novelist—she was a revolutionary. At a time when women were expected to embroider cushions and marry well, Austen wrote six novels that mocked societal norms and became some of the most cherished works in English literature. She took the world of matchmaking, awkward family dinners, and scandalous elopements and transformed it into cutting social commentary.

Her genius lay in her ability to make you laugh while revealing uncomfortable truths. Her characters are vividly human—Mr. Darcy, the romantic hero with resting bitch-face, and Elizabeth Bennet, the queen of verbal take-downs, feel as real to me now as they must have for her readers then. Beneath the humor, her stories expose some harsh realities: women's economic dependence, rigid class structures, and the threat of social ruin for stepping out of line.

Despite publishing anonymously in a male-dominated literary world, Austen thrived, gaining fans from locals to royalty. Today, she's a global icon, her face appearing on mugs, tote bags, and even British currency. But her true legacy lies in her timeless insight into human nature.

Austen's relationship with Bath was a mixed bag.

Though she was initially charmed by its elegance and vibrant social scene—it was the inspiration for settings in *Northanger Abbey* and *Persuasion*—her later years in the city were less happy. After her family moved there in 1801, Austen struggled, expressing dissatisfaction in her letters. She found Bath depressing, something we had in common, it seemed.

While Jane died at the age of 41, her legacy is firmly cemented as one of the greatest writers in history. So the idea of visiting the Jane Austen Center seemed more like a pilgrimage than a mindless tourist stop.

My maps app indicated I was only a turn away.

I arrived outside a modest Georgian terrace house, not unlike the older homes in Sydney. There I was greeted by a sign that read, in part, Jane Austen Centre Regency Tea Rooms. It wasn't exactly what I was expecting.

My hesitation deepened when I spotted the young, *Bridgerton*-loving woman from my tour walking out, clutching a souvenir bag.

"How was it?" I asked, already suspicious.

"Marvelous," she beamed, radiating Colin Firth-in-a-wet-shirt levels of joy.

I glanced past her at the price: nearly £16. My credit card cringed at the thought. Nope. Not today.

Her glowing endorsement, coupled with my mental catalog of scathing *Tripadvisor* reviews—'tacky and awful,' 'disappointed,' and my personal favorite, 'quite pricey for what it is, which is a house with a few exhibits which are mostly replicas'—only served to confirm my suspicions. I came on this trip to unearth real history, not to stare at knock-offs in a tourist trap. I could look at fake stuff back at home.

Determined not to waste £16 on a Regency-themed cash grab, I turned and walked next door to Mary Shelley's House of Frankenstein.

What I saw made my heart sink.

The signage outside described it as a 'Multi-sensory Museum & Escape Room,' promising to explore 'Shelley's unconventional life and the lasting legacy of her famous creation.' It boasted vintage artifacts, gothic curiosities, special effects, and an eight-foot (2.4 meter) tall animatronic Creature, supposedly recreated exactly as Shelley imagined.

The whole thing felt like a low-rent Disneyland—especially when Little Miss Bridgerton vanished through the doors. I wasn't about to trade one tourist trap for another.

So far, apart from its obvious visual charms, Bath-the-tourist-Mecca was proving to be almost as tragic as Shelley's own life.

Born in 1797 to revolutionary thinkers Mary Wollstonecraft and William Godwin, Mary inherited a legacy of rebellion and intellect. Her mother died shortly after childbirth, and young Mary was raised in a household steeped in radical ideas.

The original Goth girl, Mary famously lost her virginity to poet Percy Shelley on her mother's grave, then eloped with him, creating a scandal. Their life together was a storm of love, infidelity, and relentless hardship.

During a summer at Lake Geneva with Percy and Lord Byron, Mary conceived her masterpiece, *Frankenstein; or, The Modern Prometheus*, as part of the trio's ghost story challenge. Published in 1818, when she was just twenty, the novel secured her place in literary history.

Unsurprisingly, Mary's later years were no less shadowed by loss than her early ones. Percy drowned in 1822, leaving her a widow at just 24. She spent the rest of her life preserving his legacy. And that wasn't all she preserved—Mary believed she also kept Percy's actual heart. Because, clearly, she wasn't goth enough already.

According to legend, Percy's friend Edward John Trelawny snatched the smoldering 'heart' from Shelley's funeral pyre—because why the hell not? However, the charred remains he recovered were unlikely to be Shelley's actual heart. More plausibly, it was another internal organ that hadn't fully burned.

Whatever it was Trelawny handed her, Mary cherished it as Percy's heart, reportedly keeping it wrapped in silk for the rest of her life—a macabre keepsake perfectly suited to her gothic sensibilities.

It's hard to imagine a more poignant symbol of Mary's undying devotion to Percy—and her lifelong flair for the dramatic. Mary died in 1851 at the age of 53, leaving behind Percy's heart and a masterpiece that defined her legacy.

It was nearly time to meet the tour for lunch. I walked back past the never-ending line for the Roman Baths, wondering if it ever moved, and headed to the agreed restaurant. Nigel joined me, looking far more relaxed than he had on the bus.

"So, you're from Australia," he asked, before launching into his obsession with *Neighbours*—the Australian soap inexplicably adored in the UK—and his dream of visiting Down Under. Despite his awkward tour guide persona, in person Nigel was chatty and funny—a really nice guy.

Suddenly remembering his duties as tour guide, Nigel excused himself and bounced off to schmooze at other tables. I bounced off too; I only had an hour and a half to see the Roman baths. I resolved that this time, no matter how long the queue, I was goin' in.

The thing that struck me the first, second, and third times I walked past the Roman Baths was how much they resembled the surrounding buildings. Same color stone. Similar design.

I grew suspicious: Is this place really ancient?

As it turns out, there was a reason for this similarity—and for anyone seeking genuine antiquity, it was dismaying. Almost everything visible above ground, no matter how Roman it seemed, like the statues and colonnade surrounding the Great Bath, was built in the eighteenth century.

This place felt about as authentic as Mary Shelley's House of Horrors—or whatever the fuck it was called.

As luck would have it, the line had completely vanished—perhaps everyone had turned and fled at the sight of the £19 entrance fee. Reluctantly, I paid it. After all, I couldn't come to Bath and skip its namesake.

With rock-bottom expectations, I wandered in.

Once I got past my irritation at the entrance fee and the fake facade, and forced myself to see things with the eyes of an adult rather than a petulant child, my perspective began to shift. As I moved through the museum, I uncovered the real history behind the fake.

If I hadn't come to my senses, I might have missed the Temple pediment and the Gorgon's head, believed to be crafted by first-century Gallic sculptors. The Gorgon is particularly striking—a mustachioed, bearded face blending seamlessly into a mane of snake-hair. I was so captivated, I bought a magnet with the Gorgon's face, and now it proudly adorns my fridge.

One of the most relatable exhibits in the Roman Baths Museum was the collection of curse tablets—petty vengeance, ancient-style. These were appeals to Sulis Minerva, Bath's very own goddess of the springs (whose gilt bronze head is also on display), asking for divine retribution against thieves—usually for items swiped while the supplicant was bathing. One standout example reads: "Docimedis has lost two gloves and asks that the thief responsible should lose their minds and eyes in the goddess' temple."

Honestly? I hope Docimedis got his justice.

From there, I followed the well-worn path into the bowels of the building, which turned out to be amazing. I passed the changing rooms and saunas—complete with CGI recreations of massages—the Frigidarium (cold pool), and the Caldarium (the Roman equivalent of a hot tub). The path wound back up and out into the light, where the Sacred Spring and Great Bath awaited.

By now, I was hooked. No longer appalled, I was charmed. The original Roman baths had fallen into ruin by the sixth century, and the Georgians—despite their pseudo-Roman embellishments—had done what they could to preserve the site. What I'd once dismissed as fake now seemed almost sympathetic, even respectful. Hell, I even took a selfie—and I actually looked happy.

In the photo, I'm grinning with the waters of the Great Bath—a fluorescent, toxic-looking green—gleaming behind me. And yes, they really are toxic. Visitors are strongly advised not to touch the water, which is teeming with microorganisms eager to ruin your day.

Once upon a time, people actually swam in these supposedly healthful waters. That changed in 1978, when a child's death revealed the presence of *Naegleria fowleri*—a brain-eating amoeba with a 98% fatality rate.

Some might call the swimming ban nanny-state overreach, trampling our fundamental right to have our brains liquefied by microbes. But personally, I was happy to forgo the slow, agonizing death in Bath.

For the curious, though, the museum offers visitors a chance to taste a treated version of the water. Naturally, I gave it a try. It was warm, and the flavor... well, if you can imagine the taste of Satan's dirty bathwater, you're getting close.

As I passed through the gift shop—the first of many on this tour—and stepped into the street, I finally understood the allure of Bath, even if I still didn't understand *Bridgerton*.

Which was just as well. It was time to go.

Nigel pointed out another *Bridgerton*-related site as the bus eased its way through the narrow streets. The trip to Stonehenge would take about an hour, he said, and he promised to leave us in peace until we got closer to our final destination.

The last time I was this close to Stonehenge was forty-five years ago, traveling with Mum and Dad on our way from London to visit Avening, a small village in the Cotswolds where my grandfather was born. As luck—and my father's obsessive need for speed—would have it, we never made it to Stonehenge that day.

It wasn't on Dad's schedule.

We were cruising down the M4, Dad pushing the small rented car to its limit, when I saw a sign...

"Dad!" I cried from the backseat. "A turn-off to Stonehenge! Can we go?"

"No, no," he waved my suggestion aside. "I've already been there."

"Yes, but I haven't!"

Dad drove on, oblivious to my dismay, while I turned to watch the sign vanish behind us. I told myself I'd be back one day.

Well, nearly fifty years later, today was that day.

Nigel sprang to life about fifteen minutes before we arrived. He'd shaken off the last remnants of awkwardness and was now firmly in competent guide mode. He told a brief tale about the ancient megalith that seemed so far-fetched, I barely credited it as truthful—until a little fact-checking revealed it to be true.

Incredibly, this UNESCO World Heritage Site wasn't always owned by the people of England; it was once held in private hands. The second-to-last of these belonged to Sir Edmund Antrobus, who died in battle early in the First World War. With no direct heir to his title, Antrobus' estate had to be sold to pay death duties. Everything went up for auction, down to the curtains in his stately home.

And it was these curtains that Cecil Chubb's wife sent him to the auction to secure. But Chubb, a local lawyer, had other ideas. Rumor had it that an American was circling, allegedly interested in purchasing the stones and shipping them to the States—presumably to erect them somewhere gauche, like Milwaukee.

Cecil Chubb wasn't having it.

"Damned Americans, owning Stonehenge?" I can almost hear Chubb harrumphing through his walrus mustache. "This cannot be borne!"

With Britain's government too preoccupied fighting the Germans to intervene, Chubb stepped in as Stonehenge's unlikely savior. For £6,600 (about $850,000 today), he secured the ancient site—and immediately had to face his wife.

"Well, dear," I imagined him saying, "you know those curtains you wanted? Funny story..."

Though he only owned Stonehenge for a few years, Chubb allowed free public access and cared for the land. In 1918, he went a step further, donating it to the people of England.

The government, unable to grant sainthood, did the next best thing: they knighted him. Sir Cecil Chubb, 1st Baronet of Stonehenge. He even got his own coat of arms.

Lady Chubb, one assumes, was at least marginally appeased.

As the bus drew closer, I leaned forward in my seat, scanning the horizon for the first glimpse of the stones. But the landscape offered nothing remarkable—just a grassy plain stretching endlessly, dotted with the occasional rounded hill and a few sheep, grazing with complete indifference to the ancient wonder nearby.

It was still daylight when we pulled into the Stonehenge site around 7:10 pm, and part of Platinum Tours' late arrival strategy became clear: there were no other buses and only a handful of cars left in the car park. Apparently, these guys actually knew what they were doing.

Soon, we were inside the modern visitor center, which, as per Cecil Chubb's stipulations when he gifted Stonehenge to the nation, was a fair distance from the stones themselves. Nigel went off to liaise with the in-house guide, leaving our small group plenty of time to roam free in the gift shop, where I purchased yet another fridge magnet and a t-shirt. Through the floor-to-ceiling windows, I could see the light fading fast. If we didn't get to the site soon, it would be dark.

Finally, we were ushered onto a small bus and Nigel introduced us to Brenda, our Stonehenge guide. Despite the brisk temperature, Brenda was dressed in a khaki shirt-and-shorts combo like an Aussie park ranger. She gave us some interesting tidbits about Stonehenge, but I wasn't really listening. I was too antsy—the sun was nearly setting.

And then it hit me: *the sun was nearly setting!*

Soon, as the bus jolted onward, I caught my first glimpse of Stonehenge: the rock god of ancient megaliths. And in real life? It was exactly as advertised—massive standing stones crowned with horizontal lintels, their silhouette as iconic as it is mysterious.

And big. Very, very big.

If its builders wanted to leave behind something that would baffle future generations and set conspiracy theorists' brains on fire, they absolutely nailed it.

"Archaeologists believe construction started around 3000 BC," said Brenda, who looked like her every sentence should begin with Crikey! "What began as a simple earthwork ditch lined with wooden posts eventually evolved into the towering stone arrangement we see today."

But I knew this wasn't just some awesome prehistoric landscaping project—its precise alignment with the summer and winter solstices suggests that whoever built it wasn't just stacking rocks for fun. They were tracking the sun, which makes them either brilliant astronomers or deeply committed to scheduling the perfect sunrise view.

"The structure itself is made up of two types of stone," Brenda continued. "The outer sarsens—weighing up to thirty tons each—were dragged from Marlborough Downs, twenty miles away. The inner bluestones came all the way from southwest Wales. That's over 240 kilometers."

I knew this already, but it still blew my mind.

How did they do it? No one really knows. Theories range from rolling them on logs to hauling them by boat. But then it gets nutty—the conspiracy theorists are having way too much fun to listen to reason.

Meanwhile, the bus bumped along toward the usual viewing area, where visitors are typically restricted to admiring the stones from a safe, non-rock-touching distance. After a brief lecture from Brenda about not doing exactly that, we disembarked and made our way toward Stonehenge itself.

All the while, the sun was sinking lower on the horizon.

The air had turned colder, the chill brushing my cheeks and creeping down my neck. It wasn't unpleasant—if anything, it felt right. As a biological Celt, I figured this was my birthright. We approached the stones in silence, the fading light casting long shadows across the plain.

Then I stepped into the circle. And for the first time in my life, I stood in the presence of true antiquity. I was surrounded by the giant, rough-hewn stones, their forms so organic they seemed to have grown out of the earth itself. For anyone who still thinks aliens built this, standing here makes it abundantly clear that's nonsense. Such imperfect perfection could only be the work of humans.

I snapped plenty of pictures, but I never let the camera get in the way of the moment. I stayed present. And yet, it wasn't the spiritual experience I'd expected. Nor did I feel a profound connection to my Celtic roots.

Against Brenda's stern admonition, I reached out and touched a sarsen stone. It was mossy and damp beneath my fingertips, cold to the touch. And old. Not just ancient, but impossibly, profoundly old.

It was humbling.

And then, the true genius of Platinum Tours' schedule revealed itself: the sun began to set between the trilithons, eliciting a collective gasp from the fourteen of us. It streamed through just as it would have on the summer solstice, working exactly as designed.

And in that moment, I couldn't have given a shit about how much Platinum Tours had gouged me, Nigel's recycled rap, five bloody hours in Bath, or fucking *Bridgerton*.

This was magical.

This was transcendent.

This was history.

***

Unearthed

No Shitting in the Onboard Toilet

I was starting to get the hang of my CPAP machine's erratic new personality. It seemed only fitting to give it a name—something endearing yet exasperating. Meet 'Pappy.' His airflow was still unpredictable, but at least it no longer felt like mouth-to-mouth from a malfunctioning hairdryer. After a long day exploring Bath and Stonehenge, followed by a late return to Maggie and Eric's, I was out cold the moment I hit 'go' on Pappy.

Today was the day I'd catch up with CJ in London. His flight wasn't due to land until mid-afternoon, which meant I had a leisurely morning to get organized.

But why waste time?

No, I had plenty to do before meeting up with CJ. Leisure is for wimps!

We were meeting at some unique accommodation CJ had booked online: a houseboat named *Arnold*, moored on the Thames at Hampton Wick. The idea struck me as quirky and adventurous—not exactly my usual style of lodging, but I'd vowed to stop being so stuffy ages ago. Besides, how often do you get to sleep on a boat? I was genuinely looking forward to it.

That said, I knew space would be tight on *Arnold*. The last thing I wanted was to lug my massive suitcase onboard, turning the houseboat into a floating obstacle course. Clearly, a plan was needed.

I decided to offload my large luggage at the Novotel in Hammersmith, where we'd be staying the following night after joining our tour. After that, I'd travel light with just my hand luggage to Hampton Wick. It was a practical, well-thought-out plan.

After that, I had another idea to kill time while I waited for CJ's arrival.

As usual, Eric had masterminded the optimal rail journey. First, I'd need to do some fancy footwork, navigating a few Tube line changes to get to the hotel. Then, I'd combine the Tube with British Rail to reach Hampton Wick. Simple enough. My confidence in negotiating the rail network was beginning to build.

I arrived at Hammersmith Station and walked the short distance to the Novotel London West. Backpack on my shoulders and two wheelie bags trailing behind me. The hotel buzzed with activity—guests coming and going. Mostly coming. I joined a long line at reception, teeming with an inordinate number of excited children. By the time my turn came, Jamie, the young man behind the counter with a name badge pinned to his chest, looked decidedly frazzled.

"Hi. I've arranged to have my bag stored until I check in tomorrow," I said.

"I'm sorry, sir," Jamie replied, casting a nervous glance at the noisy, restless line forming behind me, "we're too busy; we can't possibly."

"But I called yesterday and spoke to..." I checked my notes. "Hannah. She said it was fine."

"Hannah's not in today," Jamie said, already starting to motion the next customer forward. Then he caught the expression on my face and seemed to think better of it. "One minute."

He disappeared through a door behind the counter and returned shortly after.

"Good news!" he said, as though he were doing me a massive favor. "We can store it back here, sir."

Relieved, I handed over my large bag and received a numbered tag emblazoned with the Novotel logo and the words *Forget Me Not*. I slipped it into my pocket, satisfied, and thought nothing more of it.

The journey to Hampton Wick was quick and painless. I now had four hours to kill before CJ landed, let alone got through customs and traveled to Hampton Wick.

Time for phase two of my plan: A visit to Hampton Court.

Perched on the banks of the Thames, Hampton Court became one of Henry VIII's favorite residences after Cardinal Wolsey gifted it to him in a last-ditch attempt to stay in the king's good graces. Wolsey had failed to secure Henry's divorce from Catherine of Aragon—his so-called 'Great Matter'—and hoped the extravagant gesture might buy him time.

It didn't. Henry took the palace, and Wolsey lost everything.

I'd visited there forty-five years previously and it was one of the places that still held vivid memories for me, particularly the maze and the Royal Tennis Court. But like so much I'd seen as a spotty teenager, I didn't really understand what it was or why I was there. It was just another old building. Now, with a far deeper understanding of Henry VIII and his world, I felt a revisit wasn't just worthwhile—it was necessary.

I could have walked the short distance from Hampton Wick Station to Hampton Court, but I opted for an Uber instead, weighed down as I was with a small wheelie bag and a backpack. Those familiar with the London rail system might wonder why I didn't simply take a train directly to Hampton Court Station. The answer is I wanted to catch sight of *Arnold* and get a feel for the area before my appointment with Henry Tudor.

As I walked through the gates of Hampton Court, the years melted away. The grandeur, the beauty, the deep sense of history—it was all so familiar.

Of course, what lay before me bore little resemblance to Cardinal Wolsey's Hampton Court, as Henry VIII had extensively remodeled it after taking possession. Even Henry, however, might not recognize the palace today. Subsequent monarchs also left their marks—none more so than William III, who destroyed large sections of the Tudor palace in his ambitious bid to transform Hampton Court into the English Versailles.

A helpful staff member at the gate pointed me to where I could stash my bags. Unlike Jamie at the Novotel London West, the staff here couldn't have been more accommodating. "Yes, of course we can store your bags, sir."

I could've hugged her.

What a difference.

When visiting a museum or historic site with someone else, I'm always polite—pausing to admire whatever exhibit has caught their eye and moving on when they're ready—unless I'm captivated by something myself. But when I'm sightseeing alone, my approach is entirely different: smash and grab, slash and burn, take no prisoners.

This solo visit to Hampton Court fell firmly into the 'no time to waste' category. I charged through the dull sections, paused to soak in key moments, then darted off again—like a demented gerbil on Red Bull.

The thought that Henry VIII might have screamed at a servant in this very spot or called Anne Boleyn a 'damnable whore' right over there completely fascinated me. No wonder anyone observing my erratic movement must have wondered what the hell I was doing.

Unlike most visitors, Hampton Court's meticulously manicured gardens, which include the famous hedge maze (been there, done that) and the Great Vine (the largest grapevine in the world, whoopee!) held little interest for me. I wasn't here for a frolic or a picnic. I was all about the main spaces: the Great Hall, the Chapel Royal, Anne Boleyn's gate, and I was still inexplicably fascinated with the Royal Tennis Court.

Henry VIII, the old dog, had managed to bring all six of his wives to this ultimate bachelor pad at various times over the years. He'd run the country from here. He'd hosted grand banquets, where I imagine him sitting at the head table, taking a single bite out of a roast chicken drumstick, then theatrically tossing it over his shoulder (a scene so memorably portrayed by Charles Laughton in *The Private Life of Henry VIII* that people think it actually happened). He'd played Royal Tennis here and, perhaps most impressively, managed not to die here.

However, Henry VIII wasn't the only monarch to live here.

Hampton Court was used by all of Henry VIII's children—Edward VI, Mary I, and Elizabeth I (who nearly died of smallpox there in 1562). James I convened a 1604 conference at the palace that led to the commissioning of the King James Bible. Later, William III and Mary II transformed it with Christopher Wren's Baroque design, and George II became its last royal resident.

The palace also witnessed some key events: Edward VI was born there, Jane Seymour died there, Henry VIII divorced Anne of Cleves and married Catherine Howard there. Some believe both *Hamlet* and *Macbeth* premiered here, though the evidence is unclear. What is certain is that Shakespeare and his King's Men performed in the Great Hall during Christmas 1603.

By the time I retrieved my luggage, the same bemused staff member raised an eyebrow.

"You're finished already?"

I nodded, grinning. "What can I say? I move fast."

Henry VIII would have hated me.

The man wanted this palace to be worshipped, to make visitors stop and marvel at his power.

I'd just sprinted through it like a courtier with diarrhea.

Although CJ hadn't touched down yet, I preemptively WhatsApped him that I'd be biding my time in *The Swan*, one of many local pubs in Hampton Wick. Perched on a sharp corner, *The Swan* exuded the kind of quaint charm rarely found in Australian pubs. I settled at a table with a frothy pint of London Pride—a name that, to me, sounded vaguely white supremacist. The beer was harmless enough though. So I ordered another.

I was the only patron in *The Swan* that afternoon. I occasionally chatted with the barman and listened to an array of vintage alternative rock playing in the background. The music might have seemed incongruous in such a quaint pub, but somehow, it fit the vibe perfectly.

My phone buzzed. One word: Landed.

By now I was pretty relaxed and it didn't seem long before CJ staggered in dragging his bags. He looked a bit rough around the edges, but not too bad considering he'd been in transit for twenty-four hours: He wore one of his extensive range of craft beer t-shirts (Eagle Brewing from New Zealand), which looked crumpled, as did his jeans and unzipped hoodie.

"Hey," I said from my seat near the door. "How was the flight?"

"Crap," CJ heaved his bags to where I was sitting and parked them. "And my fucking phone's not switched over to international roaming yet."

"If your roaming isn't working, how did you message me?"

"Public WiFi," CJ shuddered. "With no VPN."

"But..."

"I know, I know... the cybersecurity guru breaking all the rules."

"So, uh, what's with the..." I indicated the very un-CJ glasses sliding off his nose. They were either really cool or really shit—I hadn't decided yet.

"Emergency back-up glasses," he said, pushing them back into position. "The arm broke off my usual ones boarding in Melbourne."

"Smart idea to pack them."

"Would have been smarter to pack them in my carry-on," he said as they slid back down again.

"Beer?" I asked.

"I've just spent twenty-four hours wearing a pair of one-armed glasses. How is that even a question?"

Once relaxed with a pint of Guinness, CJ recounted the familiar trials and tribulations of long haul travel. After a brief chat, we downed what remained of our beers and set off to find the good ship *Arnold*.

CJ and I stood looking at a row of boats bobbing at Burgoine Quay on the Thames, very near the Kingston Bridge. We spotted *Arnold*, which looked a little like the *SS Minnow* from *Gilligan's Island*, moored next to what looked like a floating garden shed. Beside it was a wooden boat ominously named *Hemlock*.

Two dodgy-looking guys who'd been working on one of the nearby boats walked our way. They'd probably mistaken us for boat thieves.

"Gentlemen," said the first, who looked equal parts weathered seadog and man freshly ejected from his marital home.

"G'day," I replied, leaning into the Australianism to skip the inevitable explanation.

"We were looking for *Arnold*," said CJ.

"Well, you've found it," said Seadog's mate.

What followed was a meandering conversation about who we were, why we were there, the relative merits of different vessels, the correct use of the shared on-shore bathroom facilities, and finally, where to eat that night.

"*The Swan* has food," I suggested.

"*The Swan* used to be our local," said Seadog bitterly. "New owners fookin' wrecked it."

"Fookin' wrecked it," echoed the other. "Too fookin' trendy now."

"Try *The White Hart*, that's our new local."

"Er, thanks." I didn't know about CJ, but after that encounter, *The White Hart* was firmly off my list of dining options.

After extricating ourselves from this riveting conversation, we turned our attention to boarding *Arnold*. Easier said than done. First, we had to climb a ladder at the stern. Then came the real challenge: shimmying along the impossibly skinny gunwale, unlocking a sliding door, and slipping inside—all without tumbling into the Thames.

How CJ managed this with his massive bags, I'll never know. I couldn't watch. I just waited for the inevitable splash that, while it would've been fantastic for the narrative, never came.

Arnold had two beds: a small one in the bow and a larger one at the stern. Between them lay a rudimentary kitchen/dining area and a bathroom with one very specific rule.

"No shitting in the onboard toilet," CJ announced.

"Why?" I asked

"That's what the instructions say."

"It actually says 'no shitting'?"

"I'm paraphrasing."

"Where are we supposed to shit, then?" I asked.

"Apparently, there's a shared bathroom on the quayside. Toilet. Shower. All mod cons. You'll need this." CJ handed me a four-digit code. "And don't forget the toilet roll."

While CJ made use of the dockside facilities, I set up Pappy and my array of chargers: phone, watch, and additional battery pack.

Later, we wandered across the Kingston Bridge into town, stopping for drinks and a few games of pool at a bar called *The Fighting Cocks*. We capped off the evening with England's national dish—a curry—at *Moidul's Hampton Wick Tandoori*.

Finally, it was time to head back to Arnold.

I had the bed at the bow, which was comfortable enough. CJ had the larger bedroom at the stern—mainly because he had all his luggage—but it came with one major drawback: it was right next to the bathroom.

At least neither of us could shit there.

That night, I was rocked to sleep by the Thames.

The next morning we had to vacate Arnold. But before we cleared out, we wandered into Kingston for coffee and breakfast. For reasons best known to the businesspeople of Kingston, this proved almost impossible to find. In desperation, we ended up at the only place open at 8:00 am—a *Pret A Manger*—where we were served bland coffee and prepackaged sandwiches.

CJ checked his phone. "My international roaming has kicked-in—finally."

"Thank God."

We discussed the logistics of the day ahead.

"Okay, first we have to get to Baker Street Station," I said, mentally ticking off items. "Then luggage storage, then the Beatles tour. Sound right?"

CJ nodded.

"And, if we play our cards right, we'll have time for lunch first."

"And beers?"

"A beer," I said, punctuated by a sip of unimpressive Americano. "Afterwards, we head back to Hammersmith to join the bus tour."

While I still hadn't mastered the intricacies of the Tube and British Rail, we muddled our way to Baker Street Station. Baker Street's biggest claim to fame is being the fictional home of the equally fictional Sherlock Holmes.

Today's London was cold, gray, and drizzly—the kind of weather Australians expect. But this wasn't just any London day. This was the day we would step into the Beatles' world, retracing their steps through the city that defined the Swinging Sixties.

Unlike my last visit—when brilliant blue skies framed Buckingham Palace—today was far less picturesque. The other obvious difference? The sheer number of people buzzing about. Curious tourists clutching umbrellas jostled with pinstriped men, powersuited women, and midday shoppers, all colliding in a chaotic dance on the crowded streets.

After dumping our bags, a quick lunch, and a pre-tour pint at a pub called *The Globe*, we met Michael, our Beatles tour guide, under the Sherlock Holmes statue (confusingly located on Marylebone Street). Joining us were six other Beatle fanatics—a friendly American couple with two kids and a charming Turkish husband and wife duo.

Michael Purvis was a laid-back, older man with deep-set eyes and a slight Cockney accent, like a cultured version of a particular English football manager whose name I couldn't recall. He was tall and gray-haired, and I wondered if 'tour guide' had been his lifelong career—or if this was just a retirement gig. Either way, Michael was professional, knowledgeable, and—for reasons not yet clear—carried an iPad.

Our little group was as diverse as it was enthusiastic. What united us was a shared love for the Fab Four. Even the teenage kids of the American couple displayed an unexpected curiosity for such a retro phenomenon.

The Beatles weren't just a band—they were a cultural detonation. Four lads from Liverpool transformed rock and roll into something bigger, bolder, and infinitely more complex.

Their sound evolved at a staggering pace. In just a few years, they took the quantum leap from the infectious simplicity of She Loves You to the kaleidoscopic experimentation of *Sgt. Pepper's Lonely Hearts Club Band*.

From their performance on the *Ed Sullivan Show*—which countless artists have described as a personal lightbulb moment—to the rooftop concert so brilliantly depicted in Peter Jackson's *Get Back*, they defined the 1960s. They reshaped music, fashion, and even the way people thought about fame and artistry.

When I'd told people back home CJ and I were doing a Beatles tour, the inevitable question was, "Are you going to Liverpool?" While it was a valid query—and certainly something I'd want to do one day—the truth is, the Beatles outgrew their Liverpool stage quickly. By mid-1963, they were firmly ensconced in London, the city where they'd soon put the swing in the Swinging Sixties.

From then until they imploded in 1970, London was where the Beatles lived and plied their trade, mostly at Abbey Road studios, the last stop on this tour.

To truly understand their world, retracing their steps in London was essential.

The mystery of Michael's iPad was soon solved. We'd sloshed our way to a wet, side-street, which he informed us was the location of a famous scene from the Beatles' *A Hard Day's Night*. At first glance, it just looked like a stock-standard lane—nothing remarkable.

But then Michael fired up his iPad and showed us that scene. Lo and behold, there were the four mop tops being chased by a mob of girls toward the very spot where we stood. Seeing the grainy black-and-white footage overlaid on our surroundings made the moment come alive.

Michael performed similar iPad magic at Paddington Station, another key location from *A Hard Day's Night*. There, we saw the exact spot where the Beatles filmed another of their iconic chase sequences. Genius.

While mostly on foot, the tour also required us to hop on and off the Tube, carefully ensuring we didn't lose Michael in the crowd. We stopped at Ringo's flat at 34 Montagu Square in Marylebone. Michael explained that it hadn't just been Ringo's home—he'd also sub-let it to Jimi Hendrix, who wrote *The Wind Cries Mary* there, and later to John Lennon and Yoko Ono. It was in that flat where they shot their notorious nude photo for the *Two Virgins* album cover and where they were living when the Metropolitan Police raided the property for drugs.

Which, in hindsight, explains a lot.

After tour stops that spanned the Beatles' early fame and later experimentation—over which time, the rain had stopped—we arrived at the most iconic location of all: Abbey Road.

Any mention of the Beatles and Abbey Road would be incomplete without mentioning George Martin, often referred to as the 'Fifth Beatle'. He was instrumental in shaping the Beatles' groundbreaking sound, largely through their collaborations at Abbey Road Studios, where they redefined the possibilities of popular music.

Among the albums the Beatles and Martin recorded there were *Rubber Soul*, *Revolver*, *Sgt. Pepper's Lonely Hearts Club Band*, the *White Al-*

bum, *Let It Be*, and of course *Abbey Road*. Their diverse body of work showcases their evolution as artists, with each album marking a distinct chapter in music history.

I was a child of the sixties, and the Beatles had been the soundtrack of my life since before I could walk. Four men who redefined popular culture had created their magic here. For me, this pilgrimage to Abbey Road felt almost as profound as sunset at Stonehenge—hyperbolic as that might sound.

As CJ and I walked across the zebra crossing immortalized on the *Abbey Road* album cover, it wasn't just a photo op to me. It felt, in its own way, epochal. Right here, in this very spot, four of the most famous entertainers in history had once walked.

I couldn't help but think about what this place represented—not just for the Beatles, but for music, art, and the culture of an entire generation. It was more than a crossing; it was a symbol of a moment in time when creativity and rebellion collided to shape the world.

And that, too, was history.

We eventually arrived at the Novotel London West to check in. If the reception had been chaotic yesterday, today it was pure pandemonium. The crowd of hyperactive children had multiplied exponentially, transforming the place into something resembling a circus. To drive the point home, a clown car elevator spilled out an impossible number of kids in running gear, who immediately sprinted past me and out to wreak havoc on the streets of Hammersmith.

"I'd like to retrieve my bag please," I said when I got to the desk. Jamie wasn't on duty, but unfortunately the hotel had provided someone just as efficient.

"I'm sorry, sir, we don't store bags," said Jacinta, exhibiting just the right amount of disinterest for a Novotel employee.

"You most certainly do, I watched Jamie take it into that room yesterday." I jabbed a finger at the door behind the counter.

"Jamie's not on duty today."

"Humor me."

Jacinta shrugged and sloped off. She was back in seconds.

"There's no bag there, sir."

"Did they give you a claim ticket?" CJ interjected.

I checked my wallet, and there it was—the *Forget Me Not* ticket, which, of course, I'd forgotten was there.

"Here." I shoved the ticket into Jacinta's well-manicured hand.

She wandered off across the foyer—no easy task given the swarm of children. Ten minutes later, she returned, empty-handed and unapologetic.

"Is there someone competent who can help us?" asked CJ, whose jet lag, I suppose, was making him more direct than usual.

"Jenny?" Jacinta called, grabbing a passing supervisor. "This gentleman has a baggage claim ticket."

Jenny glanced at the ticket, disappeared through the door behind the reception desk, and reappeared moments later with my bag.

"We'd like to check in now," I said to Jenny through gritted teeth.

"Certainly, sir. Jacinta can help—" Jenny began.

"No," I said too quickly. "Not Jacinta."

Jenny proceeded with our check-in. She frowned at the computer screen, then looked back at me.

"We're overbooked," she said. "You'll have to take a single room."

"B-but there's two of us," CJ protested, eyes widening.

"I'm sorry, sir," she said, not sounding remotely sorry.

"Supervisor," I said flatly.

A few moments later, John the assistant manager breezed in. "It appears you have a problem."

"No," CJ and I said in perfect unison. "You have a problem."

"Look, I'm really sorry," John said, far too contritely for an employee of this establishment. "We're booked solid because of the Mini London Marathon tomorrow."

That at least explained the overly energetic children bouncing around the hotel.

"The best I can do is send up a folding bed," he said. "And give you a £100 voucher to make up for the inconvenience."

It would have to do.

After checking out our room—and discovering that a folding bed wouldn't be necessary thanks to the presence of a sofa bed—CJ and I headed to the Cosmic Tours desk. Cosmic was the tour company we'd be traveling with for the next twelve days, and we were curious to see if we might meet our soon-to-be travel companions.

Despite the fact that the tour had technically begun and the Novotel booking was in their name, Doris, the woman at the Cosmic desk—pleasant enough, if not particularly helpful—seemed completely unbothered by the fact that CJ and I had been given a single room.

"You'll just have to get to know each other a little better then," she laughed.

"So it seems," I grumbled.

We had a slow start the next morning. The details were sketchy, but we had to meet our beer tour near the Tower Bridge at noon. That should've given us plenty of time, but we spent the morning wandering around Hammersmith, trying to find a place for CJ to get his glasses fixed.

We were successful—if you call blowing a whole morning and CJ having to buy a whole new set of frames 'success'—but by the time we got back to the hotel, I realized something troubling.

"We can't get to the tour on time by Tube," I said.

"Let me have a look," CJ said, pulling out his phone. After a few moments, he sighed. "Nope. You're right."

And that was why, ten minutes later, we found ourselves in an Uber heading toward our destination.

Anderson, our driver, didn't seem to grasp the urgency of our situation. That, coupled with the thickening traffic, did not bode well.

"London Mini Marathon today, innit?" Anderson said casually.

CJ and I exchanged a look. Of course it was.

When it became painfully clear that we weren't going to make it on time, I started frantically scrolling through the tour details, hoping for a miracle. Finally, I found a contact number and fired off a text message. Thankfully, I got a quick reply: we could meet the group at the first pub if we were late.

I exhaled in relief, but the feeling didn't last long.

On Tower Bridge Road, the marathon was over and the road was open. A veritable sea of humanity was moving northwards on the footpaths of Tower Bridge—exhausted runners, spectators, and people who'd cheered them on.

Anderson, correctly, tried to drop us on the southern side of the bridge.

Somehow, I misread the map.

"We need to go over the bridge," I said.

"What do you mean 'over the bridge'?" replied Anderson, his tone suggesting he already knew this was a bad idea.

"I mean to the other side of the bridge," I said. "Near the Tower of London."

Anderson hesitated. "Okay, your call," he said and kept driving.

Halfway across the bridge, I realized my mistake.

"Oh no," I muttered.

"What?" CJ asked.

"We *were* supposed to be on the southern side," I said, trying not to meet his eyes.

CJ groaned. "Can you not read a map?"

"I'm sorry, okay?"

Anderson dropped us where I'd asked him to, and we had to fight our way back across the bridge footpath—against the tide of runners and spectators. It was like swimming upstream in a river of Lycra.

"This is a nightmare," CJ said as we dodged oncoming foot traffic.

We clawed our way back to the southern side, sweatier and even more frazzled than we'd started. Then we faced our next challenge:

getting down from the bridge to the pub below.

To our left—salvation at last—a staircase. But before we could descend, we hit yet another obstacle: a wall of marathoners, sweaty but ecstatic, dancing their way up the stairs, a boombox held aloft like some kind of victory trophy.

It was absurd, like something out of a comedy sketch—one ridiculous hurdle after another. CJ and I just stood there, helpless, laughing.

"I guess I'd be joyous too if I survived a marathon," I said.

"I wouldn't have any energy left," CJ replied.

By the time we finally reached the pub to rendezvous with our tour, the first beers were being poured.

Exhaustion and relief made them taste like nectar of the gods.

The tour took us from bar to bar, with the guide introducing a different type of beer at each stop. Most of them were good—at least, I thought so—but the nuances were lost on me. I could tell you if I liked it or not, but our guide was the one dissecting the hops and malt like a sommelier in his natural habitat.

The pale ales, he declared, had "a crisp, floral finish," while the stouts were "bold, with rich coffee undertones." I nodded along, pretending to understand, while secretly wondering why beer couldn't just taste like beer.

One of the highlights was the Southwark Brewing Company, where we had a tasting paddle that spanned the spectrum from pale ales to stouts. CJ was in heaven, nodding thoughtfully after each sip. I followed his lead, nodding too, though I had no idea what "a good balance of bitterness and floral notes" actually meant.

The tour wrapped up at *The Barrel Project*, where we sampled four different sour beers. None of us were particularly enamored with these—not even CJ. I tried to be diplomatic, but there's no way to romanticize "notes of bile with just a hint of anal leakage."

After hours of sampling everything from bitters to stouts, we ended our beer journey at the George Inn. As we sat in the courtyard with pints in hand, I couldn't help but feel a sense of history hanging in the air. Shakespeare himself was said to have drunk here, and much later, Dickens. The original buildings had been destroyed in the Great Fire of London in 1666, but *The George Inn* was rebuilt shortly afterward, and today, it still carried the weight of centuries.

"Imagine," I said to CJ, "Shakespeare might have sat here nursing an ale, jotting down notes for *Henry IV*. Or Dickens, brooding over corrections to *Pickwick Papers* with a pint in hand."

CJ raised his glass with a grin. "That's a sobering thought—we can't have that. Cheers."

We clinked glasses, and for a moment, the centuries folded into the present—a quiet reminder that some things, like a pint and a story, never change.

Once back at the Novotel, we called past the Cosmic Tours desk. Doris was on duty again and we decided to ask if there was any welcome function for our tour.

"There's a dinner tonight, but it's for three different tours," she said, scanning her booking sheet. "Only four people from your group are attending."

"But... hasn't the tour technically started?" CJ asked.

"You'll meet your guide when you get on the bus tomorrow," she replied far too cheerfully.

"And the other passengers?"

"Checked in hours ago. They're probably all in bed."

"It's only 6:15 pm!" I protested, turning to CJ. "What have we gotten ourselves into?"

CJ sighed. "A nursing home, apparently."

***

That's *Some* Erection!

As our tour group assembled at the Cosmic desk in the morning, the reason for Doris' "they're all in bed" comment became clear. Of the forty-odd people milling around in the assembly area, a solid seventy-five percent were in their mid-to-late seventies.
Granted, CJ and I weren't here to recruit partners-in-crime to pillage our way through Europe—this wasn't a Viking raid or a Contiki Tour, after all. But still…

The suitcases were lined up in neat rows, though that wasn't good enough for one of our presumed busmates—an older gentleman in a red sweater, squinting like a mole. With the intensity of a grandmaster, he began meticulously rearranging them, treating it like a life-sized game of Tetris.

"Gather around, everyone," said a fit, well-groomed man with a graying beard. "I'm George, and I'll be your tour guide."

George then explained the next few hours in slow, excruciating detail.

"First, we'll take the bus to St. Pancras Station, where there'll be time for bathroom breaks. Once we arrive, we'll check in for the Eurostar—make sure your passports are handy for that."

"St Pancreas Station?" CJ asked.

"It's St Pancras," I replied with mock exasperation. CJ's a smart guy, but I couldn't tell if he was joking.

"Whatever. I'm not a doctor."

Meanwhile, George was still monologuing: "The Eurostar is the train that'll take us to Paris. After check-in, we'll wait in the designated area, which also has toilets if needed. One quick note about currency exchange: if you're changing US dollars, don't do it at St. Pancras. They'll first convert your dollars to pounds, then pounds to euros, and you'll be charged double commission. It's better to exchange directly to euros once we're in Paris."

George continued this well-rehearsed speech for another minute or so.

Then, from the back, a quavering Midwestern voice: "Will there be bathroom breaks?"

"Yes," George said, without a hint of frustration. "At St. Pancras. Where we're going. On the bus."

Pause.

Undeterred, George repeated his entire spiel, more deliberately if that was possible. "And don't worry," he concluded, "if you can't remember any of these details, I'll explain them all again on the bus," his voice exuded the kind of endless patience reserved for kindergarten teachers and hostage negotiators.

"And then we'll breathe in," I muttered to CJ under my breath, "and then out."

Yet, as the trip unfolded, I came to appreciate the need for George's relentless precision and repetition.

As promised, once we were all aboard the bus, George repeated his instructions word for word—especially the parts about bathrooms and not exchanging US dollars for euros at St. Pancras. But this time, he added one new piece of information:

"Just before we show our passports," George said, "we're going to have to scan a QR code. Does everyone know what a QR code is?"

To my astonishment, there were murmurs of confusion. A grandmotherly woman with dark gray hair, a perm, and oversized spectacles, spoke for the group: "Q... R code? I don't know what that is..."

Not for the last time on this tour, CJ and I held a private conference—quietly, in our bus seats.

"They've never seen a QR code?" CJ looked genuinely baffled.

"'Never having seen one' and 'not knowing what one is' are two different things," I replied.

"Sure, but during Covid, we spent two years running our lives with those things."

Our disbelief, however, was not mirrored by George. It was clear he'd been through this routine countless times. With the calm air of a man long resigned to his fate, he held aloft a laminated sign bearing a QR code.

"This," he said slowly, "is a QR code."

Pause.

"What you have to do is..."

Inside St. Pancras, we lined up as if for an international flight. After scanning our QR codes—some with more bewilderment than others—we cleared passport control and stepped into what might have been a spacious departure lounge, if not for the sheer crush of humanity inside.

It was relatively modern, with cafés, bathrooms, and, of course, the infamous currency exchange lying in wait for the unprepared.

George was the very embodiment of patience as he fielded the usual barrage of questions: "Are there bathrooms?" "Are the bathrooms clean?" "Where exactly are the bathrooms?" and "Will there be bathrooms on the Eurostar?" Each time, he answered with a calm equanimity I could never hope to muster.

A little later, a few of us were chatting with George when an older American woman—white-haired, with the perpetually pissed-off expression of someone whose Dalmatians had just made a break for it—cut in abruptly. CJ and I quickly dubbed her 'Cruella'.

"Where's the currency exchange?" Cruella demanded. "I've got loads of dollars, and I need euros."

"Oh, I wouldn't do that," George replied, maintaining his Zen-like calm despite having carefully explained this at least three times. "You'll get charged double commission."

"What do you mean?" she snapped. "Aren't we in Italy now?"

CJ and I struggled to keep straight faces. Not only were we still in England, but we were about to board a train to France.

The Eurostar was comfortable and quick. We were through the Chunnel before I even realized we were in it, and the green fields of France zipped past at 300 kilometers per hour. Barely two and a quarter hours after departing St. Pancras Station, we were pulling into Paris Gare du Nord.

As we dragged our suitcases out of the station, we walked straight into chaos. Our 'Welcome to Paris!" surprise was an unholy mess of torn-up roads and footpaths.

George took charge. "In its infinite wisdom, the local council has decided this is a great time to renovate. Unfortunately, our tour bus is a bit of a walk away..."

Groans rippled through the group.

"No need for concern," soothed George. "Just follow me and I'll get you there."

And that's how a group of lumbering seniors and assorted hangers-on ended up trudging down the middle of a laneway in Paris' 10th arrondissement, dodging cars and pissing off the locals.

George was as good as his word—leading the way while somehow still finding time to assist his passengers. He was especially kind to three people I hadn't noticed before: an older African-American woman using a walking frame, accompanied by two younger women, whom I assumed were her daughters, helping her navigate the obstacle-laden streets.

When we finally arrived, the tour bus was exactly what you'd expect—not old, not new. Just serviceable. It even had a toilet, which I naively assumed would put an end to the endless stream of bathroom-related questions George had been fielding.

How wrong I was.

Once we were underway, George's tone turned uncharacteristically stern: "The toilet on board is strictly for emergencies. If you need it, you'll have to get the key from me, and we'll stop the bus. And remember: pee-pee, no ca-ca."

This potty talk drew giggles from ninety percent of the passengers.

You've got to hand it to George, he knew his audience.

Our hotel, the Ibis Styles Paris Porte d'Orléans, was a far cry from the luxury Hotel Ibis in Seoul, where I'd crossed paths with the Russian/Ukrainian Mafia boys. This was three-star budget accommodation—functional, but a considerable trek from the Eiffel Tower, where CJ and I had tickets for a tour later that evening.

This third-party tour marked the first of many times CJ and I would diverge from the main tour group. The Cosmic optional tour had the group driving through Paris, glimpsing landmarks through the bus windows as they sped by, dining on a set menu, and finally gazing up at the Eiffel Tower from a safe distance.

We, however, were cooking up something a little more boots-on-the-ground.

"Seven kilometers to the Eiffel Tower," said CJ, looking up from the map on his smartphone. "Walk it?"

"Sure," I replied.

We were happy to escape our cramped room—the beds were so close together, it felt like we'd be sharing one, so we shoved them apart as far as possible. No fridge, no safe.

After waiting an eternity for the lone, sluggish elevator, we gave up and took the stairs instead.

As we passed reception, I nodded politely at the concierge and muttered through a ventriloquist's smile: "Your hotel is crap."

And with that small rebellion, we were on our way.

I usually prefer using a taxi, Uber, or public transport at a pinch.

But I wanted to get a feel for Paris, and there's no better way to do that than by exploring it at street level. Besides, when you're with CJ, you'd better have your walking shoes ready.

Given the choice, he'd always rather go on foot.

The road from Porte d'Orléans into the city is very flat, making it an easy walk. We set off straight down the Avenue Du Maine, and along the way, we passed familiar businesses that the French language gave a fun new twist—such as Mister Minit: which promised 'tampons' among other things—as well as more niche establishments, like *The French Bastards*, a bakery that was, sadly, not open when we passed.

CJ spotted a sign forbidding public urination—essentially a no-smoking sign, but with the cigarette replaced by a stick figure of a man urinating with panache and an undeniable joie de vivre. Naturally, we couldn't resist taking a photo of CJ pretending to defy the sign.

If only he hadn't been a method actor...

About halfway into town, we turned down Rue du Sèvres and ducked into a place called *Zero Zero Sèvres*. It was more of a restaurant, but it was the bar inside that caught our attention. This was our first opportunity to test out our non-existent French.

It was a test we wouldn't take.

"G'day," said CJ, resolutely defying the conventional wisdom that, in France, one should at least attempt to speak the language.

"What would you like, sir?" replied the barman in perfect English, with not a hint of arrogance or resentment.

While we downed the beers, CJ noticed a peculiar phenomenon. "Look," he gestured toward the large window facing the street, "a glitch in the Matrix."

From our spot at the bar, we watched pedestrians walk past, only to disappear at a certain point on the sidewalk. Strangely, it also worked in reverse—people would suddenly appear out of nowhere, continuing to walk as if nothing had happened. The same thing happened with cars, vanishing and reappearing as if reality itself had been cut and pasted.

It took us longer than it should have to realize the cause: a mirror, mounted perpendicular to the wall at the 'vanishing point,' perfectly aligned to create the illusion.

Mystery solved, we downed our beers and moved on.

With time to kill, we resisted the urge to make a beeline for the Eiffel Tower—even though it teased us at every intersection, peeking out from between rows of classic Parisian apartments like it was playing hard to get.

Instead, we let ourselves wander deeper into the 7th arrondissement, pulled along by the neighborhood's charm—and CJ's unconscious momentum. It's the kind of place where cobblestone streets, wrought-iron balconies, and window boxes bursting with color make even the most aimless stroll feel like a scene from a movie.

Some genuinely historic-looking private homes took the words "shabby chic" to an extreme—their once-beautiful shutters now crying out for a fresh coat of paint.

By this stage, I was tiring and rapidly losing the will to live. CJ, however, forged ahead like a rogue Terminator, programmed only for relentless forward motion.

Doubtless, I should have planned this excursion better, but sometimes, you just fail. So, it was more by instinct than design that we found ourselves standing at the gates of the Hôtel National des Invalides.

The Hôtel National des Invalides is one of those places that sneaks up on you, its grandeur only fully hitting once you're standing at its gates. Originally built as a hospital and retirement home for war veterans under Louis XIV, it has since evolved into a massive complex that houses museums, monuments, and even Napoleon's tomb.

The Église du Dôme, where Napoleon's tomb rests, was actually constructed well before his time, between 1679 and 1706. If the glittering dome—it's coated with twelve kilograms of gold—seems a bit over-the-top for a resting place, consider two things: first, the Église du Dôme has long served as a burial site for French military heroes;

and second, Napoleon was the Emperor of France, not the Emperor of Subtlety. This is the man who crowned himself Emperor because, apparently, letting the Pope do it wasn't dramatic enough.

When Napoleon's remains were exhumed in 1840, they were transported back to France from Saint Helena inside multiple coffins, nested one inside the other, supposedly to help preserve his body. But you have to wonder: was this 'Russian doll' treatment a practical measure, or just someone taking the piss over his catastrophic Russian campaign?

The Hôtel National des Invalides is beautiful and grand—the kind of place where history feels both tangible and maybe a little too carefully curated, even if, like me, you're too tired to fully appreciate it.

At any rate, by the time we arrived after 7:00 pm, it was, of course, closed.

"Can you slow down a little?" I whined at CJ. Even to my ear, this sounded too much like a three-year-old.

We arrived at the Parc du Champ de Mars, where our eyes were dragged to the Eiffel Tower.

"It's bigger than I expected." The moment the words left my mouth, I braced myself.

"That's what she said," CJ quipped, with a guffaw that proved immaturity is timeless.

The Parc du Champ de Mars was once a humble market garden, but the construction of the École Militaire in 1765 changed its destiny. Its name, meaning Field of Mars, pays homage to the Campus Martius in ancient Rome, where the legions trained—perhaps in the hope that Roman military genius might inspire the French. Today, it's a serene park with sprawling lawns, tree-lined walkways, and picnicking visitors, offering a picturesque approach to the Eiffel Tower.

We were close to the Tower now. It was pretty impressive.

"Ever heard of Victor Lustig?" CJ asked as we gazed up in awe.

"Why? Should I?"

"The Man Who Sold the Eiffel Tower? You've really never heard of him?"

"Nope."

Clearly pleased to know something historical I didn't, he launched into the story. "In the 1920s, the rumor was that the Eiffel Tower might be dismantled, and Lustig pretended to be a government official. Convinced a metal dealer to buy it for scrap."

"Really?"

"Yep. Lustig took the money and ran before anyone caught on," CJ went on. "The scrap guy was too embarrassed to report it. Lustig pulled off dozens of scams before they finally got him. Ended up in Alcatraz."

"He ended up in Alcatraz for selling the Eiffel Tower?"

"No, some other scam."

"Oh." I was too grumpy for enthusiasm.

"Will this make the book?"

"Probably not."

We ended up at the Castel Café, near the Eiffel Tower—a spot with all the Parisian charm you could hope for, at only three times the price. We ordered one plate of French fries, and CJ went for escargot.

"The last time I ate snails," I said, "was when we were on that cruise in Noumea."

"I remember. Want some now?"

"You kidding? After forty years I still can't get the taste of garlic out of my mouth."

We washed it all down with a couple of whiskeys in sleek square highballs, then headed off to join the Eiffel Tower tour.

We met Sofie, our tour guide, in a street a stone's throw from the Tower. She appeared to be in her early twenties—and not French. Her accent sounded like it was from somewhere in the Balkans, though I didn't ask. These days, I wasn't sure if that was even appropriate to bring up.

To my relief, a group of French loudmouths waiting nearby peeled off in another direction, so there were only two other people on our tour. A young couple I guessed were on their honeymoon.

Sofie quickly ushered our small group past hundreds of waiting plebs and straight into the priority entrance line. If there's one tip I can give new travelers, it's this: always buy 'skip the line' tickets.

As we moved ahead, I glanced back at the sea of weary tourists, their patience visibly fraying as they shot us dirty looks. Sofie gave us a knowing smile, and we soon stepped into the elevator.

With a gentle lurch, it began its ascent, leaving the envious peasants far below. As the ground fell away beneath us, I couldn't help but wonder—was it this kind of casual exploitation of privilege that had sparked the French Revolution?

From inside the elevator, we could see the tower's metallic frame, its iron bones and riveted joints exposed like the skeleton of some massive industrial beast.

"This is some erection," I said to CJ.

"Monsieur Eiffel should be very proud."

The Eiffel Tower was designed by Gustave Eiffel for the 1889 Exposition Universelle, its primary purpose being to showcase the marvels of modern engineering. Its secondary purpose was to celebrate the centennial of the French Revolution, which—while not as appropriate as a festival of public guillotining—was far more socially acceptable.

The tower rose to a staggering 330 meters, making it the Burj Khalifa of its time. And it reigned as the tallest man-made structure on Earth for the next forty years—along the way it became one of the world's most recognizable landmarks.

But that wasn't always the plan. The Eiffel Tower was originally set to be dismantled after twenty years—an outcome many Parisians eagerly anticipated, convinced it was a hideous blight on their city. That widespread disdain likely inspired Victor Lustig's infamous tower scam.

However, the tower earned its keep by proving useful for scientific experiments and, later, as a radio transmission tower. Over time, its critics faded, and the Eiffel Tower became a beloved symbol of Paris. Today, it's impossible to imagine the City of Light without it.

But if something isn't done soon, there's a chance we might have to.

The Eiffel Tower, like any aging masterpiece, faces the ravages of time. Corrosion has engineers worried about its long-term stability. The tower was repainted for the Paris Olympics at a staggering cost of €60,000,000, but it seems this effort is little more than window dressing. In 2024, *The Guardian* cited an expert who warned, "At best [the paint job] will be mostly useless, but at the very worst it will make the defects in the existing layer of paint worse and result in corrosion."

But it's not all gloom and doom. Some experts remain optimistic, believing that with proper care, the repainted Eiffel Tower can last 'forever.'

But because CJ and I were halfway up in an elevator, I'd just be happy for the Iron Lady to maintain her structural integrity for the next couple of hours.

When we reached the top, the sun was setting, casting a warm glow over the city. Above us, the clear blue sky melted into purples and pinks before deepening into a rich orange at the horizon.

Had I not witnessed twilight at Stonehenge just days before, this would have been the most beautiful sunset I'd ever seen. Even so, Paris was putting on a show—lifting her skirts like a Moulin Rouge can-can dancer going commando, flaunting all her best bits for the world to see.

Below us, Paris stretched out in all its illuminated glory: Notre-Dame, the Arc de Triomphe, the Place du Trocadéro, the Hôtel National des Invalides and the Église du Dôme, the many bridges of the Seine, and, in the distance, Sacré-Cœur—where we'd be heading tomorrow.

It was bitterly cold this high up, and the wind had a real bite to it. I was finally forced to use my scarf—previously a jaunty, some might say pretentious, accessory—for its intended purpose.

By now, the honeymoon couple had melted away, presumably in search of their own romantic moment, far from the Australians who kept making dick jokes. And just like that, CJ and I found ourselves on a private tour with Sofie.

Night had fully descended, and Paris lit up in a way that left no doubt why they call it the City of Light.

'Breathtaking' is overused, but no other word captures the sea of golden light unfolding before us. We walked to every side of the structure, muscling into small gaps between fellow tourists, dodging kissing couples and rogue selfie sticks, and taking in the view from every possible angle.

It was the kind of beauty that demanded to be savored—yet all too soon, Sofie informed us our time was up.

After taking the elevator to the first floor, still over fifty meters from the ground, we bade farewell to Sofie, then ceremonially exited through the gift shop (another fridge magnet—an Eiffel Tower adorned with colorful macarons). We decided to take the stairs the rest of the way down, winding through the exposed superstructure of the tower.

And that's where we were the moment the tower's lights flickered to life.

A crowd had gathered in the Parc du Champ de Mars just for this event, and even from fifty meters above, I heard their collective gasp of delight. From our vantage point, we could only see the flashing lights—apparently part of a coordinated display.

By the time we reached the bottom, the show was over. The tower had returned to its steady, always-on glow.

That's when the real fun began.

By any measure, I was exhausted. And when I get tired, I revert to a child-like state.

My step counter's history reveals that CJ and I had walked over twenty kilometers that day. On top of that, I'd had a number of beers, a whiskey, and had earlier traveled from London to Paris in the company of people with bladder control issues.

And it was cold.

And my feet hurt.

And it was 11:00 pm.

So imagine my chagrin when CJ appeared to unilaterally decide we would walk the seven kilometers back to the Ibis. Oh, I don't think that was his intention. No, our trek began under the guise of 'finding a cab.'

But I knew CJ, so I knew how this would go. He'd march on relentlessly to a certain point, look at me, and say something like, "We're so close, we might as well walk the rest."

"Can't we just get an Uber?" I moaned after the first five hundred meters.

"I'm looking for a taxi stand," CJ said as he strode on. I began to fall behind, intentionally dragging my feet.

We'd walked at least a kilometer before I stopped dead in my tracks, refusing to follow him any further. My inner toddler had fully asserted itself.

"Uber. Now." I pulled out my phone. "What's the address of the fucking hotel?"

CJ stopped. Turned. Walked back.

Words were exchanged.

The app cheerfully informed me that my driver, Laurent, was 'two minutes away.' Ten minutes later, Laurent was apparently still 'two minutes away,' parked somewhere near a shadowy alley I couldn't locate on the map. Meanwhile, CJ stood nearby, the look on his face saying something like, 'I'm not angry, I'm just disappointed.'

The Uber ride was silent, save for the hum of the engine and my theatrical sighs of exhaustion. By the time we stumbled into the lobby of the Ibis, the day's frustrations had dulled to a faint ache, but our friendship was only slightly worse for wear.

The next morning, CJ and I came downstairs to what passed for a dining area at the Ibis—though in reality, it was just an extension of reception.

We had the foolish optimism of travelers expecting a decent breakfast to fuel us for the big day ahead. Say what you will about the Novotel London West—their hot breakfast was spectacular.

Alas, the Ibis Styles had a different perspective on breakfast.

The room was already packed with our busmates—an early-rising crowd, no doubt. We scavenged what little remained of the sparse continental buffet—a dejected-looking baguette, a few slices of processed cheese, and self-serve coffee—before finding the only available seats near Mole Man and his wife, the grandmotherly woman I'd noticed yesterday.

Mole Man was still wearing his red sweater—now enhanced with a fresh coffee stain near the collar.

After some pleasantries about the optional Cosmic tour they'd done—they were happy, but it sounded shit compared to our incredible experience—I offered an edited version of our excursion, conveniently leaving out the part where I'd acted like a spoiled brat.

George stood and addressed the group.

"Good morning, everyone! I hope you're all rested after last night's tour. It's another big day today, because we're off to the Louvre..."

"Did he just pronounce it 'Loo-ver'?" CJ asked quietly.

"...as well as Sacré-Cœur and Montmartre," George continued. "I'm afraid there's a lot of walking today..."

A collective groan rose from our busmates.

George went on to outline the trip, making special mention of when and where the toilet stops would be.

Twenty minutes later, we were aboard the Cosmic bus, en route to the Loo-ver, kicking off a day that would, more than any other, prove the folly of surrendering control to a tour group.

Mario the bus driver deftly negotiated the roundabout surrounding the Arc de Triomphe, and drove some distance down the Champs-Élysées. Blink and you'll miss it. He then powered-on to the Place du Trocadéro, where, mercifully, we got out of the bus for a short photo op.

"But hurry back," George said. "Mario can only park the bus for fifteen minutes."

Here we saw views of the Eiffel Tower from the opposite side to the Parc du Champ de Mars. I can't speak for all the travelers, but as spectacular as the tower is, I'd seen an awful lot of it yesterday.

Our next stop was at the newly reopened Notre-Dame de Paris.

Well, no. Actually, it was at *Shakespeare and Company*, the world-famous bookstore in the Latin Quarter. From there, we could see Notre-Dame on the L'île de la Cité across the Seine. However, the real purpose of our stop was, of course, a bathroom break.

Missing Notre-Dame stung more than I expected. Could CJ and I have broken away from the group? Sure. But I knew from the start that Cosmic's breakneck itinerary left no room for second chances. I just hadn't realized how much I'd regret it until we were already gone.

In my judgment, splitting our time—self-guided one day, coach tour the next—was the best way to maximize what we could see. It was a trade-off, and while it stings to have missed Notre-Dame, the plan made sense at the time.

Of course, Notre-Dame had already come close to being a miss that could never be remedied, after being tragically gutted by fire in 2019. Restoring it required over a thousand artisans, stonemasons, and engineers, painstakingly reconstructing its medieval grandeur using centuries-old techniques, salvaged relics, and hand-carved oak beams to resurrect what history nearly lost.

It reopened in 2024, and while I missed it, at least it was there to go back to.

Built between 1163 and 1250 AD, this building is heroic in scope.

The interior of the cathedral is 130 meters long by 48 meters wide, with the roof 35 meters above. Two hulking gothic towers flank the western facade.

To achieve this truly epic construction, the architects and engineers pioneered the use of flying buttresses (graceful arched structural supports) and rib vaulting (arched ribs that enable a ceiling to cover a large open area), which allowed Notre-Dame to effortlessly soar (with the addition of the spire) to a height of ninety-six meters. Its enormous stained glass rose windows are, on their own, amazing artistic statements. Clearly, given the splendor of this cathedral, the restoration team had undertaken a daunting task, but this wasn't the first major renovation rescue performed on the old girl.

During the French Revolution, Notre-Dame was desecrated and left in disrepair. It took public interest in the building spurred by the publication of Victor Hugo's *The Hunchback of Notre-Dame* to rally Parisians behind their fallen icon, and the old girl was restored between 1844 and 1864.

Yep, turns out Quasimodo was the real hero of Notre-Dame.

Though I was bummed about missing Notre-Dame, the failure taught me a valuable lesson: I wouldn't make that mistake again.

Bathroom break complete, there was no time for regrets—we had spots to hit. Our crew was back onboard, doing Paris drive-bys like a bus full of decrepit gangstas.

We rolled past the Grand Palais—Pop! Pop! Pop!

We cruised by the Musée d'Orsay—Pop! Pop! Pop!

By the time we hit the Louvre, I was ready to up the stakes. Maybe it was the dangerous look in my eye that spooked the guard in front of the Mona Lisa.

But I'm pushing a metaphor too far, and getting ahead of myself.

Mario eased the bus past the famed glass pyramid and into the Louvre's underground car park, where it disgorged its load of self-funded retirees and misfits. Once lined up outside the bus, George stepped up, flanked by a red-haired woman of indeterminate age.

"Okay folks, this is Lily, our Loo-ver guide.," He indicated the woman, in case we weren't sure. "I'll be taking a backseat here, and she'll lead you through to see the *Venus de Milo*, *Winged Victory*, and, of course, the *Mona Lisa*."

"And whatever else we pass along the way," Lily added in a surprising accent. "And yes, I'm an American. I came ten years ago to do post-graduate work in Paris, and never left."

We dutifully followed Lily into the Louvre—skipping the line, of course. Security was intense—bags were x-rayed, bodies were scanned, and the guards looked amped up enough to tackle a museum heist.

Then, Lily was out of the blocks like a ginger Usain Bolt, daring her aged charges to keep up. We blazed past paintings I'd studied in my art-history days—*Bacchus*, one of da Vinci's lesser-known works, *St. Francis of Assisi Receiving the Stigmata* by Giotto, *Venus and the Three Graces* by Botticelli, and others I recognized but couldn't name.

Lily crossed the finish line in front of the *Venus de Milo*, the ancient Greek sculpture that launched a thousand dad jokes: "Don't mind the *Venus de Milo*—she's 'armless!"

The *Venus de Milo* is a marble masterpiece from ancient Greece's Hellenistic period, and is believed to date to the second century BC. It was unearthed on the island of Milos in 1820; it has been on display at the Louvre ever since.

And yes, she has no arms, but it wasn't that detail that grabbed CJ's attention. He circled her a couple of times, then said:

"Look at her feet."

I looked. "So?"

"Look how big they are compared to her body."

"Yeah," I admitted, "those hoofs would've done justice to Hercules."

This sent CJ spiraling down a rabbit hole of his own making. He examined Venus from every conceivable angle—he'd have up-skirt-ed her if he could. Finally, he said: "See? See that line there? I think they've put two different sculptures together!"

It was an interesting theory, but one we couldn't test then and there, because Lily was already setting a cracking pace toward *Winged Victory*.

The *Winged Victory of Samothrace* is rightly famous as a stunning example of two-thousand-year-old Greek sculpture, but even a history nerd like me struggled to get too excited about it. Sure, what remained was impressive—the wings were exquisitely carved by a master craftsman—but too much was missing to truly captivate me. Knowing what else the Loo-ver held, I had to question why we were lingering here when there was so much more to see.

"Well, that's shit," was CJ's verdict. Unfortunately, I had to agree.

"We'll have a lunch break now," said Lily. "I'll meet you back here at 2:00 pm."

Brilliant.

CJ and I had already spotted a McDonald's in the Louvre's food court, and before we left France, there was one crucial mission we had to complete:

We needed to confirm the veracity of an iconic line from *Pulp Fiction*:

"And you know what they call a Quarter Pounder with Cheese in Paris?... They call it Royale with Cheese."

Clearly, this was the kind of vital research we were born to do.

There are a couple of things I can confirm about McDonald's in the Louvre.

First, it had, without a doubt, the slowest service of any McDonald's I've ever encountered.

Second, the food probably didn't meet McDonald's international quality standards—the burger was small and greasy, and the fries were overcooked and came in a half-empty box.

And as for *Pulp Fiction*? The quote is only partially true. A Quarter Pounder with Cheese is not called a 'Royale with Cheese' in Paris. It's called a 'Royal Cheese'—or at least, that's what it said on the wrapper.

That's Some Erection!

You heard it here first.

We were on time, waiting near the inverse pyramid in the vestibule directly beneath the glass pyramid with a number of our busmates, while Lily began corralling the stragglers. Once they were assembled, she stepped out in front of the group.

"I'm taking you to the Mona Lisa now," she said. "Once we get to the line, if you can call it that, my job will be over. After you've seen it, you have about thirty minutes until you have to meet George in the carpark."

She then sprinted off at her customary pace.

I'd heard the stories about the constant crush of humanity that moves inexorably toward the Mona Lisa, but nothing prepared me for the reality. Of course, the painting's fame guarantees the chaos—but fame is a strange thing. It doesn't always reflect merit.

Sure, the Mona Lisa is a da Vinci, and that adds to its luster, but let's be honest—there's more to it than that. Earlier, I'd seen da Vinci's Bacchus—arguably a better painting, with its dynamic composition and playful sensuality—but I was the only person paying attention.

Not so for the Mona Lisa. Maybe it was the history...

It had been commissioned by Francesco del Giocondo, a wealthy Florentine merchant, as a portrait of his wife, Lisa Gherardini, and da Vinci painted it between 1503 and 1506. However, Signore del Giocondo never got his portrait. Instead, Leonardo carried it around with him, obsessively working on it until two years before his death in 1519.

Art historians rightly praise da Vinci's meticulous attention to detail, his pioneering use of sfumato, the blurred lines that give it that dreamy, soft-focus effect, and his genius for capturing human expression. But even these technical marvels don't fully explain the Mona Lisa's cultural dominance.

But the Mona Lisa wasn't an overnight phenomenon.

For centuries, she hung quietly in private collections and royal palaces, including the French court after King Francis I acquired her in the sixteenth century. Her rise to fame started in the nineteenth century, thanks to French Symbolist poets obsessing over her 'haunting beauty.'

But her global renown skyrocketed in 1911, when Vincenzo Peruggia stole her from the Louvre, believing she belonged in Italy. Her whereabouts remained a mystery for two years—until Peruggia tried to sell her in Florence.

It was this theft that turned the Mona Lisa into a global sensation—nothing boosts artistic fame like a good heist.

In recent years, she's been the target of protests, even taking a can of soup to the face. Luckily, the bulletproof glass didn't flinch.

Does the Mona Lisa deserve this level of attention? Not really. But fame works in mysterious ways—once something goes viral, it's unstoppable. Today, she's more meme than masterpiece—an icon people recognize but rarely engage with beyond snapping a selfie at the Louvre.

Maybe it's just the famous smile—that enigmatic expression acting like a mirror, reflecting whatever meaning we bring to it. Call it sacrilege, but I've never understood what the big deal is.

But for me, the real enigma of the Mona Lisa wasn't the smile, the sfumato, or even her over-the-top fame—it was why the guard locked onto me like a heat-seeking missile.

One second, I was angling my phone for the perfect selfie. The next, he was storming toward me, eyes locked, jaw clenched, like I'd just brandished a can of Campbell's Pea & Ham.

Forty-five minutes after my narrow escape—whatever crime the guard had mentally convicted me of—I was back with the Cosmic crew, making our own getaway en route to Sacré-Cœur.

At the base of Montmartre Hill, we looked up and saw what awaited us—a steep climb that seemed to stretch endlessly toward the sky.

Luckily, the Funiculaire de Montmartre spared us the ordeal. This little cable railway whisked us up the hill in no time, delivering us to the top with minimal effort and maximum gratitude.

And then, George did what George does best: he pointed out the bathrooms.

After that, he gave us time to explore Sacré-Cœur before regrouping for a guided walk through Montmartre.

The Basilica of Sacré-Cœur de Montmartre is hard to miss. It's undeniably beautiful, with its high domes, arches, and intricate mosaics done in a Romanesque-Byzantine style. The whole thing practically glows, thanks to the bright white travertine stone that somehow cleans itself.

For a building that looks so timeless, Sacré-Cœur isn't actually that old. Construction began in 1875 and it was completed in 1914. Perched at the top of Montmartre Hill, it offers some of the best views in Paris. And, as CJ was quick to point out, it's also where they filmed that epic fight scene on the stairs in John Wick: Chapter Four.

But here's the thing—no matter how beautiful it was, I just couldn't warm to it.

It made no sense. What's not to love? It's iconic, beautiful, and the views are spectacular.

At first, I thought maybe it was because Sacré-Cœur wasn't old enough to intrigue a history nerd like me.

But then it hit me—it wasn't the basilica itself.

It was what it represented.

Sacré-Cœur felt like a stand-in for what I'd really wanted to see—Notre-Dame. Seeing it so close yet untouchable was a wrenching reminder of what I'd missed. Standing there at Sacré-Cœur, all I could think about was the experience I'd lost.

It wasn't Sacré-Cœur's fault, but it could never fill the Notre-Dame-shaped hole in my trip.

Or maybe I was just tired—a grumpy hangover from last night. Because I felt the same sense of 'meh' about Montmartre—which, considering my art history background, I really should have loved.

Yes, Montmartre is charming and historic. Yes, it has cobblestone streets and deep artistic roots, tied to Picasso, Van Gogh, and Toulouse-Lautrec.

But that so-called bohemian vibe? I think it packed up and left long ago, replaced by overcommercialization, crowds, and souvenir shops.

The Place du Tertre—which the guidebook said was a: "bustling square filled with artists offering portraits and paintings, surrounded by cozy cafés perfect for people-watching"—felt more like a movie set than a living, breathing neighborhood.

It lacked authenticity.

I couldn't help but imagine Picasso, Van Gogh, and Toulouse-Lautrec's disappointment at seeing Montmartre as it is today. I think they'd have given it a wide berth and found somewhere more real.

It was a relief when George finally announced it was time to head back to the Funiculaire. But on a whim, CJ and I decided to skip the train and walk down the iconic 'John Wick' stairs instead.

"You boys must be energetic," Mole Man said, watching us head toward the steps.

"I can't believe it," said Cruella.

"It's not like we're walking *up* them," CJ pointed out.

"I hope you make it," someone else chimed in.

"Don't fall!" came another voice.

"See you down there," I said with a grin.

As it turned out, we beat the train down—despite stopping a couple of times to reenact scenes from the movie. We really were just big kids, and at least the Montmartre trip ended on a high.

On the bus back to the hotel, I tried to pinpoint the source of my malaise.

This wasn't *Paris Syndrome*—that infamous wave of disappointment some tourists feel when the city doesn't match their romanticized expectations. I wasn't disappointed in Paris. I regretted not seeing *enough* of it. I'm no Francophile, but Paris had more than surpassed my expectations—it was glamorous, historic, chaotic, and alive.

And yet, I felt like I'd been holding my breath the whole time, ticking off one tourist site after another without ever truly being there.

No, this wasn't *Paris Syndrome*. It was something stranger, more specific.

This was *Tour Bus Syndrome*™—the frustration of being dragged through one of the world's most beautiful cities, with every landmark reduced to a Gaussian blur.

I wasn't angry at Cosmic Tours. They'd delivered exactly what they promised—hitting most of the spots I wanted to see. In George, we had a friendly, obliging, and endlessly patient guide.

As for the busmates? Well, that was the luck of the draw.

I certainly wasn't angry at CJ, whose relentless, metronomic walking had dragged me further into the city's heart than I would've ventured on my own. In hindsight, his stubborn pace had shown me more of Paris than the tour ever could.

No, the fault lay squarely with me.

I'd chosen the limitations of a bus tour, knowing full well what that meant. My much-pored-over plan hadn't accounted for the reality of it. Notre-Dame still stung.

And don't even get me started on missing Versailles.

In the end, bus tours are an exercise in letting go. You don't control the pace, the itinerary, or the people you're stuck with. All you can do is embrace the chaos, take what you can from the experience, and move on.

Next time, I'd do Paris differently.

But for now, it was enough to have been here at all.

***

Is Anything Alright?

Over another underwhelming Ibis breakfast the following morning, CJ and I decided to do the Ibis chain a favor and brainstorm a new, more appropriate tagline:

"Ibis: it's French for shit," I offered.

"Ibis: when only the worst will do."

"Nice... what about, Ibis: Our inadequacy makes everything else seem better?"

We amused ourselves like this for a few minutes until George mercifully put the Ibis out of its misery.

"We have a long journey today," George began. "But don't worry, we'll have plenty of bathroom breaks."

"Thank Gawd," came a voice from the back, prompting a ripple of quiet, embarrassed laughter.

"Now, the one thing you have to know about bathrooms in Europe is," George continued, "you have to pay. Usually one euro, but sometimes two."

"What? You have to pay to pee?" The same voice cut in again, louder this time. I turned my head and finally identified the source.

It was Cruella.

"But George," she went on, her tone teetering between outrage and desperation, "what if I don't have any quarters, or whatever they call them?"

"That's why I keep a supply of one-euro coins," George's calm, practiced tone was yet more proof that this was not his first rodeo. "If you don't have any, come and see me, and I'll fix you up."

"Well, that's just ridiculous," Cruella muttered, loud enough for everyone to hear. "Paying to use the bathroom..."

This precipitated murmurs of agreement from many on the bus.

George, ever the professional, nodded sympathetically but stuck to his script. "I know it's not what you're used to, but that's Europe for you. Think of it as just part of the experience."

CJ leaned toward me, smirking, "Cruella's going to have a tough time in Europe."

"I think Europe's going to have a tough time with Cruella."

Today's Cosmic schedule was tight. We only had one day to get from Paris to Lucerne, cutting through a massive swathe of France. Six hundred kilometers, give or take, which should take around six and a half hours. But, of course, that estimate didn't account for rest stops.

The drive was only in its second hour when, bored, CJ and I started naming the passengers. It was a game born out of equal parts amusement and desperation to pass the time.

We already had Cruella ("I don't usually complain, but...") and Mole Man (whose customary red sweater had acquired yet another stain over breakfast). His wife, the grandmotherly woman with iron-gray hair and oversized specs, we'd simply dubbed Grandma—not our finest work, but it fit.

Then, a loud, loaded sniff came from across the aisle.

CJ and I turned to investigate.

There sat a man wearing the most obvious wig I'd ever seen—jet black, poorly blended, and clinging to the last remnants of his real graying, hair like it was holding on for dear life.

As we watched, he took another deep, phlegmy sniff, loud enough to make the hair on the back of my neck stand up.

His wife, seated beside him, was unmoved. She stared straight ahead, her face a mask of practiced indifference, as though this was a sound she'd long since accepted as background noise in her life.

"That's going to get old real fast," I said

"Mr Sniffy?" CJ suggested.

"Sure," I muttered back, "although if we workshop it, I'm sure we can get something in there about the toupee."

"Mr Sniffy works for now," he said. "But give it time, it's a long trip."

As if on cue, Mr Sniffy let out another deep, guttural snort—it was like his skull was filled with oysters. His wife, who must've been even more patient than George, didn't even flinch.

She just kept staring out the window like she was meditating through it.

At the first bathroom stop, in a roadhouse just off the freeway—where two euros was the going rate for the loo—we overheard a couple from our tour speaking in New Zealand accents.

I nudged CJ, nodding in their direction. "How have we not noticed them before?" I asked under my breath.

CJ shrugged. "No idea. They look around our age, too."

It was true. On a bus apparently full of retirees, this couple stood out.

"Have they been here the whole time?" CJ asked, incredulous.

"So it seems," I said.

"G'day," CJ said.

"Kia ora. You guys Aussies?" she asked, her tone warm and curious.

"Yep. Kiwis?"

"Yep."

She was Karen, and he was Kevin, and they were from Christchurch. It turned out they'd only just made the tour in time after arriving from Liverpool, where they'd also done a Beatles tour.

We bonded over our shared love of the Fab Four, they told us about Liverpool, and we mentioned our Daytripper tour with Mike.

"How was it?" Kevin asked. "We're thinking of doing that when we get back to London."

"Magic," I said.

As we walked out of the roadhouse, we spotted Cruella, lips pursed as tight as a drum, desperately dragging on a cigarette. It looked like she was trying to vacuum in every last microgram of nicotine.

If only she had a jeweled ivory cigarette holder and a sack full of puppies—it would've completed her aesthetic perfectly.

"That checks out," said CJ.

"She's a weird one, eh?" said Kevin.

"Hey," said Karen, "have you talked to those people yet?"

She nodded toward a sour-faced man with ruddy cheeks and gray-flecked hair and beard, striding toward the bus. A few steps behind, at a careful distance, followed a pear-shaped woman with a towering beehive—who I assumed was his wife.

"No," said CJ. "Should we?"

"Only if you feel like arguing," said Kevin. "We sat next to them at dinner our first night in Paris."

"I made an innocuous remark about what an idiot Trump is," said Karen, "and how the rest of the world thinks he's a piece of shit."

"He turned even redder and stayed quiet," said Kevin. "Then she pulled out her phone, showed us a meme she'd saved to her camera roll, and started lecturing us on why he's the best president since Lincoln."

"This could be a whole bus full of MAGA nuts," I muttered. "Better to keep our mouths shut."

Kevin laughed. "Then you clearly don't know Karen."

The bus cruised down roads flanked by impossibly green fields. From time to time, we caught glimpses of stone châteaux, castle-like in their grandeur, or the occasional church spire—the only hints of history on this leg of the journey.

About an hour later, we crossed into Switzerland.

By now, George's banter over the mic was routine—a mix of where we were, how long until the next stop, a little local trivia, and the occasional wee or poo joke.

But around this time, he introduced something new: managing expectations.

"Now that we're in Europe, things are going to be a little different," he said. "We already know you have to pay to use the bathroom. And, well, hotel standards won't always match what you're used to back home, either. Customer service might feel different too. My advice? Roll with it and enjoy the experience."

I wasn't sure if this was George responding to grumbles about the Ibis in Paris or if he was preemptively bracing us for something even worse down the road.

Probably both.

We stopped for lunch at another roadhouse—a peculiar structure that straddled the freeway. Identical entrances on either side made it alarmingly easy to get turned around—walk out the wrong door, and suddenly your car was a distant mystery on the other side of the freeway.

Or worse—your bus.

Once again, George's experience came to the fore. He made sure to warn everyone about the potential for confusion. And to my surprise, his advice worked—we didn't have to send out a search party before getting back on the road.

This roadhouse was our group's first encounter with bathrooms staffed by human attendants. Their role seemed... redundant. They'd take your money, insert it into the coin slot on the turnstile for you, and then hand you a receipt.

The receipt, as far as I could tell, entitled you to a free something-or-other.

No one was sure what, because the details were in French.

Walking out of the bathroom, I ran into yet another new busmate around my age—a guy from California named Gerry, who bore an uncanny resemblance to Kevin, the New Zealander.

The biggest differences? A) Gerry was American, and B) he was wearing an orthopedic boot.

"I did that a few days before the trip," he explained, glancing at his moon boot. "I'm an electrician, and, long story short, I fell off a ladder."

As we talked, an attractive Asian woman joined him, followed by an African American woman who appeared to be single.

"This is Sandy," Gerry said, motioning to the Asian woman. "And this is Kate."

We greeted each other politely.

"Honey," Sandy said, handing Gerry the bathroom receipt/special offer. "I think this gets us something for free. Can you find out what it is?"

Gerry dutifully hobbled off to do her bidding.

Later, he told me the 'special offer' turned out to be 25% off a very expensive fruit juice they didn't even want.

Anyone not watching the road signs—half the bus was asleep, so there were quite a few—would've had no idea we'd crossed into Switzerland until George announced the momentous event.

The rest of the trip passed in relative silence.

By the time we arrived in Kriens, a suburb just outside of Lucerne, the sun was disappearing behind the mountains.

Off the bus, the air was brisk—not as cold as the top of the Eiffel Tower, but chilly enough that if you looked into the surrounding hills, you could see snow falling. We retrieved our bags and took shelter in the foyer of our base of operations for the next couple of days: the Holiday Inn Express.

Even at first glance, it was a noticeable upgrade from the Ibis Styles in Paris. However, checking in such a large group was slow, so CJ and I parked ourselves in some lounges and grabbed a couple of beers from the bar.

Some of our busmates followed our lead, and for the first time, we socialized with the group. CJ and I split up and chatted with different people, proving once and for all that we weren't joined at the hip.

As the queue to check in dwindled, our convivial little group began to melt away to retrieve their room keys.

About forty-five minutes after our arrival, we dumped our bags in the room. It was clean and had everything you'd expect from a three-star hotel.

And the beds were a generous distance apart.

Bonus.

After unpacking, CJ and I went foraging for dinner.

As with anything CJ-related, this meant walking about fifty percent more than absolutely necessary in search of craft beer.

Not that there's anything wrong with that.

I'd come to appreciate that, short of being murdered by street thugs (an unlikely scenario in sleepy Kriens), this rambling was an integral part of the experience. By now, darkness had settled, and the cold had grown a little sharper.

After a couple of false starts, including being the only two patrons in the far-too-upmarket-for-us *Alag Bar*, we ended up at the *Bar und Restaurant Ranch*. While there were a few customers inside, they seemed surprised to see us, particularly when we proved to be from Australia. We were hungry and demolished a shit ton of chicken wings, and the local Ittinger Amber Ale washed it down a treat.

However, the undoubted highlight of the evening came when the waiter approached our table and asked, "Is anything alright?"

To which we enthusiastically replied, "Yes! Everything."

The next morning, as we boarded the bus for a tour of Lucerne and St. Stanserhorn, I finally caught a glimpse of the real, unsanitized George.

I stood a couple of meters from the bus, watching my breath turn to condensation, when George strolled up—hands in pockets, a wicked grin on his face. With a slight tilt of his head, he gestured downward.

I followed his gaze.

Is Anything Alright?

At my feet lay an empty Viagra blister pack.

"Looks like that guy had a good night!" George winked and walked off.

From that moment on, CJ and I shared an unspoken bond with George.

He understood the frustrations of being among the youngest on this tour because—as someone close to our age he was facing them too—with the added disadvantage of being in charge of the whole thing.

The cool, calm, and impossibly kind George? That was just a role he played for the benefit of his audience.

The bus trip from Kriens to Lucerne was brief.

Mountains loomed above the old city, their jagged peaks like something lifted from a Toblerone box—a reminder of how surreal this landscape felt compared to my home in Australia.

Below them, Lake Lucerne lay glossy and still, its surface a perfect mirror for the patchwork of buildings—medieval stone, baroque facades, and sleek modernity—crowding its shores.

Unlike Montmartre or Bath, Lucerne felt real—a place people lived in, not just a backdrop for someone's Instagram feed.

Near the shores of Lake Lucerne, I encountered the Cosmic tour's curious 'pee-for-profit' system for the first time.

The arrangement was simple: drop off a busload of incontinent tourists at a business—in this case, a large souvenir shop—and in return, the business grants free access to their toilets.

No purchase necessary.

A win/win—though I imagine the janitor handling post-tour cleanup might have had a different opinion.

With this essential service complete, George led us on a quick walking tour, the first stop being Lucerne's star attraction: the Kapellbrücke, or Chapel Bridge.

Built around 1365, the Kapellbrücke is the oldest wooden covered bridge in Europe, spanning 204 meters across the Reuss River. Its two sections jut out at odd angles from opposite shores, meeting at the Wasserturm (Water Tower)—an octagonal relic that has, over the centuries, served as a prison, a torture chamber, and, perhaps its darkest role yet: a tourist gift shop.

Beneath the bridge's roof, Lucerne's history once unfolded across more than 150 paintings by Hans Heinrich Wägmann. But in 1993, a devastating fire destroyed two-thirds of them, leaving the bridge in need of a $3 million restoration.

The result? A mix of old charm and difficult-to-detect new construction.

At the bridge's entrance, we spotted a 'no dog peeing' sign—a delightful Swiss twist on the Parisian anti-public-urination sign CJ had discovered a couple of days ago. Picture a no-smoking sign, but instead of a cigarette, it's a dog cocking its leg.

I need one for the living room.

Turning west, we strolled along the waterfront, where some of our group peeled off for an optional cruise on Lake Lucerne. We, however, continued north along Zürichstrasse, passing a coffee shop called *Äss Bar*.

Yes, you read that right.

And no, it's not a one-off—Switzerland boasts an entire chain of these unfortunately named establishments.

Our final stop was a small, picturesque park housing Lucerne's other major attraction: the Lion Monument.

Carved directly into a rock wall, the Lion Monument is a stunning, somber relief sculpture of a dying lion, its head bowed, and a spear lodged in its side. It was designed by Danish-Icelandic sculptor Bertel Thorvaldsen and carved between 1820–21 by Lukas Ahorn.

The carving commemorates the bravery and sacrifice of Swiss Guards, who were slaughtered in 1792 while defending Louis XVI during the French Revolution.

And what were the Swiss Guards doing in Paris? Their jobs. These guys were the elite special forces of their time. From the beginning of the sixteenth century, the Royal Household of France had employed a regiment of Swiss Guards as mercenaries. As many as seven-hundred and sixty guards died in the fighting at the Tuileries Palace, and this poignant sculpture is a fitting tribute to their heroic deaths.

Mark Twain once called the Lion Monument 'the most mournful and moving piece of stone in the world,' and standing there, it's hard to argue. Even CJ—whose emotional range usually extends to mourning the closure of his favorite craft breweries (he still hasn't gotten over the demise of Deeds Brewing)—seemed uncharacteristically pensive.

As moving as the Lion Monument undoubtedly is, what made it truly special for me was knowing that Mark Twain once stood here, reflecting on it too. Just the thought of sharing the same spot with one of history's great humorists and travel writers was, well, pretty damn awesome—because, y'know, history.

When the brief walking tour concluded, George unleashed the group for a couple of hours. "Remember, meet the bus outside Casagrande Souvenirs no later than 11:30 am."

CJ didn't need the starting gun—he was off, and I was left scrambling to keep up. He had no idea what he was looking for, but by god, he was going to find it, no matter how far we had to walk.

So it was surprising when he found it almost around the first bend.

West of the Kapellbrücke, we stumbled into a used clothing shop—the kind of place where a bell tinkles as you enter—and CJ discovered the vintage leather jacket he never knew he had to own.

The woman running the shop was the kind of airy bohemian you'd expect to find in a seventies rock documentary. She wore Stevie Nicks-style flowing robes over a Clash t-shirt, paired with scuffed black Doc Martens, and her enthusiasm for sales was about what you'd expect, given her attire.

"Clothes were much better made back then," she said dreamily as CJ held up the jacket.

"How much for this?" he asked.

"I saw the Clash in 1979," she replied vaguely, as if that answered the question.

"The jacket?"

"It really suits you..." she said, before floating to the other side of the shop to straighten a display of vintage t-shirts.

"How much for the jacket?" CJ asked again, this time with a hint of impatience.

"How much do you want to pay?"

"Nothing," CJ said flatly. "But seriously, how much?"

Eventually, after a negotiation that felt like bartering in a parallel universe, they settled on a price. But as CJ pulled out his credit card, she recoiled like a vampire confronting a crucifix.

"It's cash only," she muttered, rummaging around for proof. Eventually, she unearthed a faded cardboard sign that had been lying face down on the counter. "I'm sorry."

And that's how we ended up spending the next thirty minutes wandering Lucerne in search of an ATM. But we eventually found one and the jacket was purchased.

After a quick bathroom break at Casagrande—and the purchase of a fridge magnet (note to retailers: pee-for-profit works)—I dutifully returned to the bus, waiting for George to announce our next move. CJ sat in the seat next to me, the blank expression on his face perfectly mirroring my feelings.

Somewhere along the line, we'd relinquished all responsibility.

Normally, I like to stay one step ahead—knowing what I'm going to see and why it matters. But not today. I had no idea what to expect at Mount Stanserhorn. And honestly, I didn't care.

Somewhere over the course of the morning, I'd become a tourist zombie—shuffling from landmark to landmark, brain half-functioning, snapping photos on autopilot. I'd seen the type: eyes glazed over, lanyards hanging limply from their necks, staggering from photo op to photo op. Now, I was one of them, numb to the routine.

And yet, as the bus rumbled away from Lucerne, I found myself at peace with the unknown ahead. Maybe it was exhaustion, or maybe I'd finally realized that not every moment needed to be crammed with purpose or meaning. For once, I wasn't searching for a story to tell.

For once, it was refreshing to just be curious about what might happen next.

We arrived at the base of Mount Stanserhorn and stepped onto a cobblestone forecourt in front of what looked like a quaint little train station—the kind you might see in Disneyland. The air was brisk, and I kept my hands jammed deep in my jacket's fleece-lined pockets. Above us, fast-moving clouds still obscured the mountains, offering only fleeting glimpses of their splendor.

My eyes followed the train tracks as they curved gently upward into the mist. This wasn't just a train—it was another funicular. As we waited, a wooden carriage emerged from the near-whiteout, its open sides exposing passengers to the elements. The returning tourists didn't look horrified or particularly impressed. A few smiles, maybe, but mostly just blank faces.

Zombies, like the rest of us.

While we stood in the cold, waiting for the carriage to unload and for George to give us the go-ahead, Gerry stumped up to me. His moon boot, for once, must've been an advantage, keeping his lower left leg toasty warm.

"Hey," he said. "I hear you guys are writers."

"Who told you that?"

"I saw CJ writing and asked him," he said. CJ was like that—totally unafraid to put himself out there. Me? I was terrible at self-promotion.

"Yeah," I admitted. "CJ writes fiction, and I write history."

"That's great." Gerry leaned in, clearly interested. We ended up talking for a while about my *Lightbulb Moments* series.

"I'll have to check it out," he said, then raised an eyebrow. "Hey, are you gonna write about this trip?"

"No, of course not."

"Will I be in it?"

"I'm *not* writing about this trip."

A few hundred meters into the funicular ride, the gradient steepened, and the temperature dropped. George had advised CJ and me to stand at the rear of the carriage for the best views. As usual, George was right.

The higher we climbed, the more the clouds parted, revealing mountains that now stood sharp against the gray sky. The grassy landscape alongside the tracks gave way to fir trees, their branches flecked with snow. The air grew colder with every meter.

At the halfway point, we pulled into another station, where an enormous hangar-like structure loomed beside us. This was where we'd switch to our next mode of transportation: the Cabrio cable car.

If the Cabrio's publicity is to be believed, it's the world's first open-top aerial cable car. Passengers normally ride on the open upper deck, accessed by a spiral staircase from the lower cabin, to enjoy breathtaking, unobstructed views. However, for reasons best known to the Cabrio staff, it had been left out of its shed overnight.

The result? The upper deck was buried in snow. So much for unobstructed views. Never mind—what we could see from the enclosed lower cabin was spectacular enough.

Beneath us, lower peaks and checkered green fields stretched out in every direction. Lake Lucerne glowered in the distance, its surface a deep steel-blue. Above, the clouds began to lift, revealing flashes of brilliant blue sky.

The Cabrio glided through a corridor of frosted fir trees, the ground below dusted with snow. Then, at a certain elevation, the scenery transformed. We ascended into the kind of 'winter wonderland' I'd heard so much about but had never seen.

We passed over a small alpine house, its roof thickly coated with fresh snow. It looked like something from an old-fashioned Christmas card, the kind with glitter sprinkled around the edges. Near the summit, the Cabrio slipped back into thick clouds.

At the top, we disembarked into a modern building that housed the Cabrio's mechanism, a gift shop, a restaurant, and a viewing platform buried under the deepest snow I'd ever seen. Outside, the world dissolved into an almost total whiteout.

I stepped gingerly onto the snow-covered platform, unsure how to move in this strange, silent environment. It felt like I'd been transported to a world that didn't belong to me—like Heidi dumped in the surf at Bondi Beach, her boots sinking awkwardly into the sand.

I wasn't a zombie any more, the stunning otherworldly environment had shocked me out of my stupor. I was filled with a kind of childlike wonder.

It took me a while to realize that, despite the heaps of snow around me, it wasn't all that cold up here. Nor was it slippery—at least, not at first. This was my first encounter with deep, powdery snow, so different from the icy, hard-packed stuff I knew back in Australia.

The soft snow lulled me into a false sense of security. It felt forgiving, almost playful, crunching beneath my boots with none of the solid slickness I'd come to associate with 'snow'. But as I ventured toward a high-traffic area—like the stairs—I discovered, to my near peril, that the powder had been trampled into a dense, glassy surface.

The slip, when it came, was quick and unforgiving. My boots skidded out from under me, and for a brief, heart-stopping moment, I was sure I'd go down. Only my white-knuckled grip on the handrail saved me from disaster.

Chastened, I retreated to the safety of deeper snow, where I promptly sank up to my knees.

Meanwhile, CJ was making snowballs and tossing them over the handrail of the viewing platform, watching them explode on the snowdrift ten meters below. He soon graduated to finding thick piles of snow that had built up on the railing and pushing them over the edge—rather like a naughty cat batting objects off a table.

It looked like fun, so I joined him.

After maybe half an hour of this frivolity, during which we circumnavigated the platform that enclosed the building, we ventured inside. There we retrieved our Cosmic-branded 'Cabrio' caps, which had a top section that could be zipped off making them into visors. We then joined the queue for the famed rotating cafe.

CJ and I both ordered the "Stanserhorn Sausage with French Fries on Dark Sauce with Mustard Seeds," because it seemed appropriate (and because nothing else on the menu sounded remotely appealing).

When my plate arrived, the sausage was comically oversized, curving almost halfway around the plate, and drowned in a runny brown liquid that looked suspiciously like gravy. The fries were a Chernobyl yellow, verging on green.

Yet, despite its revolting look, it smelled incredible.

We carried our red plastic trays to a seat near the window on the stationary lower deck of the restaurant. As I watched, the circular middle section of the restaurant, complete with its diners, rotated slowly.

There we were joined by Mole Man—whose sweater had accumulated more food stains since we'd met last—and Grandma. Not long after, Cruella slunk in to complete the awkward quintet.

"Have you been outside?" CJ asked.

"It's amazing," I said through a mouthful of Stanserhorn sausage.

"No. It's freezing," said Granny. "Too cold for us, right dear?"

Mole Man nodded, a thin line of gravy escaping the corner of his mouth.

"I was outside for a while," said Cruella—probably smoking, I figured. "And you can't see anything. Plus, it was too cold."

An awkward silence followed.

"You can really tell we're rotating," said Grandma, breaking the tension.

"Yes," CJ said, "if you look at the—"

Cruella cut him off. "Oh yes," she said, with the absolute confidence of the ignorant. "The whole building is rotating, I can feel it!"

This was patently absurd.

"But, look," I said, gesturing toward the rotating central platform of the room.

"No, no," Cruella insisted. "It's definitely the building."

I opened my mouth to argue but decided against it. Let her have her magic spinning building.

While we were inside, the clouds had cleared, revealing the full majesty of the view. It was breathtaking. From this height, we were above all but the tallest peaks, with the valleys below spread out like a patchwork quilt of fields and forests. Lake Lucerne shimmered in the distance, its surface reflecting the now-blue sky.

It struck me that this was the highest altitude I'd ever been while not airborne. For a moment, I let the absurdity of Cruella's rotating-building theory fade into the background and just took it all in.

The trip back down on the Cabrio was enhanced by the top deck—now free of snow and actually being open. The view was, indeed, amazing, but I'd already seen it all from the top, so it had lost some of its impact.

We boarded the bus and were back in Kriens before we knew it.

CJ and I decided to skip the Cosmic optional Swiss 'cultural dinner,' where attendees were promised, among other things, a "display of alphorns, cowbells, flag throwing, and yodeling."

"Entertainment-wise, I literally can't imagine anything worse," I said to CJ.

"Beer then?"

"Obviously."

We decided to head back to Lucerne, where we'd scouted a few potential spots earlier in the day. The Kriens train station was conveniently close to the Holiday Inn, and with only two stops to Lucerne, we were there in no time.

Looking for a James Bond-style European casino experience, we made a beeline for the *Grand Casino Luzern*. Located in a neo-baroque palace on the shores of Lake Lucerne, the building certainly looked the part—it was easy to picture a tuxedoed Daniel Craig beating the crap out of one of Blofeld's goons on the ornate steps.

Unfortunately, reality didn't match the fantasy. Entering through the back door, we found ourselves in a quiet, empty vestibule. It felt more like the lobby of an underwhelming conference center than an international casino. We wandered aimlessly in search of excitement—slot machines, green baize tables, even a stray croupier—but found nothing. No people. No games. Not even a hint of where such things might be.

After several minutes of fruitless exploration, we gave up and moved on.

To cut a long story short, we walked four kilometers—punctuated by a couple of false starts—before settling on *Bierliebe & Friends*, a busy craft brew pub with a cool vibe.

I ordered a Hazed and Confused, a cloudy New England IPA that sparked my new obsession with hazy IPAs. CJ opted for a Happy End pale ale.

At least, that's where we started.

"This is infinitely better than yodeling," CJ said, raising his glass.

"Infinitely," I agreed, clinking his glass a little too hard.

One of my photos from the night shows a table with two mouthwatering burgers and a plate of what I assume were mozzarella sticks. Sadly, I can't tell you how they tasted—or what else we drank.

Since Bill Cosby wasn't in attendance, I can only attribute this memory gap to excessive beer intake.

What I do know is that we made it back to Kriens without incident.

If I'd been in any fit state to reflect on the day, I might have thought about how easily I'd slipped into—and then out of—tourist zombie mode. There's a strange comfort in surrendering to the rhythm of a tour, letting someone else plan your steps—unless, of course, those steps involve yodeling and cowbells.

Sometimes, I realized while fumbling with Pappy's mask, it's okay to let go—to follow the herd for a while.

As long as you never forget: *you're* the black sheep.

***

I Slept Through George Carlin

"Do you remember much about last night?" I said, pinching the bridge of my nose.

"I remember you snored," CJ said in a bitter tone.

"Oh. Sorry."

That wasn't supposed to happen with a CPAP, but it seemed with Pappy's intermittent malfunctions, all bets were off. In fairness to my beleaguered machine, drinking as much beer as I had last night must've made its job nearly impossible.

"You sounded like a fucking chainsaw," he added.

Clearly, Pappy wasn't working properly. Maybe that was why I was so exhausted.

Or maybe it was walking fifty kilometers a day to drink ten pints of beer. Whatever was causing it, it was the kind of bone-deep exhaustion I'd only felt a couple of times in my life.

"Haven't felt this tired since we were in Vegas," I said, rubbing my face.

CJ groaned. "You mean the time you slept through George Carlin?"

"I didn't sleep through *all* of it."

"You slept through enough."

Las Vegas: May 1986

The Contiki West Coast USA tour had pulled into Vegas over a day-and-a-half before, and since then, I hadn't slept. The first night, the tour took us through the main casinos—*Caesar's Palace, Dunes,* and

Circus Circus—as well as the smaller, seedier joints like *Sassy Sally's* and Glitter Gulch.

When the bus returned to the hotel and the sensible people went to bed, CJ and I stuck around the in-house gaming rooms. Why not? The longer we played, the more free drinks we got. Breakfast was free too—at least I think it was breakfast.

I'd budgeted $500 to blow in Vegas—a holiday expense. So far, I was only down $100, and the way things were going, I wouldn't be sleeping for a while. CJ was in the same boat.

But it wasn't because we were great gamblers.

The way we figured it: casinos hooked their customers with free drinks and small wins on the slot machines, grooming them to graduate to the tables—where the real money was lost. Between the free food, free drinks, and hours of 'entertainment,' I was getting my $100 worth.

The rumors were true. Vegas casinos never displayed clocks, and hours could just vanish. I looked at my Seiko calculator watch—surely the pinnacle of wrist-worn technology—it was 8:00pm.

"I need a shower and clean clothes," CJ said, sniffing his armpits. "We should get back to our room. Carlin's on at 10:30pm."

"I need sleep," I replied. But there was no time. I'd been living on No-Doz, but caffeine tablets had their limits—the label was very clear: No more than six tablets should be taken within twenty-four hours. I'd taken seven.

George Carlin had been a default choice. We could've seen Wayne Newton at the Hilton (a hard no from both of us), the Pointer Sisters at Caesar's (I was ambivalent, but CJ vetoed it outright), or George Carlin at the Riviera.

"Never heard of him," I said.

"You haven't heard 'Seven Words You Can Never Say on Television'?" CJ raised an eyebrow. "That's a classic. We gotta see Carlin."

"I'll take your word for it. Carlin it is."

And so it was, showered and dressed in the cleanest clothes we had, CJ and I began the trek from our hotel (off the Strip, naturally) into Vegas proper. The neon lights felt close enough to touch, a garish twinkle just four, maybe five kilometers in the distance. An easy walk for two young men in their early twenties—or so we thought.

We were sharp dressed men that night: I went for a 'classic' look—cream sports jacket, white shirt, blowfly green tie, and black pants. In contrast, CJ was going through his *Miami Vice* stage—a linen suit with the jacket sleeves rolled up.

Disaster struck a kilometer in. CJ, limping, stopped dead and rubbed his thighs.

"I need to change these fucking pants."

"Did you shit them?"

"No. They're chafing."

"Baby powder?"

"Fuck you."

The detour added another couple of kilometers to our trip, and as the minutes ticked by, we started to realize the Strip was much farther than it looked. The neon lights that had seemed so close taunted us from the horizon as we trudged along, sweating and swearing under our breath. We finally stumbled into the *Riviera* with just ten minutes to spare—and I was already running on fumes.

The room was a blur of cigarette smoke and neon light. This was a dinner show, and instead of being in auditorium seating, we were at long tables with strangers.

The crowd roared as Carlin walked onto the stage—a living legend, or so CJ told me.

And yet, as the first punchline landed, I felt my eyelids grow heavier. The adrenaline and caffeine of the past thirty-six hours had finally run out. Somewhere between his riff on religion and his rant about the seven dirty words, my eyes closed.

I'd fought it as hard as I could, but in the end, I surrendered to the void...

... and slept through George Carlin.

Europe: Present day

All these years later, I'd learned to appreciate George Carlin. But the Great Man was gone now, and I'd missed my one chance to experience his brilliance. I'd been there physically, not mentally—too drained to take in what was right in front of me.

That memory lingered, a quiet reminder of how easily exhaustion or distraction can steal moments that matter.

The stretch between Lucerne and Venice was a long one, winding through the Alps—first up and over them, then beneath them, through a tunnel that seemed endless. When we emerged on the other side, it was as if the world had shifted. The cool alpine air gave way to warmth, the clouds dissolved, and the sky opened into a brilliant, sunlit blue. It felt full of promise and something distinctly Italian.

Passing through the northern outskirts of Milan, the Cosmic tour bus rumbled on toward Verona, where we had a major stop planned. I was looking forward to it—Verona, the city of Romeo and Juliet, romance and history. But as we pulled into town, it became clear we hadn't arrived alone.

It seemed like the whole of Italy had descended on Verona that day. The streets were packed with people waving flags, cheering, and spilling out of cafes and piazzas in a cacophony of festive energy.

"These guys seem happy for a Thursday," said CJ.

"It's Liberation Day," said George who was walking nearby, "a national holiday."

"What were they liberated from?" I asked.

"They're celebrating their freedom from the fascists at the end of World War II," George explained.

"But they *were* the fascists in World War II," I said, dodging a man waving a flag so absurdly large that even Mussolini would've considered it overkill.

"I wouldn't tell *them* that," CJ indicated the crowd surrounding us.

The atmosphere was electric, but with the energy came anarchy.

Every cobblestone street was jammed with revelers, every café was bursting at the seams, and, of special significance to Cosmic Tours travelers, every bathroom had lines running around the corner.

With difficulty and no little skill, George led us into town, and we eventually found ourselves—along with thousands of others—outside the Verona Arena, an ancient Roman amphitheater that predates the Colosseum by fifty years. Unlike the Colosseum, however, the Verona Arena remains a living venue, regularly hosting up to 22,000 patrons for concerts and events. In its heyday, it could hold 30,000 Romans, eager to witness gladiatorial combat and other blood-soaked spectacles.

I'm ashamed to admit I had no idea the Verona Arena even existed. It was just another glorious surprise that came with being a tourist zombie—wandering from site to site, phone in hand, only half-aware of the history I was stumbling into.

"Because of all these people," George shouted, trying to be heard over the exuberant crowd. "It will be impossible to give you a brief tour as I hoped."

"I can't hear you, George!" Cruella screeched, her voice slicing through the noise like a dagger. Thirty other Cosmic heads nodded in agreement, their faces a mixture of confusion and mild panic.

George took a deep breath, repeated himself louder, then added, "I suggest you head in this direction. It's the way to the Juliet House and Museum. We'll meet back here in two hours."

He may as well have yelled, "Every man for themselves!" because within moments, people scattered in every direction, clutching tourist maps, valuables, and only a vague idea of what to do next.

CJ started walking in the general direction of the Juliet House. I struggled through the crowd to keep up.

We wandered into the Piazza delle Erbe, a square that had been the heart of Verona since Roman times. Surrounded by colorful medieval buildings adorned with faded frescoes and bustling market stalls, it was easy to imagine the centuries of life that had unfolded here—from gladiators to merchants to tourists like us.

In the center of the square stood a small, four-pillared stone structure. Unassuming at first glance, it was undeniably antique. It looked like an old whipping post, complete with a rusted metal chain still attached. The chain ended in a manacle—its purpose unmistakable and unsettling.

What caught my attention, though, was the child playing with it. He tugged and swung the chain back and forth, laughing as if it were a playground toy.

I stared for a moment, struck by the absurdity: a relic of punishment turned into a plaything. Once, someone had been shackled there, bleeding to death. Now, centuries later, a child giggled as he twirled the chain.

Shaking off the thought, we continued our walk, making our way toward Juliet's balcony.

The whole concept of Juliet's balcony seemed absurd. *The Most Excellent and Lamentable Tragedy of Romeo and Juliet* was a play by William Shakespeare—a work of fiction. How could this balcony be anything but a tourist trap?

And yet, Shakespeare's tale was inspired by an earlier poem, which in turn drew from even older Italian works. Maybe, just maybe, there was a sliver of truth buried beneath the legend.

Not really.

The balcony in question was a twentieth-century addition to a thirteenth-century house—a blatant attempt to cash in on Verona's most famous fictional lovers. The whole thing felt less about history and more about selling tickets and vague romantic fantasies.

As if the rampant commercialism of the balcony weren't bad enough, the courtyard beneath it was dominated by a bronze statue of Juliet. According to local tradition, rubbing her right breast supposedly brought good luck.

There were pictures online: she stands frozen mid-gaze, her expression wistful, and her right breast polished to a high shine from years of being groped by tourists. Honestly, I would've loved to see it—if only for the kitsch value.

But alas, the crowds had us beat. We had less than an hour until George's assigned meeting time, and this rabble—it certainly wasn't a line—wasn't moving.

Groping Juliet's boob would have to wait. Time was up, and the crowd wasn't moving. We turned back toward the rendezvous point, weaving through Verona's packed streets.

On the way, we spotted a knot of Cosmic busmates lined up for the bathrooms, their faces etched with varying degrees of urgency and despair.

As we watched, Kate from the Cosmic tour reached the front of the line. She approached the bathroom attendant, a stern-faced woman stationed by the door with a cash box, taking the two-euro entry fee.

What happened next was a masterclass in cultural miscommunication.

There was some disagreement—perhaps over the exact amount, or Kate's apparent lack of small change. Frustrated, and no doubt desperate to pee, Kate pushed a handful of coins across the counter in what she must have thought was a gesture of goodwill.

The attendant did not see it that way.

With a look of pure indignation, she swept the coins back at Kate in one dramatic motion, sending them clattering to the floor. A tense silence fell over the line as everyone froze, watching the exchange like it was the opening act of a Shakespearean tragedy.

"How darest thou cast thy vile coinage upon me, thou frothy, fat-kidneyed, incontinent knave!" might have been the attendant's lines.

"I dost spit upon thee, for thou art an errant, plume-plucked lewdster!" might have been Kate's Bard-scripted reply.

Instead, our bus mate simply stood there, stunned, while the attendant glared, arms crossed and unmoving. In the end, some manner of truce must have been reached, for Kate was granted passage into the Holy of Holies.

And in something else approaching a miracle, the entire group reconvened with George at the assigned hour. Despite the day's chaos, we had somehow managed to corral ourselves—a small victory in the grand circus that was Cosmic Tours.

I was reluctant to leave Verona. It deserved far more time than we'd given it. Its history, beauty, and, yes, even its absurd tourist traps warranted a slower, more appreciative visit. But Cosmic waits for no one, and soon we were back on the bus, leaving the holiday crowds behind as we made our way toward Venice.

Well, sort of Venice.

Because, as with all things Cosmic, there was—of course—a catch.

"We're now going straight to our accommodation at Hotel Poppi," George announced over the bus's crackling PA system, "which is just outside Venice."

I frowned.

Venice is, famously, an island.

What could "just outside Venice" possibly mean? I imagined our hotel teetering on the edge of a canal or perhaps tucked away on some obscure neighboring islet. As it turned out, "just outside Venice" meant a mainland location—a fifteen-minute drive to the dock.

Hotel Poppi, however, was a world unto itself.

Imagine *The Shining* as a goofball comedy. Now imagine the Overlook Hotel in that universe. It wasn't that the hotel or service was bad, per se. It was just that everything felt slightly... off. The food, the decor, the service—none of it was outright terrible, but all of it was just a little wrong, like a painting hung slightly crooked on the wall.

I wish I had some grand anecdote about Hotel Poppi's eccentricities, but its weirdness was maddeningly subtle. No glaring issues. No spectacular comedic mishaps. No Basil Fawlty-style meltdowns. Just a persistent, low-grade hum of oddness—a nagging sense that something was always just a little off.

The hotel was located near a supermarket and liquor store, but getting there required a death-defying trek. No footpath, just a hundred meters of dodging Italian traffic on a very busy road.

Even CJ, usually unfazed by such things, thought better of it.

So we ate and drank at the hotel bar instead. The food was… fine. Nothing wrong with it, but nothing worth mentioning either—except for one surprise standout. CJ had the crème brûlée for dessert, and in his words, it was "exceptional."

I was at the bar getting another round when the unmistakable whiff of stale cigarettes hit me. I turned.

Cruella.

To my credit, I didn't scream. I didn't gasp. I didn't even flinch.

"Gerry tells me you're writing about this tour," she said.

"Gerry's mistaken," I replied. "I'm writing about the historical sites we visit."

"Will I be in it?"

'Well, you are a crumbling ruin from a bygone era,' was what I *wanted* to say.

Instead, I just smiled and shook my head.

The next morning, after winding through a seedy industrial area, our bus pulled into the marina. In the distance, Venice shimmered on the horizon, its buildings floating on the water like a mirage. The dockside, however, was decidedly less poetic—a briny tang mingled with the unmistakable stench of rotting fish.

Lined up at the dock was an array of sleek, modern vessels—shiny, streamlined, and clearly equipped to whisk us to Venice in style. But by now, we all knew better. Not even Cruella harbored the illusion that one of those boats was meant for us.

Sure enough, as soon as we stepped off the bus, George directed us straight past the luxurious crafts to a low-slung, white-and-blue wooden ferry—the kind that inevitably shows up in catastrophic tourist disaster reports.

Looking at the vessel, I could almost hear the news anchor's voice: "Sixty-five people drowned today after a Venice-bound cruise took a deadly turn."

The gangplank was narrow and wobbly, a genuine test of balance for many in our group. And the struggle didn't end there. After stepping onto a small, flat landing, we were met with five steep, rickety steps leading to the cramped seating area below deck.

It was shaping up to be yet another classic Cosmic experience.

For Gloria, the African-American lady with the walking frame, this was a bridge too far.

"I'm *not* going down there," Gloria said.

"Well, you can't stay up here, Mom," said Sharon, one of her daughters, with a note of exasperation.

"I can sit right here," Gloria declared, unfolding the padded seat attached to her walking frame.

"It's not safe," Liz, her other daughter, countered.

I jumped in, "I'm staying up here. I'll make sure she doesn't go over the edge!"

"See, girls?" Gloria said with a laugh, a girlish sound that seemed to defy her years. "I'll be fine."

Gloria was everything I hoped to be in twenty-five years—resilient, adventurous, and unflinching, even as her body was letting her down. But more than that, she still had all her marbles and her sense of humor, qualities lacking in too many of the Cosmic crowd. Her daughters were wonderful too—kind, supportive, and willing to travel with her and look after her.

Gloria had it right.

Once the entire Cosmic group had clambered aboard the low-ceilinged ferry, George took to the microphone. In his familiar, calm way, he outlined the plan for the day.

"So," George said, "Glass-blowing first. Optional tour meets at Dock A at 1:00. Everyone else, same place at 5:00 for the ferry home. Questions?"

Mole Man raised his hand. "Will there be bathrooms?"

"There are bathrooms when we get to the glass-blowing demo," George replied. This, of course, was to be the second coming of the infamous pee-for-profit deal, this time at the Murano Glass Shop.

For the first time since Paris, CJ and I had signed up for the optional tour. We actually had no idea what it was, but for reasons I can't fully explain, neither of us had high expectations for Venice. We figured we'd need the tour to help pass the time.

As our ferry continued toward Venice, the skyline sharpened into focus. The Campanile di San Marco, the bell tower of St. Mark's Basilica, rose high above the city, flanked by the majestic dome of Santa Maria della Salute. The Doge's Palace came into view, its intricate façade a promise of grandeur, followed by St. Mark's Square and, finally, the Lion of Venice column.

We cruised past the entrances to narrow canals, and if you looked closely, you could spot some of Venice's famed bridges arching gracefully over the waterways.

But it wasn't always like this.

"Venice shouldn't exist," I muttered as we pulled into the dock.

"Well, that's promising," CJ said.

"I mean, who looks at a swamp and thinks, 'Let's build a city here?'"

Turns out, desperate fifth-century Romans did. Their empire was collapsing, barbarian hordes were storming through Italy, and the Venetian Lagoon was the one place nobody wanted to invade. So they built on it.

And somehow, it worked. By the Renaissance, Venice was the Dubai of its day—dripping in gold, silk, and power-hungry merchants. If they could've built the Burj Khalifa, they would have.

And they certainly could've afforded it.

Then, like all good monopolies, they got complacent.

Trade routes changed, and the city became the eighteenth century equivalent of a Blockbuster Video. By the time Napoleon's troops rolled in, it was so past its prime that the French army took it without a fight.

But Venice refused to drown—literally.

Even now, the city reeks of both grandeur and decay.

Our ferry pulled into the dock, full of people already trying to leave.

"Still think this place shouldn't exist?" CJ asked.

I glanced around at the sinking buildings, the murky canals, and the absurd number of overpriced souvenir stands.

"I stand by my assessment."

Once on dry land, George led us along the docks, past the Doge's Palace and into St. Mark's Square, which was already bustling. There were too many people and, it seemed, not enough time for tour guide speeches.

We bustled across the square, through a colonnade, into a lane, across a bridge, through another lane, up some stairs, and finally arrived at Murano Glass.

Even CJ and I needed the bathroom after that.

Once refreshed, we assembled in a stifling room with tiered seating facing a glowing kiln. Heat rolled off it in waves, making the already heavy air feel even thicker. Nearby the kiln sat a bald-pated man with a spade-like beard and glasses. He wore gray cargo pants, an old gold sweater, and was seemingly impervious to the heat. Beside him stood a smooth-talking Murano Glass representative, narrating the glassblowing process while the craftsman demonstrated.

With the effortless precision of a man who had absolutely done this a thousand times before, the craftsman blew a glowing bubble of molten glass through his long blowpipe. The orange-red sphere swelled, wobbling slightly, before he seized a set of metal tongs and began shaping the fragile orb like a sculptor working in fast-forward.

Within moments, it was a delicate glass flower—intricate, beautiful, and so impossibly perfect that it felt like it should be displayed in a museum.

The crowd murmured in admiration.

And then, with zero hesitation and the casual indifference of a man discarding an old sandwich, the craftsman plunged it straight back into the fire.

A collective gasp rippled through the audience.

Someone behind me whispered, "What a shame."

But before anyone could fully process the artistic murder we had just witnessed, our guide smoothly stepped forward, hands clasped, his smile unchanged.

"Some beauty is fleeting," he intoned, as if his underling had not just emotionally traumatized half the audience. "But I'm about to show you some beauty you can take home. Follow me, please."

Glassmaking had been a Venetian specialty since at least the eighth or ninth century, but by the late 1200s, it was *the* place for it. There was just one problem: the furnaces. One stray spark, and Venice's wooden buildings could go up like a medieval bonfire.

In 1291, the authorities decided they'd rather not deal with that and exiled all glass furnaces to Murano, a nearby island. It turned out to be a brilliant move—not just for fire prevention, but for keeping Venice's glassmaking techniques under wraps. These artisans were so valuable they were forbidden to leave the Republic under penalty of death.

Because nothing says "we appreciate your craftsmanship" like a government-mandated travel ban.

From there, Murano took off, churning out impossibly intricate goblets, chandeliers, and enough delicate trinkets to keep noble households drowning in fragile opulence.

Once the demonstration ended, we were funneled into the adjoining showroom, where things took a sharp turn into infomercial territory. The room was packed with shimmering glassware, most of it leaning toward the 'expensive but gaudy' end of the spectrum.

Our host—a man who had definitely sold things before (used cars, photocopiers, his soul)—picked up a delicate tray lined with vividly colored wine glasses and a matching pitcher, holding it aloft like it was the Holy Grail.

"How much would you expect to pay for this?" he asked, in his best Italian approximation of an infomercial host.

Nothing, I thought. It doesn't interest me at all. No one else ventured an opinion either.

Unperturbed, he pressed on. "We usually charge €3,000 for this, but for you today, only €1,800—delivered to your home, undamaged!"

"Well, that's a relief," CJ muttered under his breath.

Our busmates, most of whom I guessed were on modest incomes, didn't seem tempted by the offer. Sensing the lack of enthusiasm, Mr. Murano quickly pivoted to lower-priced items. We drifted through the displays, admiring the craftsmanship required to create such over-the-top pieces.

One, however, caught CJ's eye: a large blue glass ornament that must have weighed nearly ten kilograms. Unlike the gaudy trinkets surrounding it, this piece was strikingly elegant—sleek, modern, and undeniably chunky.

CJ beckoned me over but stopped me before I got too close.

"What do you reckon it's worth?" he asked.

"I don't know... €4,000?" I guessed, based on Mr. Murano's previous pricing.

"Nope... €15,000! That's..." he paused for a quick mental calculation, "around $24,000 Australian!"

I gulped. You could buy a compact car for that price.

Meanwhile, Mr. Murano had finished wringing all he could out of our group. A significant number of our busmates now clutched Murano bags filled with ten-piece sets that, I was sure, would become sixty-piece sets by the time they got home. Somehow, CJ and I had escaped empty-handed.

"That stuff really isn't my style," CJ said. "Even if I could afford it."

"Same for me. Impressive skills, though."

"Obviously, some people love it," said CJ.

"It's a bit like Venice, really," I said, "Beautiful and historic, but not to my taste."

"I thought you were the history guy."

"Even I have my limits."

Once freed from the Murano shop, CJ and I wasted no time distancing ourselves from our busmates. We made our way back to St Mark's Square, soaking in as much of the atmosphere as we could. Even with the crowds, one thing was impossible to miss: the Winged Lion.

This is the Lion of St Mark, the symbol of the Venetian Republic, and you can't escape it. It's perched on the pinnacle of the Basilica of St Mark, it decorates building facades, it's stamped on t-shirts, and most impressively, it takes the form of a 4.5-meter bronze statue standing atop a column in the square.

Napoleon himself couldn't resist swiping it during his 'international art thief' phase. However, after his defeat at Waterloo, the Lion of St Mark was returned to Venice. But Venice isn't its original home. It's now believed this three-metric-ton sculpture was cast in China between the seventh and tenth centuries.

Venetians are obsessed with St. Mark the Evangelist. He's their patron saint, and, according to tradition, he—much like CJ and me—passed through Venice during his European tour.

That, however, is where the similarities end.

Neither CJ nor I are likely to meet our end being dragged through the streets of Alexandria with ropes around our necks. Nor is it likely that our followers would steal our remains from Alexandria and smuggle them to Venice.

But that's exactly what happened to St. Mark. Today, whatever's left of him rests inside the Basilica of St. Mark.

Yet, despite our shared credentials as European travelers, CJ and I decided not to make a pilgrimage to the bones of the saint. Instead we left St Mark's Square and ventured into the winding laneways of Venice, dodging oncoming tourists with aplomb.

We crossed bridges, wandered through archways, stopped for a beer at the 'venerable' *Devil's Forest Pub* (est 1991!), scuttled down laneways, and—of course—passed countless souvenir shops. Along the way, we each grabbed a slice of thick-crust pizza-slash-focaccia called a pizzaccia.

Then, by sheer luck, we emerged at the Grand Canal and the Rialto Bridge.

Built in the late 1500s, the Rialto Bridge is the oldest bridge across the Grand Canal. It's a stone arch spanning the canal's narrowest point; it sits in the heart of Venice, with a wide, rectangular deck that holds two rows of shops flanking three walkways.

It also holds an alarming number of people, as CJ and I discovered. We shouldered our way to the handrail to snap the obligatory photos of gondolas gliding below. Then we fought back through the crowd to reach the other side.

The bridge was designed by Antonio da Ponte, who won a competition to replace the Ponte della Moneta—a wooden bridge that had collapsed and been rebuilt countless times. Critics argued that a 25-meter single stone arch was far too ambitious and would soon join its predecessors at the bottom of the canal. Over 400 years later, though, it's still standing strong—proving the doubters wrong.

"Did you know," I asked as we walked, "in Casanova's time, Venice was the Vegas of Europe, full of loose women and gambling houses?"

"He'd hate it now, then,' CJ said.

It was true. We'd passed all manner of tourist-oriented boutiques, cafes, the ubiquitous souvenir shops, and so many old churches I lost count.

But there were no loose women in sight.

This was thirsty work, so we ducked into the *Ciak Bistro* where we each had a couple of pints of Birra Moretti IPA. We sat outside right next to the Campiello San Toma, a seventeenth-century baroque church.

"I'm going to ask you a question," I said to CJ. "I think I know the answer, but I don't want to influence your response."

"Okay..."

"What time do we have to meet George for the tour?"

"1:30 pm" CJ responded with confidence.

"Good, that's what I thought too."

"We better start getting back."

We left the *Ciak Bistro* and began to navigate our way back to the rendezvous point when after a few minutes CJ suddenly said, "Where's your backpack?"

"Shit!"

I'd hung it on the chair at the bistro, keeping it close for safety—only to forget it entirely in a city notorious for thieves and pickpockets. We sprinted back, bracing for the worst, but to my relief, the backpack was still draped over the chair, untouched.

Without missing a beat, we turned and raced back to the dock, miraculously arriving just before 1:30. But there was no sign of George or the Cosmic crowd. We waited. A few minutes passed. Still nothing.

CJ messaged George: *We're at Dock 1B. Are we at the right place?*

George's response: *Right place, wrong time. We left 30 minutes ago.*

"I could've sworn he said 1:30," said CJ.

"Me too."

"We have a couple of hours to kill, and I can't go back there," CJ said, nodding toward the throngs of people surging toward St. Mark's Square.

"Agreed."

"Let's head up this way," CJ said, already moving in the opposite direction toward the Castello district. We followed, and the bustling crowds began to thin, though the architecture and canals remained just as stunning.

Before long, Venice felt almost deserted. Clotheslines stretched between rustic buildings over narrow canals, their fabric swaying gently in the breeze. We wandered through quiet laneways, where the romantic disrepair was interrupted only by the occasional faint smell of sewage.

So why does Venice smell—let's be blunt—like actual shit?

Sure, shit plays a role, but the real culprit is the canals. In summer, stagnant water brews a pungent cocktail of organic matter and pollutants. Add an overworked sewage system struggling to handle battalions of excreting tourists, sluggish low tides that let everything linger, pollution from boats, and the occasional algal bloom, and voilà—Venice's infamous eau de canal.

Yet here, on the quieter side of town, while the occasional unpleasant waft still hit, it was intermittent. And here, at least, it was easy to distract oneself from the odor.

"Check that out," I said, pointing across a canal to a third-floor window. Framed as if by an old master was a young woman—her back resting against one side of the window frame, a leg dangling indolently out the window, completely absorbed in her book.

I thought he hadn't heard me, so I repeated myself. But he had. He stood still, almost like one of the statues we'd seen earlier, before slowly raising his phone toward the window.

"No point," I laughed. "She has clothes on."

CJ snapped the photo anyway and turned to me.

"You know the 'mindless wandering' you say I'm always leading you on?"

"I prefer 'relentless, metronomic marching,' but sure, go on."

"That's why." He inclined his head toward the window. "We've seen the landmarks, the history, the crowds. But that? That's the Venice people live in. The one that's not for sale."

"Wow, didn't realize you felt that way."

"What can I say?" CJ gazed off into the middle distance. "I'm a complex human being."

This was the side of CJ I rarely encountered.

Sure, he can be reflective, even deep when the moment takes him, but this felt different—more contemplative, as if Venice had stirred something in him beyond the usual curiosity.

For a guy whose lifelong devotion to Kiss was as loud and unapologetic as their music, it was surprising to see him captivated by something so quiet and understated. But maybe that's what made him tick—he could switch from Gene Simmons vomiting fake blood to moments like this, which hit just as hard.

He took one last glance at the window, then shook off his reflective mood. "Now, where was that grappa bar, again?"

But before we could get there, we had to get back to the touristy side of Venice. We moved into a district that was hosting part of La Biennale di Venezia, the city's annual art festival. We checked out an exhibition by Sam Spratt called *The Monument Game*, which featured a series of digital paintings paired with written psalms that tell a 'story about the rediscovery of our most ancient human values in a post-historic world.'

I may not have fully grasped Mr. Spratt's work, but it *was* cool.

Eventually, we made it back to the dockside area. On our way to the bar, we passed a doorway with an inscription: 'Franz Kafka stayed here in September 1913, writing love letters to Felice Bauer.'

It was a reminder of Venice's ghosts—and of why I'd come here in the first place: history.

How many legends had passed through these dockside lanes?

Had Marco Polo walked this way before setting off for China? Had Casanova seduced a barmaid in that doorway? Had Vivaldi wandered here, humming an early version of The Four Seasons? What about painters like Titian, Tintoretto, or Bellini?

More importantly, had any of them drunk at the grappa bar?

The place turned out to be called *Snack Bar Arcobaleno*—Rainbow Snack Bar. A tiny, no-frills hole in the wall, it felt like the kind of spot locals forgot existed. We were the only customers. We downed a couple of rocket-fuel grappas, steeling ourselves for the inevitable reunion with the Cosmic crew.

Just as we were about to leave, a woman's voice erupted from a nearby apartment. She was screaming at a man in rapid-fire Italian, her tone sharp enough to cut Murano glass. A man's voice shot back. From the little I could catch, it sounded like he'd done something unforgivable.

It was heated—thumps of heavy objects, the crash of glass. For a second, I wondered if we were about to be ear-witnesses to bloody murder.

But as suddenly as it began, it died down.

It felt like the perfect counterpoint to the woman in the window—two sides of Venice, both more real than anything we'd seen on the tourist side of the island.

"What happened?" Kevin asked when we met the tour group at the dockside.

"Yeah, I thought you guys were coming with us," said Karen.

"We were," I said, "but we both forgot the meeting time."

"A good thing too... you didn't miss anything," said Kevin.

"We went to a lace-making factory on Burano," Karen added, letting out an exaggerated yawn. "I think I aged fifty years just standing there."

"Well," CJ said with a smirk, "at least now you'll fit right in on a Cosmic tour."

We boarded the same blue-and-white ferry, and once again, I stood in the open air with Gloria, watching the skyline of Venice fade into the horizon, its spires and domes dissolving into the mist.

I thought back to CJ's epiphany—the young woman reading in the window. At the time, I'd laughed it off, but now I wondered—why hadn't I felt the same way? Maybe I'd been too focused on the surface, too caught up in checking off sights and stories to let the city truly sink in.

Maybe I was just too shallow to get it.

The jury's still out.

Venice had been worth the visit—its beauty undeniable, its history palpable. But would I return, like so many others?

Maybe Venice keeps its secrets for those who come back, willing to look beyond its surface. Or maybe, like the woman in the window, it's best admired from afar—perfectly framed and left untouched.

I wasn't sure.

Like I told CJ—even I have my limits.

***

Dante's Leather Emporium

As I lay in bed waiting for the alarm, I already knew today was going to be tough.

Paris had hammered the lesson home: some places demand more than a cursory glance.

Florence was one of them.

The Cosmic tour was scheduled to breeze through the city today, and I already knew the included tour wasn't going to cut it.

This time, though, I was prepared for the crushing disappointment. I'd seen the itinerary. I knew before even booking the trip that this part of the tour would feel laughably inadequate.

One day in Florence?

Who were they kidding?

No one who loved art and history could possibly do justice to Florence in one day. It was absurd—but I'd signed up for it.

I consoled myself with a plan. Today would just be reconnaissance—a smash-and-grab raid. I'd see what I could, make mental notes, and come back for the rest another time. Florence wasn't going anywhere.

Still, knowing this didn't make it any easier.

There wasn't even time for CJ and me to break off and explore on our own. No, we were stuck with Cosmic's patented Scratch-the-Surface tour.

I even had a checklist of the 'must-see' items I would not see:

The *real* Statue of David in the Galleria dell'Accademia di Firenze
The inside of the Duomo
And everything inside the Uffizi Gallery

It was a short list—unless, of course, you itemized everything inside the Uffizi. Then it became a very long list.

And as if that weren't enough, the entire day was on a tight schedule, because Florence wasn't even our final destination. It was just a stop-off on our way to Montecatini, a small Tuscan town near Pisa, where we'd be staying the night.

I steeled myself. I didn't want to ruin another day with regrets.

I was going to enjoy whatever this day gave me and—with luck—make up for it another time.

Across the hotel room, CJ lay motionless. Asleep, I assumed—blissfully unaware of all this agonizing. Like Lucerne and Venice, he had zero expectations.

He'd roll with it.

I had no choice but to do the same.

Breakfast at Hotel Poppi was as inexplicable as everything else about the place. Alongside the usual continental fare, there was an attempt at hot options. I say attempt because nothing on offer resembled what an American, English, or Australian visitor might recognize as 'breakfast.'

CJ and I headed down to the dining room, where two Cosmic groups were in residence. Ours, and the group we'd encountered on the ferry yesterday. This was their last day, and there was an unmistakable air of sadness at their table. They'd clearly formed real connections, and now they were parting with genuine regret.

Then I looked toward our group.

One table sat twenty-odd generic old people, including the MAGA couple, Mole Man and Granny, and Cruella.

No regrets there.

At the table we chose, Kevin and Karen sat with Gerry, Sandy, and

Kate. They were nice enough people, but we hadn't formed any deep connections. No email addresses had been swapped, and there'd be no reunion. When our tour ended in three days, it wouldn't be like the other group's wistful goodbye.

But there was another couple at our table—one I'd noticed before but never really paid attention to.

The man was middle-aged and overweight, with heavy-lidded eyes and thick down-turned lips that gave him a perpetual look of sadness and disappointment—as if life and luck had conspired against him.

His wife—or at least, the thickset woman I assumed to be his wife—had a pleasant, if somewhat vacant expression. But, his bad juju negated her innocuousness, and together they radiated a negative vibe.

"—but we'd paid for a romantic gondola ride," the man moaned in an Australian accent that made me want to apologize on behalf of my entire country.

Somehow, he managed to look both sleepy and angry at the same time.

"And they put another couple with us!"

Karen, not known for her diplomacy, decided this was the perfect moment to drag us into it.

"Have you met CJ and Scott?" she said, dumping us straight into the line of fire.

The indignant guy turned his mournful eyes toward us.

"You're the writer guys, yeah?" he asked.

Sad Sack. That's what I'd decided to call him.

"Something like that," CJ replied.

"Well, you should write about this," he said, his voice rising with indignation.

"All Danielle and I wanted on this fucking tour—"

He paused for dramatic effect.

"—was to have a romantic ride in a fucking gondola."

I silently prayed for a quick death.

"It's pretty hard to do that," Sad Sack added, his outrage growing, "when you have to share it with a couple of Yanks who fall asleep!"

"It was disappointing, sweetheart," Danielle said gently. "But I don't want to make a big deal of it."

Just then, George appeared, swooping in like a reluctant savior to take one for the team.

"What seems to be the problem?" he asked, with the air of someone obligated to listen, whether he cared or not.

Sad Sack launched into his story again, and CJ and I bolted.

"Thanks for dumping us in that," I muttered to Karen as we passed her in the lobby.

"Those two are always whining about something," she said with a shrug. "I figured it was your turn to listen."

"The guy has a point, though," CJ said.

"Yeah," Kevin agreed. "If it were anyone else, I might even be sympathetic."

"Did you guys have a gondola ride?" I asked.

"Don't be fucking ridiculous," Kevin said.

It was on the road to Florence that I became convinced there'd been a death on board. I'd been quietly afraid of the possibility for some time, and there were a number of potential candidates: Mole Man didn't look well, and there were at least three people I regarded as more-bewildered-than-most.

The truth is, the Cosmic trip maintained a grueling schedule. I knew how exhausted I was, but for people fifteen to twenty years older than me, it must have been a real test of endurance.

So, when the man seated in front of CJ slumped forward in his seat—held upright only by his seatbelt—I couldn't help but feel a stab of concern.

"CJ... CJ..." I shook him.

"Yeah?"

"The guy in front of you... is he... okay?"

"One moment, caller." CJ leaned into the aisle and craned his neck to get a better look. "Unclear."

"His wife doesn't seem concerned," I pointed out, watching the woman calmly flip through a guidebook.

"Maybe she's relieved," CJ said.

Just then, the man gave an explosive gasp, jerking upright and repositioning himself in a more natural manner.

"Cancel 'Code Dead,'" CJ said in his best walkie-talkie voice. "I repeat: Cancel 'Code Dead.'"

"You know what I like most about you, CJ?" I said. "Your compassion for others."

The countryside we'd been barreling through had been green and flat but otherwise unremarkable—until it transitioned into verdant rolling hills, farmlands, cypress trees, and the occasional quaint farmhouse. Then, as if on cue:

"Ladies and gentlemen, we are now in Tuscany," George announced.

At this, people straightened in their seats, eyes turning eagerly to the windows. This, I realized, was what many of these people had come to see.

Over the years, I'd spoken to countless people who, when asked about international travel destinations, would answer confidently: Tuscany. When pressed, they'd offer something vague like, "It's apparently very beautiful," or, "There's a romance about the place," or my personal favorite: "I don't know, it just sounds nice."

Under the Tuscan Sun had a lot to answer for.

Tuscany was indeed very beautiful, but did it live up to the hype? The countryside was not illuminated in golden shafts of ethereal light beaming down from above. The land was not blessed with ambrosial springs or orchards heavy with forbidden fruit. Nor did a host of seraphim descend from Heaven to herald me onward.

But Tuscany didn't need divine intervention to earn its reputation—it had history on its side.

Tuscany was the land of the Etruscans, a pre-Roman civilization renowned for their art, architecture, and sophisticated culture. It also gave the world some of its greatest minds and creators: Leonardo da Vinci; Michelangelo; Dante Alighieri; Galileo Galilei; Niccolò Machiavelli, the devious political thinker; and Giacomo Puccini, the celebrated opera composer—just to name a few.

Above all, it was home to Florence—the birthplace of the Renaissance, and a city that changed the course of history.

When we arrived in Florence, our long-suffering driver Mario faced the same challenge all tour bus drivers encounter in Europe: like every other tourist site, there was nowhere convenient to park the Cosmic bus.

He dropped us off within easy walking distance—or at least, easy for some of us—of the Piazza Santa Croce, where we were immediately greeted by a statue of one of Florence's favorite sons, Dante Alighieri, of *Dante's Inferno* fame, standing proudly in front of the Basilica di Santa Croce.

Apart from being a significant and beautiful construction in its own right, the Basilica is also the final resting place of Michelangelo, Galileo, and Machiavelli.

I would've loved to go inside and pay my respects at the tombs of these Renaissance giants, but as always on a Cosmic tour, there was simply no time.

Or at least that's what we were led to believe.

No sooner had the Cosmic group gathered in front of Santa Croce, a light drizzle misting my glasses, than George herded us—ostensibly for a bathroom break—across the piazza to the final stop in his pee-for-profit circuit: a sprawling leather store I'll call *Dante's Leather Emporium*, for reasons that will soon become clear.

There, our group was essentially held hostage while Satan the salesman spun a seductive tale, determined to lure us into purchasing €1000 leather jackets.

Most of us just needed the promised bathroom, but this demon wouldn't reveal its location until he'd finished his devilish sales pitch. Despite the rich, calming scent of leather, I could feel my blood pressure rising. Here I was, in one of the most beautiful and historically significant cities in the world, wasting precious time in a leather shop.

"This guy needs to shut the fuck up," I muttered to CJ, aiming for a quiet aside but apparently loud enough to draw a few glances.

"The jackets are nice, though," CJ said, running his hand over a sleeve. "Feel how soft the leather is…"

"Which way is out?" My eyes darted around the room, searching in vain for an exit sign.

Satan had now zeroed in on the tour member most likely to look good in a particular red jacket, parading them around like a ritual sacrifice.

"It looks *good*, doesn't it?" tempted Satan.

"It does look good," CJ agreed, already halfway to selling his soul.

"I swear, if you start trying them on, I'm going to lose my shit," I warned.

For the tenth time, I mentally reviewed today's itinerary. After this ordeal, we'd have a couple of hours before the Cosmic walking tour began. If we were going to get a feel for Florence, we'd need to move quickly—and luckily, fast walking was CJ's superpower.

I'd already written off the Uffizi Gallery. I'd Googled tickets after the Paris debacle and found they were sold out for our date. Disappointing, sure, but it made planning easier.

You can't see what you can't see.

Being on foot further limited our range, narrowing our choices even more. I'd made my peace with that.

But I couldn't do anything until I escaped this fucking leather shop.

Once Beelzebub had finished working his dark retail magic, CJ decided to buy a monogrammed leather notebook for his daughter. While I was impatient to get moving, this felt like a reasonable thing to do in Florence, so the delay didn't bother me.

What *did* bother me, however, was the attitude of the staff member tasked with engraving it.

When CJ handed over the notebook, the engraving guy—clearly a demon overseer of the Eighth Circle—fixed him with a withering glare and said, in heavily accented English,

"You must wait. I go."

And then he vanished.

Minutes ticked by.

Was he off tormenting corrupt souls in a boiling pit of tar?

Or just taking a dump?

Around fifteen minutes later, the engraving guy reappeared. Without apology, and still glowering, he performed an outstanding job branding the initials on the notebook, the smell of seared leather filling the room.

Purchase completed, we stumbled bleary-eyed into the Florentine streets, like damned souls escaping the Inferno—CJ's credit card singed, but our spirits intact.

To emerge from *Dante's Leather Emporium*, with its pungent air of seared hides and impatient commerce, and step into the shadow of the Duomo is to feel the full paradox of Florence: A city where the banal and the sublime collide.

The Duomo is big—one might even say unnecessarily big. It's the architectural equivalent of a midlife crisis sports car, except instead of a Ferrari, Florence set about building a marble-and-terra-cotta megastructure with no idea how to actually finish it.

When construction began in 1296, there were precisely zero plans for the dome. That was *future* Florence's problem. It took them one hundred and twenty years to figure it out. A medieval version of 'we'll fix it in post.'

Enter Filippo Brunelleschi, an irritable genius with no formal architectural training and a bad habit of starting fights with his coworkers. He single-handedly solved the dome problem with a system of herringbone bricks that made the whole thing self-supporting—which he refused to explain to anyone until after it was built.

"Imagine Brunelleschi," I said to CJ, staring up at the dome. "No training. Bad attitude. Telling anyone who'd listen: 'Relax, I've got this.'"

"That's a hell of a thing, ain't it?" said the man next to me.

I turned, shocked to see it was the Cosmic bus mate I had been fairly certain had died on board.

"It's a miracle," I agreed.

Imagine the generations who have gathered beneath this structure, drawn to its grandeur and sheer defiance of gravity. How could they not have been moved, as I was now?

Michelangelo stood here once, gazing up at this same dome. Leonardo da Vinci did too—though, in true Leonardo fashion, he was probably also sketching improvements on the spot and writing in his my-brain-is-broken mirror reverse script.

The dome even inspired Michelangelo's later work on St. Peter's Basilica.

I could almost picture them—Leonardo squinting at the brickwork, Michelangelo shaking his head at the Baptistery doors, muttering, Nice, but I could've done better.

"Think about it," I said to CJ, as we both gazed up. "Michelangelo and Leonardo both stood right here, looking at this very sight."

"What about Donatello and Raphael?" CJ asked.

"You're an idiot."

We moved into the Piazza della Signoria, where our attention was immediately drawn to its centerpiece: the Palazzo Vecchio, or 'Old Palace.' With its cuboid design, towering battlements, and crenellated walls, it looked less like a city hall and more like it was waiting for a medieval siege.

It was also home to one of Florence's most notorious buzzkills—Girolamo Savonarola, a religious nutjob who, in 1494, briefly turned the city into a Renaissance theocracy—because if there was one thing Florence didn't need, it was less fun.

His greatest achievement? The Bonfire of the Vanities, where he and his overzealous disciples convinced Florentines to toss their sinful belongings into a massive fire. Books, jewelry, fine clothing—anything that screamed too much enjoyment—was torched in the name of purity.

"Imagine a Renaissance-era Marie Kondo," I said to CJ. "But instead of thanking your possessions, you just set them on fire."

"Savonarola didn't spark joy. Did they throw him in?"

"Funny you should mention that..."

Savonarola was eventually condemned as a heretic—and in a chef's kiss moment of irony, he was hanged and burned in the very same square where CJ and I were standing right now.

Not long after Savonarola's fiery downfall, the Palazzo Vecchio took on a new role. In 1540, it became home to the Medici family, the influential dynasty that ruled Florence from the fifteenth to the eighteenth century.

"Florence basically went from being ruled by the Taliban to the Trumps," I said.

"That sounds a little more fun," CJ replied.

"The Medici family ran Florence like their personal Renaissance startup for centuries."

"So, they bankrolled the Renaissance?"

"Exactly. They funded Michelangelo, Leonardo da Vinci, and Galileo. But they were also huge drama queens."

"How so?"

"One of them called himself Lorenzo the Magnificent—"

"Say no more."

"It gets better. Another was known as Piero the Gouty. Yet another got assassinated during mass. And the last Medici died drunk and alone in 1737."

"What I'm hearing is they went from the Trumps of the Renaissance to a cautionary tale about bad life choices?"

"So... nothing ever changes."

One of the most enduring symbols of this legacy is Michelangelo's *David*. For centuries, the statue stood proudly in the Piazza della Signoria, right outside the Palazzo Vecchio. But in 1873, concerns over weather damage led to its relocation indoors to the Galleria dell'Accademia di Firenze, where it has been kept safe ever since.

Well, sort of...

Bringing the real *David* inside shielded him from the elements, but it certainly didn't protect him from humans. In 1991, a man with a small hammer hidden in his clothing lunged at David's left foot, hammering and shattering one of the big guy's toes before horrified museum patrons managed to stop him. Since then, *David* has been confined behind plexiglass—it seems humanity poses much greater risk to art than weather or time.

The closest CJ and I got to Michelangelo's masterpiece was the replica now standing in the piazza. It's an impressive stand-in, but it's hard not to miss the Michelangelo was here magic that only the original could provide.

That said, there's absolutely nothing wrong with this *David*. At 5.17 meters tall, just like the original, he's identical to the untrained eye. It's fantastic that someone commissioned this copy and returned it to its historic place.

But CJ had a complaint.

"He's not very... well-proportioned, is he?" CJ said, tilting his head.

"Michelangelo designed him to be viewed from below," I explained. "His hands and head are bigger than they should be."

"It's not his hands or head I mean," CJ said, raising an eyebrow. "It's his... you know..."

"Oh," I said as the penny dropped. "Maybe it was cold in Florence that day."

Alongside the replica *David* is Bandinelli's *Hercules and Cacus*, a piece with such a strong homoerotic vibe it feels borderline NSFW. But even that isn't the weirdest statue in the piazza.

To the right of the Palazzo Vecchio's entrance lies a courtyard that feels like the garden center of an eccentric aristocrat. Here, Benvenuto Cellini's *Perseus with the Head of Medusa* shares space with a chaotic mix of other sculptures. Brilliant yet unrelated, the collection added a touch of whimsical disorder to the piazza's grandeur.

Giambologna's massive bronze *Equestrian Monument of Cosimo I* dominates the center of the piazza. It's a grand, heroic depiction of Cosimo, which really goes to show just how much ego-stroking you can buy when you have enough money.

With a little time to spare, we grabbed lunch at the Osteria de' Peccatore in Piazza San Firenze—which included pizza and a Granda Dangerous Imperial Stout (which, at 10% ABV, lived up to its name). Refueled, we met the Cosmic crew for our official guided tour.

Our guide, Allegra, was an Italian woman in her forties. Her blue-patterned dress featured a decidedly untour-guide-like plunging neckline that scandalized the more conservative members of our group. To make matters worse for them, her thick accent and the ever-growing crowds left the hard-of-hearing exasperated at her commentary.

Cruella and Granny took turns yelling, "We can't hear you!" until they realized Allegra didn't care. The swelling crowds in Florence only added to the chaos, making it nearly impossible to get close enough to hear her. This didn't seem to bother Allegra, who carried on as if nothing had happened, much to the distress of some of our busmates who started falling behind.

Not everyone struggled to keep up, though. Mr. Sniffy—whom I'd successfully avoided for several days—made his unpleasant presence known with a deep, phlegmy sniff, followed by a wet hock-tua that made lunch sit uneasily. I tried to edge away, but the crowd was too dense, trapping me within earshot of his next expectoration.

If Allegra noticed this disturbance—and she didn't seem to notice much about her tour group—she had the grace not to flinch.

The walking tour turned out to be nearly identical to the one CJ and I had done earlier, hitting all the major public spaces. The main difference was the sheer number of people crowding the Duomo and the piazza. For those who could hear her, Allegra's commentary was informative and interesting, and she even deigned to answer a couple of questions.

The biggest difference between our morning walk and the guided tour came when we passed into the colonnade outside the Uffizi Gallery. Some of the greatest masterpieces of the Renaissance were tantalizingly close inside, but they might as well have been in Australia.

No matter—I'd already made my peace with that.

Lining the exterior of the Uffizi were statues of Florence's home-grown heroes: heavyweights like da Vinci, Machiavelli, Giotto, and Dante, alongside lesser-known Florentines like Amerigo Vespucci.

It was at Amerigo's statue that CJ provided a graphic demonstration of how differently our minds worked.

"Who's that Amerigo dude?" CJ asked.

"He's the guy America is named after. He—" I began, ready to dive into the history of his voyages and the naming of a continent.

But CJ, as always, had other priorities.

"Why is he missing a finger?"

"What?"

"His little finger is missing."

Sure enough, Amerigo's statue was indeed short of a digit.

Why?

My historical deep dive abandoned, I shrugged and followed CJ, who had already moved on. For him, the missing finger was the story.

For a moment, I allowed myself to fall into CJ's rabbit hole. Was it sculpted that way because Amerigo Vespucci actually had a missing finger? Or had it broken off in some accident?

Was this what it was like inside CJ's head?

Once we passed the Uffizi, we found ourselves on the banks of the Arno River. If anything, the crowds had only gotten worse. Allegra pointed down the river toward what looked like a cross between an elegant colonnade, a cluster of ramshackle overhanging buildings, and an arched bridge that seemed to defy time.

"The Ponte Vecchio," she shouted above the noise, her voice nearly lost in the crush of bodies and sound.

The Ponte Vecchio is one of Florence's most iconic landmarks, dating back to the fourteenth century in its current form. The buildings perched atop it are famously lined with jewelers and goldsmiths, making it a tourist hotspot. It has survived floods and wars, and legend claims that Hitler personally ordered retreating German troops to spare it—unlike the other bridges in Florence—due to its artistic significance.

Tourist hotspot the Ponte Vecchio may be, but Cosmic Tour's relentless itinerary waits for no man. George elbowed his way through the throng to where Allegra stood, her blue-patterned dress just barely visible amid the chaos.

"Thank you, Allegra," George bellowed, effortlessly drowning out whatever historical fact she was mid-sentence on. "We have to get on our way."

And just like that, our Florentine experience was over.

But my mental preparation had paid off—I had no regrets. Sure, I left with only the faintest taste of its grandeur, but when I return—and the gods willing, I will return—I'll stay as long as it takes.

After twenty minutes of struggling through the crowds and past Santa Croce—so tantalizingly close to the tombs of Michelangelo, Machiavelli, and Galileo—we were on the road again.

From there, it was on to Montecatini, the Tuscan town that would serve as our launching pad for Pisa. There's no doubt the scenery was incredible—rolling hills quilted with olive groves and vineyards, cypress trees and rustic farmhouses scattered across the landscape, some of which wouldn't have been visible from a car.

Honestly, I could make a strong case that the elevation and oversized windows of the tour bus made it the perfect viewing platform.

We barreled along with no scheduled bathroom stops, when Cruella decided to call George's bluff about the onboard toilet.

"Oh George," she said, unleashing her paintstripper voice at full volume, "I have to use the bathroom."

He turned in his seat, visibly unimpressed. "We're only an hour out of Montecatini."

"I can't wait that long!"

George leaned across to Mario and instructed him to park the bus in a convenient spot. Gravel crunched under tires and the bus came to a halt on the hard shoulder.

Cruella took the walk of shame down the aisle to retrieve the key from George, then back toward the small cubicle near the stairs.

"I can't get the lock to work!" she yelled over the sound of frantic rattling "...oh... yes I can."

"I almost feel sorry for her," CJ said, while an entire busload of people waited for the woman to pee. "It's not like she's a criminal."

The absurdity of having an off-limits bathroom on the bus was irritating, but it was the one point where George refused to compromise. But he'd made his point.

After Cruella's public shaming, no one dared speak of the bus bathroom again.

At first glance, Montecatini looked like the kind of Tuscan town that could make a bored homemaker fake her own death, assume a new identity in Italy, and fall in love with a retired sculptor named Enzo. The streets were quiet and unassuming, the kind of place where life seemed to move at a slower, simpler pace.

We were dropped off at the Hotel Settentrionale Esplanade,

tucked into the northern outskirts. After checking in, CJ and I decided to explore the town on foot. We walked through an outdoor marketplace, where half the stalls were already closed—probably because of the late hour.

From there, we wandered into an area where narrow streets were lined with weathered homes, their faded façades leaning more toward neglect than charm. It was a shabbiness born of necessity, where things endured because they had to—unvarnished, unpretentious, and real.

One abandoned house caught my eye. Unlike the others, it carried its history more heavily. Ivy clawed at its crumbling walls, small plants pushing stubbornly through fractures, their green defiance a sharp contrast to peeling paint.

Entropy had long since claimed victory.

In a wealthier place, the building might have been lovingly restored. Here, it stood quietly resigned to decay, its beauty fading into ruin. We moved on, but the image lingered—worn, resilient, unmistakably Italian.

The Hotel Settentrionale Esplanade was, without doubt, the classiest place we'd stayed on the Cosmic tour. The lobby had retained its old-world ambience, even post-renovation, and while the rooms weren't exactly new, they were serviceable—and charmingly worn. The furniture had seen better days, but it all fit the vibe perfectly.

"Y'know, this hotel isn't bad," I said to CJ as we were going to the breakfast buffet the next day.

"There's nothing weird here," he agreed. "Which probably makes it the weirdest hotel on the tour."

The dining room, like the lobby, was new but appropriately old-fashioned, with high ceilings, hanging chandeliers, and Roman columns. We'd arrived late for breakfast, and after scanning the room, we spotted the only available seats—right next to Sad Sack and Danielle.

"This'll be a hoot," muttered CJ as we slid into our chairs.

"Good morning," Danielle said politely.

Sad Sack grunted, focused entirely on shoveling scrambled eggs into his mouth.

Next to us, a table of eight Asian tourists buzzed with energy. Their conversation flowed in a language I couldn't identify, often culminating in gales of laughter. The contrast to the heavy silence at our table was stark.

Another burst of laughter erupted from their group, louder this time. Sad Sack froze mid-bite, his fork hovering over his plate. His face soured as he turned toward them and said, loud enough for them to hear:

"Speak English and we can all get the joke."

The words hit like a slap. I stared at him, stunned, my mind scrambling for something to say. Berating this idiot might turn the last days of the tour into a minefield of awkwardness, but staying silent felt like giving him permission.

Before I could decide, CJ stepped in.

"Well," he said, his voice calm but deliberate, "just as well they weren't speaking to us."

Sad Sack grunted again, his fork pausing for a moment before he went back to his eggs. It was impossible to tell whether CJ's words had landed or not. Danielle gave a tight, apologetic smile.

"We better get our bags downstairs," she said, her voice clipped.

I glanced at the group next to us. They didn't seem fazed—maybe they hadn't noticed, or maybe they were too smart to let a bitter stranger ruin their morning.

"Like I said, a hoot," CJ muttered, his voice low and bitter.

For someone obsessed with history, today was destined to be unforgettable. At long last, I would finally have boots on the ground in Rome.

But first, there was Pisa.

From Montecatini, the Cosmic tour would take us to Piazza dei Miracoli, home to the world-famous Leaning Tower. After that, we'd continue straight to our final destination—Rome: Nirvana for any history nerd.

Unlike Paris, which I'd drastically underestimated, I knew exactly how significant Rome would be. Early in the planning stages, I'd taken full charge of our itinerary. I had decided to completely abandon the Cosmic tour program in favor of our own plans for the Eternal City.

That meant today marked the last full day we'd spend with the tour group. Sure, we'd still bump into them at the hotel, maybe over breakfast, but Cruella, Sad Sack, Mole Man, and the rest of the jolly crew would no longer figure in our plans.

After today, Rome would be ours.

In fact, at my insistence, we'd added two extra days in Rome after the tour ended. The debate I'd had with CJ over this was laughable.

"Isn't two days in Rome enough?" CJ had asked. "Is there even enough to do?"

I nearly did a spit-take. "Two days? In Rome? Are you fucking kidding me?"

"I thought we might take a couple of extra days in Amsterdam," CJ looked as if this was the most reasonable proposition in the world—and maybe it was to someone who wasn't a massive history nerd.

"You want to spend four days in Amsterdam and only two in Rome?"

"I just thought we'd run out of things to do..."

"I'm spending four days in Rome." I said, emphatically. "You can go to Amsterdam whenever you want, and I'll meet you there later."

"No need to get your knickers in a twist," CJ had said. "Four days in Rome it is."

It was a short bus ride to Pisa, once again passing through the gorgeous Tuscan countryside. Upon arrival, George pulled off yet another small miracle—corralling a scattered group of tourists, dispensing the necessary information, and then leading us through a tent-city of souvenir stalls toward the entrance of Piazza dei Miracoli.

The tower and cathedral had been hidden by a high wall. But as we walked in the entrance, the whole piazza was laid out before us, and it was amazing. The cathedral was beautiful, but it was the Leaning Tower that immediately drew the eye—it was so familiar—yet in real life, its lean made it seem unreal.

At that early hour, Piazza dei Miracoli was still sparsely populated, but George had warned us that, like Florence, this wouldn't last.

"Better get your 'holding up the Leaning Tower' pictures in before the crowd grows," he advised.

CJ and I set to work. Of course, being us, we weren't interested in the predictable shots. I opted for the 'pushing over the Leaning Tower' pose, while CJ—ever the contrarian—deliberately botched the perspective in increasingly absurd ways.

Naturally, we also did the classic pose. We weren't total idiots.

But even as I framed CJ's photos, I couldn't help but marvel at the tower itself. Its lean wasn't just a quirky photo op—it was a story of survival.

The Leaning Tower of Pisa wasn't meant to be a curiosity, but it quickly became one. Construction began in 1173, but by 1178, the poorly designed foundations and unstable subsoil caused the tower to start sinking. A nearly century-long pause in building, brought on by Pisa's constant wars, ironically saved the tower, allowing the soil beneath it to settle.

When construction resumed in 1272, builders tried to compensate for the tilt by making one side of the upper floors taller than the other. Instead of solving the problem, this only gave the tower a subtle banana shape. Another war halted progress again in 1284, and the seventh floor wasn't finished until 1319—by which time the lean had reached 4 degrees.

Since then, Pisa has endured four major earthquakes—any one of which could have toppled the tower. Ironically, the same unstable soil that caused the lean may have also saved it, absorbing shocks through 'dynamic soil-structure interaction.'

But where engineers—and everyone else—saw a problem, Galileo Galilei saw an opportunity. According to legend, he climbed the tower and dropped two cannonballs of different masses, proving that objects fall at the same rate regardless of weight—blowing Aristotle's centuries-old theory to bits.

"So Galileo was a Medieval Mythbuster?" CJ was still trying to come up with an even more absurd way of posing with the Leaning Tower.

"A *Renaissance* Mythbuster," I corrected.

"I mean, he busted medieval myths," said CJ.

"Fair comment—I'll pay that."

I would have loved to climb the tower's 294 steps and stand where Galileo had supposedly conducted his experiment, but the line was already stretching into eternity. There was no way we'd make it to the top before our meeting time.

If today had been just about the Leaning Tower, I'd have been seriously bummed. But today was about Rome.

And for Rome, sacrifices had to be made.

By the time CJ and I rejoined the Cosmic group, the entire piazza was buzzing with the absurd spectacle of tourists striking the same, overplayed pose—arms outstretched, pretending to hold up the Leaning Tower.

There was something almost mesmerizing about it, the way people from all over the world seemed compelled to take part, as if caught in some unspoken, collective instinct. Who even started this trend—and how had it become a global phenomenon?

George herded his sheep through the maze of souvenir stands, a chaotic shearing shed in full swing—these vendors were relentless. Every few steps, another Cosmic tourist was plucked from the flock and fleeced of their euros with startling efficiency.

Yet somehow, George got everyone back on the bus—a minor

miracle, considering the battlefield of cheap trinkets and aggressive sales tactics we'd just waded through.

At last, the moment had arrived: Rome, here I come.

Rome—Roma, the Eternal City, the City of Seven Hills, the Holy City. Whatever you called it, I'd been obsessed since childhood. I devoured books about it, mapped its ruins in my mind—hell, I even took a shot at ruling it as Caesar in *Civilization* VI. Though, in fairness, with limited success.

And now? Fantasy time was over.

But could reality possibly live up to it?

I wasn't worried. Rome is too legendary to disappoint.

George walked up the aisle toward CJ and me, clipboard in hand.

"You guys aren't coming on the optional excursion tonight?" he asked.

"No," said CJ.

"I didn't think so," George laughed. "You guys missed the only optional excursion you signed up for."

"Actually, we won't be on the bus tomorrow," I said, realizing we hadn't let George in on our Rome plans.

"Oh? What are you doing?"

"We're doing a day trip to Pompeii and Positano," I said. "Then we're in Rome for two days after the tour ends, doing the Vatican, Colosseum, Forum and everything else we can fit in."

"Good move," said George.

Eventually, the landscape began to change. Lining the roads were unusual trees with tall, slender trunks that spread into wide, flat canopies, their shapes casting dappled shadows on the pavement. They weren't relics of ancient Rome, as one might imagine, but they had a surprising story.

"We're now beginning to pass the famous Italian Umbrella Trees, which means we're getting close to the Eternal City," George announced from the front of the bus. "And you can thank Mussolini, who had them planted all round Rome."

"Well," CJ quipped, "say what you will about Fascists—they're great at landscaping."

Well, to a point.

What the Fascists hadn't been good at landscaping was the area surrounding the Hotel Oly, which was to be our home base for the next two nights. It was austere and a little decrepit.

A sad, modern-looking church stood nearby, and further down Via Antonino Pio, a concentration of large apartment blocks—each clearly past its prime.

Directly across the road was a complex of buildings that looked like it should be the headquarters of a significant business. Except there was no signage. And many, many security cameras.

Once CJ and I had checked into our modest room—complete with a balcony directly overlooking the mystery facility—we began to wonder.

"It looks occupied," CJ observed, "but no one ever goes in... and no one ever comes out."

"Like Willy Wonka's factory."

Intrigued, we passed the building on our way to find dinner. Out back, a couple of black-suited men were smoking, but they offered no clues about the facility's purpose.

"Clearly not Oompa Loompas," I noted.

"No... maybe headquarters for the Italian MI5?" CJ suggested.

Eventually, we got some genuine Italian pizza—sold by weight. It was okay, but one slice was more than enough. After a beer run and a second recon of the mystery facility—still no clues—we called it a night and headed back to the hotel.

Finally in bed—my head at the wrong end thanks to a lack of powerpoints for Pappy—I let my aching body relax. It had been an exhausting day, and moments like this gave me a newfound respect for my elderly busmates.

As Pappy intermittently blasted air into my face, my mind drifted over the last couple of days. Florence and Pisa had been beautiful, frustrating, overwhelming—offering just enough to whet my appetite while reminding me how much more there was to see. They weren't finished with me. And I wasn't finished with them.

I didn't feel cheated. I'd be back. Places like these endure.

Or do they?

I'm sure the people of Pompeii thought their city would last forever. And in a way, it did—buried, waiting, for nearly two thousand years.

Tomorrow's visit wouldn't be just another tourist stop. It wouldn't be a tease or a taste.

Pompeii would be the real deal.

***

Unearthed

The Professor of Pompeian Graffiti

Freed from the rigid confines of the Cosmic Tours schedule, CJ and I set out early for Rome to join our Pompeii tour.

On the way into the city, our taxi drove by countless buildings daubed in sprawling graffiti. The sheer volume was staggering, a chaotic tapestry of spray paint and scrawled messages. If there was one clear takeaway, it was this: the Lazio football team is shit.

Soon, we passed ancient buildings—not internationally famous, but ancient all the same. At first, CJ and I pointed out every ancient marvel—until we realized they were everywhere.

On arriving at Piazza del Popolo, the first thing that caught my eye was a strangely out-of-place artifact standing proudly at its center.

"Why is there an Egyptian obelisk in the middle of Rome?" asked CJ.

"Ancient imperialism," I answered. "Emperor Augustus stole it from Egypt and erected it in the Circus Maximus."

"So is this where the Circus Maximus was?"

"No... but over time the obelisk became buried and forgotten."

"How could something that big just go missing?"

"One thousand years is a long time," I said.

"Yes, but—"

"Anyway, Pope Sixtus V unearthed the obelisk in 1589 and had it moved here."

"I didn't realize popes could moonlight as archaeologists."

It appeared a number of tour groups were meeting at this spot, making things more difficult than expected. Eventually, we met our guide, Aurora, who bore an uncanny resemblance to Allegra, our guide in Florence—same hairstyle, same accent, and a similar fondness for revealing outfits.

Our new tour companions were, in general, a much younger bunch than the ones we'd left behind at the Oly. Still, as I scanned the group, they felt a bit generic: families with young kids who'd be bored by Pompeii, a cluster of European backpackers weighed down by massive packs, a few older couples who would've fitted right in on the Cosmic bus, some individual travelers, and a quiet Japanese couple who kept close to each other.

In the piazza, an old woman—apparently cosplaying as a medieval crone—approached us. She muttered to no one, compulsively crossed herself, and exuded just enough creepiness to make interaction feel like a poor life choice.

She held out a gnarled claw, hopeful for a few coins.

"Sorry, I gave at the cathedral," I said.

Unfazed, she shuffled off to try her luck with some nearby tourists.

Not far away, an attractive young woman was posing for a photographer. We were immediately drawn by her beauty—after all, *hello, attractive young woman*—but her carefully practiced poses soon felt too staged and professional.

"There's nothing more off-putting than a self-aware beauty," CJ remarked.

Later, as we headed for the bus, we noticed the old crone and the young model had teamed up, approaching tourists in tandem. Whatever scam they were running was innovative enough to blend fear of God with Instagram.

A hustle so ingenious it deserves its own hashtag: #CroneGlamScam

Before we knew it, we were on yet another tour bus, heading southeast toward Naples.

"This bus is nice," said CJ. "More modern than what we're used to."

"Agreed."

"The tour guide is more attractive too," CJ added with a grin.

"Feels a little like we're cheating on George."

"I'm sure he'd understand."

As we pulled out of the city, the bus cut a straight line through lush, green hills south of Rome. It was a long trip, so naturally, Aurora had scheduled a toilet stop—and, in true bus tour fashion, it came with reciprocal perks. This time, however, the stop wasn't at a gaudy glass factory or a satanic leather shop.

Instead, it focused on the essentials: food.

There were snacks for the road, sit-down meals of meatballs and pasta. The works.

Then, to cap it off, we were herded through a labyrinthine gift shop that boasted, among other oddities, intentionally penis-shaped bottles of hot sauce wearing little spotted bows—proof that in Rome, even the souvenirs have a sense of humor.

Back on the road, Aurora drew our attention to a cluster of buildings perched on a hill to our right.

"That's the monastery of Monte Cassino," she said in her charming accent. "It was founded in the sixth century by St. Benedict and is the birthplace of the Benedictine Order."

"Rings a bell," CJ whispered.

"Me too," I replied.

"Over the centuries," Aurora continued, "Monte Cassino has been sacked and destroyed by invading armies multiple times—only to be rebuilt and sacked again."

"It's almost like God *wasn't* protecting them," CJ muttered.

"Finally, toward the end of World War II," Aurora went on, "the Allies mistakenly bombed it, thinking there were Germans there."

"That's what I remembered," CJ said. "Pretty sure there was a movie about it."

"After the war, the monastery was reconstructed yet again," Aurora concluded.

"Until someone blows it up again," I added.

Soon, in the distance to our right lay the sprawling city of Naples, and to our left, Mount Vesuvius loomed, a stark reminder that it's still an active volcano. Another half-hour of bouncing along on the bus passed before we finally entered Pompeii.

It was close now.

I had expected Pompeii to hit like a sledgehammer—a place where history's weight would obliterate my detachment from the past. Instead, our first impression barely made a dent. Rather than stepping into the shadow of an ancient tragedy, we found ourselves wading through a gauntlet of tacky souvenir stalls, gimmicky restaurants, and the unmistakable air of a cheap roadside attraction.

I suppose I'd imagined a grand forecourt, flanked by monumental architecture—a fitting entrance for a World Heritage Site. Instead, I found myself in a dusty, ramshackle town that felt more like a tacky holiday camp than a gateway to history.

After battling through the gauntlet of overpriced stalls and shameless upselling, the bus finally neared something that vaguely looked the part: the Parco Archeologico di Pompei.

Out front, we armed ourselves with headphones for the tour and prepared to enter the ruins.

I should have felt a shimmer of anticipation. Instead, I was thrown off by the weird, carnival-like atmosphere.

Our tour group passed through the turnstiles and got our first real glimpse of the ruins. This was more like it. An ancient stone wall stretched out before us, but little else was yet visible.

I took a deep breath—this was why I had come.

But again, any budding sense of reverence I felt was promptly banished when we met our tour guide, Antonio.

Antonio was not the tweedy, elbow-patched scholar I'd imagined. Instead, he looked like he'd survived a massive bender and had dragged himself to work through sheer obligation. He was unshaven and wore a dirty *Simpsons* t-shirt, a baseball cap, faded jeans, and a sweater lazily tied around his waist. Oversized black sunglasses completed the look, obscuring any hint of enthusiasm—or eye contact.

Suffice it to say, my hopes for the tour hit rock bottom.

"I am Antonio, your guide today," he said in good but heavily accented English. "Welcome to the Parco Archeologico di Pompei."

Antonio briefly outlined how the tour would operate, his delivery as flat as his expression.

"How much are we going to be able to see?" asked a young American woman.

"Not much," Antonio replied bluntly, unfolding a large map of the park. "We are here, yes?" He jabbed a finger at a tiny corner of the map.

"I guess..." the woman said hesitantly.

"And this tour lasts an hour, yes?"

"Yes, I think so."

"Well, I can show you this much," Antonio said, indicating less than ten percent of the map with a dismissive flap of his hand.

"Have we taken the wrong tour?" I whispered to CJ.

"I could show you the highlights in around four hours," Antonio continued. "But it takes two full days to tour the entire park. And that's just the parts that are open to the public."

He regarded us with the authority of Mussolini, as if daring us to complain. Then, without another word, he said, "Follow me, please," and took off at a brisk pace—leaving us scrambling to keep up.

We walked past the Quadriportico and the Amphitheater of Pompeii, each time accompanied by Antonio's surprisingly professional narration in our headphones.

Then he said something that completely upended my first impression.

"To me... Pompeii... it is not just a ruin," he said, his voice quieter now, speaking from somewhere deeper. "It shows us nothing lasts forever. But the past speaks... if you know how to listen."

I had been put off by Antonio's appearance, but now I realized I'd underestimated him. The supposed 'flatness' of his voice wasn't boredom—it was just a man carefully navigating his second language.

His commentary was sharp, vivid, and deeply informed.

Turned out this guy was a kindred spirit. He had 'history nerd' written all over him.

He might have looked disheveled, but his knowledge—and his passion for protecting this site—were undeniable.

Particularly when he saw a preteen boy climbing through what, two thousand years ago, had been a window.

"Hello, excuse me," he suddenly yelled. "Mister! Hey!"

The kid bolted back to the safety of his mother.

Antonio scowled, then said—loud enough for the mother to hear—"We're in a museum, madam."

The woman hurried her son away down the cobbled street.

"Some parents," Antonio muttered to himself, and then to us: "Where were we? Ah, yes—" he resumed his descriptions of the shops and buildings surrounding us.

From Antonio's vivid explanations and the well-preserved streetscape, it was easy to reconstruct the Pompeii of 79 AD: merchants haggling in the forum, bakers pulling fresh loaves from their ovens, children playing in the streets.

A city full of life—until, suddenly, it wasn't.

The locals probably found it odd that Vesuvius had been belching smoke for days, but Latin didn't even have a word for 'volcano.' How could they have known it was about to explode? No one thought to run—at least, not until it was too late.

The rest of the story was all too familiar.

Of course, Vesuvius wasn't just belching; it was loading up for one of the most infamous eruptions in recorded history. By mid-afternoon, the volcano exploded with all the fury of the god Vulcan having an absolute shit of a day, raining hellfire on an unsuspecting populace.

People ran screaming through the streets as ash blanketed the city in darkness so complete that it felt like night had fallen early. By the morning, Pompeii was buried under meters of ash and pumice, its bustling streets silenced and its people entombed in the tragic tableau of a city caught mid-life.

"And the next time Pompeii saw light was one thousand five hundred years later," Antonio said, "when its ruins were discovered by the architect Domenico Fontana."

"They didn't know it was here?" asked a bearded man in a German accent.

"No. It had passed out of human memory." Antonio replied. "It didn't even have a name until 1763 when an inscription was found that read Rei publicae Pompeianorum."

It was a chilling thought. How could a city so full of life simply vanish, leaving nothing but silence?

Easy, really. It happens all the time.

The jobs we perform, the lives we lead, even the memories we cherish—none of it truly endures.

In a strange and terrible way, Vesuvius had given these Pompeians the only kind of immortality that lasts. Their tragic end ensured they would never be forgotten.

Memento mori.

Antonio led us down the cobbled streets, guiding us past Pompeii's earliest finds. Many were instantly recognizable from books, their familiarity lending them a haunting resonance.

My mood had shifted, now appropriately reverent—here, the veil between past and present felt thin.

And then it grew thinner still.

Antonio led us into a sheltered area where a crowd had gathered around a series of glass cases. As we shuffled closer, the reality of what they contained came into focus—the famous body casts of the victims, frozen in the moments of their deaths.

"There were two phases of death in Pompeii," Antonio began. "Those who died in the initial rain of pumice and ash, and those who were killed by the pyroclastic flow."

"Pyroclastic flow?" someone asked.

"A pyroclastic flow is a wave of superheated gas and volcanic matter that rushes down at speeds of up to seven hundred kilometers per hour," Antonio explained, his tone suggesting this was a well-practiced script.

"Shit," someone muttered under their breath.

"No time to shit," Antonio quipped with a wry smile. "Those caught in the pyroclastic flow died instantly from thermal shock."

He gestured toward the glass cases. "Their bodies were frozen in place, buried beneath layers of ash."

"These guys?" one of the backpackers asked, pointing at a cast.

"Yep," Antonio said. "After their bodies decayed, all that was left were their bones and a human-shaped void in the hardened ash where they had once been."

"How did they cast them?" asked another voice.

"Around one hundred and fifty years ago, a man named Fiorelli drilled into one of these voids and poured in plaster. When it was excavated, voilà—a model of the victim in their final moments. He made many."

"Was this one of his?"

"No, his are all in the museum," said Antonio. "These are more recent. Nowadays, they try to keep the casts in the places where they're found."

"So this is where these guys died?" I asked.

"Yep," Antonio replied simply.

We moved from one cast to another, but I lingered at one—a woman lying face down, her head resting on her right arm.

Beneath the layers of plaster were the bones of a real person, someone who had once carried hopes, dreams, and lived a life of ordinary moments. Someone caught in the chaos of that day, roasted alive in a brief, inescapable inferno.

One moment alive. The next, gone.

Her final breath—still trapped in ash.

"We have to move on," Antonio said.

So much for this tour being a waste of time.

Pompeii was one of those rare places where the past felt palpably alive, preserved in a way that made history tangible and immediate.

Back outside, the streets stretched ahead of us. Everywhere, echoes of daily life remained frozen in time. At several points along the road, a cluster of large stone blocks jutted up—like a three-dimensional pedestrian crossing.

Which was exactly what it was.

These 'crossing stones' allowed pedestrians to cross without soaking or soiling their feet—a simple, ingenious solution to ancient street grime.

An idea struck.

"Let me get a picture of you walking across," I said to CJ.

"Like Abbey Road, 79 AD?" CJ nodded. "Nice callback."

It was a lighter moment, but the feelings of awe and melancholy still lingered.

The mood, however, was about to shift in a way none of us could have predicted.

"This," Antonio said, gesturing toward a surprisingly intact building nearby, "is one of twenty-five brothels unearthed in Pompeii."

A slow-moving line filed inside. The dim interior swallowed us, and it took a moment for our eyes to adjust.

The room was divided into cramped cubicles, each equipped with a stone bed that looked as unforgiving as the lives of those who had worked here. Above the cubicles, erotic frescoes decorated the walls—intercourse, fellatio, cunnilingus, anal sex—each scene vividly illustrated.

"You might think these frescoes were just to set the mood," Antonio said, his tone straddling the line between humor and seriousness. "But they served a practical purpose. Most people back then couldn't read, so think of these as a menu."

He let the weight of that sink in for a beat before adding, "Like the pictures at McDonald's—'I'll have a Quarter Pounder with Cheese, hold the mayo.'"

CJ and I burst out laughing, the comparison cutting through the awkwardness of the scene.

Most of our companions didn't laugh—whether from confusion, discomfort, or an unwillingness to mix Roman history, sex work, and fast food, I couldn't tell.

But Antonio brought us back to reality.

"Most of the prostitutes here were slaves," he said, the humor in his voice gone. "Stolen as children. Used until they weren't useful anymore."

The weight of his words settled over us, a shadow lingering even as we stepped into the sunlight.

Outside, Antonio stopped beside a weathered stone wall on the opposite corner, pointing to graffiti carved into the rock.

"Here's an example of the wit and wisdom of ancient Pompeii," Antonio said, gesturing toward a single carved word: fellatrix.

I snorted, recognizing it instantly—it was basically the Roman equivalent of "cocksucker."

Antonio smiled. "Ah, there's a man who knows his graffiti."

He was even more amused when CJ pointed out a 'dick and balls' etched into the footpath: "Care to explain, Antonio?"

"I wondered if you guys would notice," Antonio chuckled. "That's basically an arrow pointing to the nearest brothel."

"Subtle," said CJ.

In truth, I didn't know Pompeian graffiti as well as Antonio imagined.

Later, on a deep dive into the topic, I'd discover that the city's walls were an unfiltered window into the lives of its citizens. Among the gems were the bittersweet:

"Weep, you girls. My penis has given you up. Now it penetrates men's behinds. Goodbye, wondrous femininity!"

The straightforward: "I screwed the barmaid."

And the masterpiece: "Amplicatus, I know that Icarus is buggering you. Salvius wrote this."

Among many, many others.

These scribblings revealed a city that was vibrant, crude, and deeply human—more similar to today than we like to admit.

I thought back to the 'Lazio Merda' graffiti I'd seen earlier on the way to Piazza del Popolo. Maybe I didn't need to spiral into an existential crisis over modern graffiti—it was just an ancient Roman tradition.

Later, we moved to an open square and had time to explore alone before meeting back up. CJ and I chose to chat with Antonio.

"You had us fooled," I said. "I thought the real tour leader was off sick, and they dragged in a homeless guy to fill in."

Antonio shrugged. "Pompeii is a dusty place. No point wearing your best clothes."

"Seriously," CJ cut in, "does that 'the past speaks… if you know how to listen' line actually work on the ladies?"

Antonio grinned. "Charms their panties right off… History is sexy. Who knew?"

"I'll have to try it," I said.

Antonio gave me a knowing look. "You must have a passion for the past. Otherwise, it doesn't work."

"I write about history," I said.

"He's writing about this trip," CJ added.

I turned to Antonio. "So, you think I can pull it off?"

Antonio clapped a hand on my shoulder. "You also need the accent, my friend."

The tour concluded with a visit to the Pompeii Antiquarium, a museum housing many of the treasures unearthed during the site's excavation. Among them was the famous plaster cast of the watchdog of Vesonius Primus—a dog frozen in agony, mid-struggle, trying to free itself from its chains.

I felt a lump in my throat. He'd been a good boy until the very end.

The Antiquarium was extraordinary, but after walking even a fraction of Pompeii's streets, it couldn't compare to the raw, haunting impact of the ruins themselves—the visceral power of standing where life had been so suddenly and irrevocably snuffed out.

As we bid farewell to Antonio, he grinned, shaking our hands.

"When you write about this, just don't make me sound like a homeless guy, okay?"

I laughed. "I promise, Antonio. I'll make you the Professor of Pompeian Graffiti."

Soon, we were back on the bus, hurtling toward the Amalfi Coast.

Aurora had warned us this would be quite the drive, so we settled in for the long haul. Outside, the Bay of Naples shimmered in the afternoon light.

CJ snapped a photo. "Not bad. I wonder what the Cosmic people are doing now?"

"If I had to guess? Driving past the Colosseum at seventy kilometers per hour while George points at it."

"Cruel."

"Accurate," I said.

"Think they'll slow down at the Vatican?"

"Only if Cruella needs a bathroom break."

The combination of winding roads and the deep-fried pizza abomination we'd grabbed before getting back on the bus was not sitting well.

To make matters worse, the roof of my mouth had been scalded by the pyroclastic flow of molten cheese.

CJ, of course, had finished his without incident.

"Survival of the fittest," he said with a smirk.

It was an experiment I wouldn't be repeating.

The main road down the coast was a narrow, twisting ribbon of asphalt, clinging precariously to the cliffs. I sat in the window seat on the right-hand side of the bus, and more often than I liked, I could look straight down—hundreds of meters—to the sea below.

Of course, this meant the views were beyond spectacular.

I had rarely seen the sea so vividly turquoise—perhaps I never would again. One small error, one misjudged turn, and it might very well be the last thing I ever saw.

As we neared Positano, the road narrowed to the point where our tour bus could go no farther. We were decanted into smaller buses for the final stretch.

Somehow, the sea grew even brighter, glimmering under the afternoon sun.

Below us, Positano tumbled toward the water, its buildings terraced into the hillside in a cascade of peach, yellow, and soft terracotta. Sunlight bathed their pastel facades, framed by bursts of bougainvillea and the deep green of cypress trees.

Once the minibus stopped, we did what any self-respecting tourist would do: wandered down the winding laneways, past a higher class of souvenir shops than we were used to, and made our way toward the waterfront—nearly five hundred meters below.

The first thing I noticed—besides the dazzling blue sea—was the volcanic gray beach. For those used to golden sand, it looked dirty, even uninviting, but that didn't stop hundreds of tourists from gallivanting along the shore and wading into the water.

CJ and I found a spot on the terrace of *Ristorante Bucca di Bacco*.

With a chilled Peroni in hand and a magnificent view stretching before me, I was completely relaxed. Even CJ, so captivated by the scenery, forgot to complain about the lack of craft beer options.

For about an hour, our whirlwind trip through Europe slowed, transforming into a brief, sun-drenched beachside holiday.

All too brief.

Before we knew it, we were back on the bus, winding our way up the Amalfi Coast and heading toward Rome.

After a long drive, punctuated by another pee-for-profit visit at Montecassino, we arrived back at the hotel exhausted—10:30 pm, long after our Cosmic cronies had gone to bed.

A quick scotch—or maybe two— and I followed suit, once again inverted thanks to the curious placement of the Oly's power sockets.

In the morning, CJ and I, like the rest of the Cosmic tour group, had to check out. For many, this was the end of the line—they'd be boarding the bus with George to head for Rome's Fiumicino Airport to fly back to the States. Others, like Kevin and Karen, were continuing their adventures; in their case, onward to London.

"Do we have to go downstairs?" CJ asked. "We don't have to say goodbye, do we?"

"We should," I said. "We need to thank George at least."

"True," he shrugged. "Let's get it over with."

The moment we entered the lobby, Cruella made a beeline for us. "Someone said you quit the tour in protest."

"Who—" I spluttered.

"Dissatisfied with George. Full meltdown," she added, stepping closer. The stench of cigarettes clung to her like a bad memory.

"Nothing of the sort," said CJ, beating me to the punch.

"No," I agreed, "we just took a day tour to Pompeii."

"We would've said goodbye if we were leaving the tour," CJ lied effortlessly.

Mole Man and Granny wandered over. "It was a pleasure meeting you boys," he said.

"Someone said you'd quit the tour," Granny glanced at Cruella whose face had an unrepentant look.

"It's amazing how rumors start." CJ said, already pivoting. "Must grab some breakfast."

"Yes, must grab some breakfast," I echoed, seizing the chance to escape into the dining room alongside him.

Over breakfast, we chatted to Kevin and Karen, who told us our worst fears about yesterday's Cosmic tour were well-founded.

"You were better off in Pompeii," said Karen. They talked about their plans in London.

"Might end up doing that Day Tripper tour," said Kevin.

Gerry, Sandy, and Kate were also flying back to the States, as were Gloria, Sharon, and Liz. They were all nice people with whom we could've, maybe should've, spent more time. But we'd had other plans.

At a far table, isolated from the rest of the group, sat Sad Sack and Danielle. It seemed they'd finally alienated everyone on tour. I had no idea what they were doing next, and, frankly, I didn't care.

At a nearby table, Mr. and Mrs. Sniffy sipped their coffees. It occurred to me that I hadn't heard his phlegmy nasal inhalations in a while.

Had he finally stopped?

Or had I just grown used to it?

We caught George just before he was swallowed by the mass checkout mayhem.

"We had a great time—basically thanks to you," CJ said.

"Absolutely," I said. "I'm not sure how we would've managed otherwise."

George gave a wry smile. "Next time, travel by yourselves. These tours aren't for guys like you."

"Where are you off to next?" CJ asked him.

"I begin a tour in Amsterdam in four days," he said.

"We'll be in Amsterdam then as well," I said.

"Maybe we could catch up," George suggested.

"That would be great," I said. "We'll see if we can swing it."

CJ handed George an envelope. "You really deserve this. Sorry—it's in Swiss francs."

George laughed, tucking it into his pocket. "It all spends."

We shook hands and left 'calm George' to corral his charges one last time.

Our checkout time was the same as everyone else's, but there was no point in joining the long queue. We nodded politely at a few of the Cosmic crew—including the man I thought had died. A handful of half-hearted goodbyes, a few handshakes, and then, suddenly, George was leading them toward the bus.

"I'll enjoy reading your book!" Cruella called over her shoulder as she crossed the road.

"I guarantee you won't," I muttered.

CJ let out a breath. "Well, thank God that's over."

As we checked out of the Oly, I glanced back at the lobby. It wasn't much—just a place of small, strange memories. But it had been part of our journey, if only for a moment. A footnote in the story.

Like Pompeii, like the Amalfi Coast, like George and his Cosmic herd—it was already part of the past.

"We never did find out what the mystery facility across the road was for," I murmured as we got in the cab.

CJ frowned. "Just as well. Otherwise we'd be in Tuscany digging our own shallow graves."

I laughed but didn't answer. Instead, I looked ahead, toward the Airbnb waiting on the other side of Rome.

One cliché closes, another opens.

"Ready?" CJ asked.

I nodded. "As I'll ever be."

As the cab pulled away, I caught one last glimpse of the Oly in the rear window.

And just like that, it too slipped into the past.

***

Vatican Airways: Join Our Kids Club!

"Oh?" The woman's hand flew to her mouth as if she'd just been told the Pope wasn't a Catholic.

"You want *both* beds made up? *Scusa!*"

After weeks of traveling together, CJ and I had learned to laugh through misunderstandings like these. But this one felt like a fitting start to the next chapter of our trip.

It wasn't the first time someone had assumed we were a couple—I was fairly sure Cruella had spent the entire tour assuring everyone we were—but it was definitely the funniest.

We exchanged a look. And then, before we could stop ourselves, we lost it.

"We should just start telling people we're married," CJ said. "It'd save a lot of awkward explanations."

"Sure," I replied. "But only if you put a ring on it."

"No. Just no."

The Airbnb host, still flustered, muttered something in Italian that I didn't quite catch—probably something along the lines of 'Idioti'—before bustling off to fetch extra bedding.

She'd met us outside the old apartment block in Il Borgo, the area of Rome just outside Vatican City, and it hadn't gotten awkward until she'd made her... assumption.

The beds in question were part of a hulking double-bunk setup—yes, a bed stacked on another bed. Once again, I'd let CJ handle the booking, and once again, he'd chosen something... unique.

"It's got character," CJ said.

"That's *one* word for it," I replied.

The flat had an attractive parquet floor, a large bookcase, a serviceable kitchen and bathroom, and furniture that fully committed to the bright orange retro theme.

But dominating the room, like a shrine to Eros, was the bed itself: a pine colossus that seemed engineered to withstand a Vesuvius-level eruption—or something much, much worse.

Affixed to the structure in large, blaring orange letters were the words 'LOVE' and 'DREAM'—as if offering life advice to anyone daring enough to lay their head there.

At this point, I'd have been happy with 'SLEEP.'

I'd claimed the bottom bunk because of Pappy, and it had plenty of headroom. The top bunk, though—which our Airbnb host was still wrestling with—was so close to the ceiling it felt suffocating.

Worse, the ceiling was decorated with garish, oversized artwork of the sun, moon, and stars—a Sistine Chapel of kitsch.

Her job done, the host bid farewell, still apologizing for her misconception.

CJ closed the door behind her, with a thud that sounded like a bank vault sealing shut. "Whoa."

"That's the chunkiest door I've ever seen." It had to be at least six centimeters thick with enough locks to make Fort Knox look vulnerable.

"Why do they need this much security?" CJ asked.

"I'm not sure I want to find out."

Still, we didn't have time to dwell on the mysteries of our very own Fortress of Solitude. Our tour of the Vatican met in thirty minutes.

As a humanist, the idea of being at ground zero of Catholicism didn't move me—at least not in a religious sense.

And yet, standing outside the imposing walls of the Vatican, I couldn't help but feel awe—not for its spiritual significance, but for its sheer influence, its history, and the treasures it held within.

The Vatican is more than a religious center; it's a cultural and political powerhouse, a fortress of creativity, power, and ambition that has shaped the world for centuries. But the weight of history isn't always noble.

For all its grandeur, for all the beauty it has fostered, the Vatican's legacy is shadowed by darker truths.

It has safeguarded not just priceless masterpieces, but also predators within its priesthood. Its insistence on celibacy—a doctrine engineered centuries ago—created an environment where abuse thrived and victims were silenced. The same institution that nurtured Michelangelo and Raphael also nurtured systemic corruption.

And yet, my awe remained—not for the institution, but for the art it has preserved, the genius it had patronized.

These works, gathered through centuries of wealth and power, are a testament to humanity's relentless pursuit of beauty—even in the shadow of deeply flawed systems.

Standing there, I felt a strange mix of reverence and unease. How could one place embody both humanity's highest aspirations and deepest failings?

Today, I'd see three of Michelangelo's greatest works: the ceiling of the Sistine Chapel, the dome of St. Peter's, and the *Pieta*. A small consolation for missing the real *Statue of David* in Florence.

CJ, on the other hand, had other things occupying his mind.

"Thank Christ for skip-the-line tickets," said CJ. "Look at those poor suckers!"

Indeed, our shortened line was moving four or five times faster than the walk-up ticket line, which snaked far out of sight.

"Look at the hate in their eyes," he said to me.

"It might not be hate—"

"Agreed, it's more like pure, undisguised jealousy. Envy is a sin, you guys!"

We passed through the glass doors into the modern entrance of the Vatican Museum.

"Is it just me, or does this look like an airport terminal?" I said.

"Welcome to Vatican Airways," CJ announced. "Why not join our Kids Club?"

"Vatican Airways: We Touch More Than the Clouds."

"Vatican Airways: Altar Boys Fly Free."

"Lightning bolt in 3... 2... 1..."

CJ glanced upward, smirking. "If we haven't been struck down by now, I think we're okay."

Today's tour guide couldn't have been more different from Antonio in Pompeii. Matteo was a man in his mid-twenties, with the clean-cut look of a Mormon missionary—neat haircut, white shirt, and a tie. His voice crackled through the radio earpiece—high, precise, and unwavering.

"We are going to have a bathroom break before venturing into the museum," he said. "Please meet me here in ten minutes."

Even though the Cosmic Tour was over and we were starting afresh, it was good to know that some things never change. In the world of tourism, the need for a toilet stop was a universal constant.

"Now, if you'll all walk this way please," Matteo, as I was realizing, was more usher than guide.

After the obligatory security check, we followed him up a long staircase, through some corridors, and stepped out into the bright sunlight. The first thing I saw was a Michelangelo—the Dome of St Peter's Basilica—dominating the middle distance. It was a view the great master never lived to see, as he died before its completion.

"This is the Cortile del Belvedere," Matteo's reedy voice crackled in my ear, "a courtyard designed by Bramante for Pope Julius II in 1505—" He then launched into a long-winded explanation of its significance that failed to hold my attention for more than a few seconds.

"I already miss Antonio," CJ muttered.

"Yep," I said. "I don't think Matteo's got any dick jokes in him."

Already, I could see the problem with this tour—and it had nothing to do with Matteo or the lack of adolescent humor. It was the sheer volume of breathtaking architecture and artwork. We'd barely begun, and I was already overwhelmed. Everywhere I turned, there was something stunning, something extraordinary, something demanding my attention.

Amid this overabundance of riches, missing something significant was inevitable. After all, the so-called Musei Vaticani is actually a collection of fifty-four museums—an impossible feat to conquer in a three-hour tour.

But there was no point focusing on that. There was—quite literally—too much to see.

And too many people to see it with.

"If that guy in front of me doesn't stop elbowing me—" CJ said through gritted teeth.

"I think it's gonna get worse before it gets better," I said.

"You always know the right thing to say."

Matteo led us into the Octagonal Court of the Pio Clementino Museum, where I turned a corner and suddenly stood face-to-face with one of the greatest pieces of ancient Greek sculpture ever discovered. It depicted an impossibly muscled man and two smaller men locked in a desperate fight to the death with a massive, coiled serpent.

"That's *Laocoön and His Sons*," I said to CJ in awe.

"Who and his what-now?"

"A Greek legend. Laocoön's the guy who warned the Trojans not to accept the wooden horse: 'Beware of Greeks bearing gifts.'"

"Okay, so why the snake?"

"Laocoön angered the gods—some say by warning the Trojans, others say by screwing his own wife in Poseidon's temple. Either way, Poseidon and Athena were pissed off and they sent serpents to attack Laocoön and his sons."

"That's a bit harsh."

"That's how the Greek gods roll."

"Still, it's a pretty amazing sculpture."

"That's what they thought when it was dug up during the Renaissance. Michelangelo himself was summoned by the Pope to witness the unearthing. It's super famous."

"Thank you, Mr. Wikipedia," CJ said.

Then we stepped inside the Pio Clementino Museum, and once again, I was overwhelmed by the sheer abundance of antiquity. *The Apollo Belvedere. Antinous*, the lover of Emperor Hadrian. The Belvedere Torso. The bronze-coated *Statue of Hercules. The Bath of Nero*—not really a bath, but reputedly worth two billion dollars.

The treasures just kept coming.

We were corralled down what was ostensibly a hallway but was, in truth, an artwork in its own right: the Vatican Gallery of Maps. The walls were adorned with frescoed maps of Italy, every detail meticulously painted, while the high vaulted ceilings soared above us, covered in intricate, exquisite decoration.

"Not as convenient as Google Maps," said CJ, "but pretty amazing."

We moved deeper into the Vatican Museums, passing through spaces that felt like a labyrinth of masterpieces, until we arrived at the Raphael Rooms. And there it was—I was blindsided by one of my all-time favorite works of art: *The School of Athens*.

"This—is in my book," I stammered.

The Sistine Chapel had been my focus, but suddenly, this was everything.

I'd seen it in books, analyzed it, admired it. But standing before it? It hit differently.

The selfie I took conveys this to perfection: I'm standing open-mouthed before the painting, which depicts Socrates, Plato, Aristotle, Pythagoras, Archimedes—a veritable who's-who of Greek thought.

"Not only that," I said to CJ once I'd regained my composure, "Raphael included cameos by Michelangelo, Leonardo, and even added a self portrait—and no, there's not a Donatello in sight."

"An unfortunate missed opportunity," CJ said with mock sadness.

"Sorry to history-nerd all over this," I said, "but Michelangelo, Leonardo, Raphael, and Donatello weren't even all alive at the same time."

"Really?"

"Donatello died when da Vinci was fourteen," I said, aware I'd crossed over into know-it-all mode, "and before Michelangelo and Raphael had even been born."

"I feel like you've just told me the Beatles never met each other," CJ said, shaking his head.

I turned back to the painting—In that moment, nothing else existed, not even the *Teenage Mutant Ninja Turtles*.

Matteo then gathered us together: "Now we are about to enter the Sistine Chapel. I must remind you that photographs are forbidden, and you must only speak in a whisper."

He motioned us to follow.

We walked into an extremely noisy space that, to begin with, didn't look much like the Sistine Chapel I'd seen in photographs. Everywhere I looked, Vatican employees were shushing us—not that our group needed shushing. It was the angle which had fooled me. It turns out we had entered from a door at the altar end of the chapel underneath the *Last Judgment*.

Inside, the chapel was packed. Hundreds of people stared upward, chattering like they were in a food court. Vatican employees shushed in vain.

My blood boiled.

"I wish these selfish bastards would shut up," I hissed.

Then I looked up.

The shoving, claustrophobic crowd vanished. The obscene noise fell away. There were no more shushing guards.

It was just me and Michelangelo.

And it was perfect.

At the exit of the Sistine Chapel, we bade farewell to Matteo, handing back our earpieces. He hadn't exactly been a barrel of laughs, but his job was very different from those of Antonio, Allegra, and Aurora. The very nature of the museum meant that everyone on the tour was always looking at something different, making a cohesive commentary nearly impossible.

Next stop: St Peter's Basilica.

I'd only ever seen St. Peter's Square on TV, packed with hundreds of thousands of people—cheering for the Pope or waiting for a puff of smoke. What I walked into was a very different place. There had been more people in the Sistine Chapel than there were in St. Peter's Square now. I even took a selfie from the steps of St. Peter's—and there was no one within two hundred meters.

It was almost eerie.

Inside the basilica, however, was a different story. It was busy, but manageable. Once within, it was impossible not to look upward—eyes drawn to the massive marble columns and the soaring, intricately detailed vaulted ceilings. If the intention was to inspire reverence—and it most certainly was—then even this old atheist was drawn in.

It was time for the one-two knockout punch: the *Pieta*.

It's not like I hadn't seen Michelangelo's sublime masterpiece before. I'd pored over it in a Time-Life book I'd owned since I was a kid. It was everything I expected. And more. Quite apart from the ghost of Michelangelo that seemed to haunt it, experiencing that beauty in person, moved me.

"Are you crying?" CJ asked incredulously.

"I'm not crying. You're crying!"

"Clearly, Michelangelo stirs up strong emotions," CJ said, indicating the bulletproof glass. "Like the guy who went after the *Statue of David*."

"It was worse here," I said. "In the 1970s, some guy yelled, 'I'm Jesus Christ risen from the dead!' then attacked the *Pieta* with a hammer."

"Shit." CJ shook his head ruefully.

"He broke off Mary's arm, nose, and even one of her eyelids."

"And that," CJ said, "is why we can't have nice things."

"Well, if he really was Jesus, he definitely had Mommy issues."

After that, we roamed around, gawking at waxy-looking Popes inside glass coffins—Pius X and John XXIII—before taking in the grandeur of the Chair of St. Peter and Bernini's Papal Altar. But it was the inside of St. Peter's Dome that truly captivated me. I stood there, utterly enthralled, so much so that I didn't even think to take a photograph.

By the time we walked outside, the sun was setting behind the Dome of St. Peter's Basilica. Like sunset at Stonehenge or the Eiffel Tower, it was special—albeit a little subdued by the clouds. Even so, the way the sunlight filtered through them cast an ethereal glow over the square, giving the scene a, dare I say, Heavenly majesty.

A religious person would have left the Vatican today reinforced in their faith.

But me? I came in awe, and I left in awe.

There was only one thing for it.

"Beer?" I asked.

"I thought you'd never ask."

Another day. Another tour.

We'd planned to walk from our studio apartment near the Vatican to the Colosseum, discovering Rome on foot. But the rain had started before dawn, streaking the windows and filling the air with the smell of wet stone. The weak sunrise and continuing drizzle put a damper on the walking idea.

CJ seemed disappointed, but I was secretly relieved. I wasn't up for a long walk this morning, even though I knew it would be the best way to see Rome.

Uber it was.

It didn't help that we'd started early, still groggy from last night. Be.Re., a craft beer pub with the obligatory polished brass and warm wood fittings, had lured us in after our Vatican tour, and we'd stayed longer than planned. The beers may—or may not—have been on par with the brewpub in Lucerne, but whatever they were, they went down a treat. I'd love to give you details about the hazy IPA, but I'm afraid the whole night is a little hazy.

What I definitely remember is that we also discovered trapizzinos, a Roman street food that's basically pizza meets hot pocket. They came in a range of tasty meat fillings, artfully suspended on a stainless steel frame.

"Do you think they deliver trapizzinos?" CJ asked as we climbed into the Uber.

"I need to finish digesting last night's first," I said, yawning.

The tires of the Uber hissed on the wet streets, and the wipers smeared away constant drizzle as we sped toward the Colosseum. Everywhere I looked, the ground floor walls of buildings were covered in—what I now saw as—traditional Roman graffiti.

"Walking would've been shit," I said, based on the evidence before me.

"Wuss," said CJ.

We were to meet the tour in a backstreet that looked quiet, but a little dodgy. Between the buildings, the Colosseum was visible in all its moody magnificence.

"I need coffee," I said.

"Ditto."

With only fifteen minutes left before meeting our tour group, we finally stumbled upon an open café, grabbed paninis and Americanos to go, and hurried toward the rendezvous point.

About twenty people were waiting outside the small tour office, with staff calling groups in one at a time to complete registration.

The ones still outside were being treated to a show.

"Here... take this," slurred a guy in passable English, trying to shove a Rome guidebook into the hands of a middle-aged tourist.

"No thanks," the man said, placing the book on a nearby table next to a box of plastic water bottles.

"I'm only trying to be nice!" he yelled, before hurling the book into the street.

One of the male tour staff must've heard the commotion and came outside.

"Vaffanculo!" he yelled at the drunk.

"See? See how he treats me?" the man shouted to the crowd, shaping up to the tour guy. This might get ugly. Just as I was wondering whether CJ and I should get involved—definitely a terrible idea—two more tour employees stepped out of the office.

"I'll just go and... get the book," the drunk guy muttered, turning toward the street. He took one step, then slipped down a short flight of stairs onto the wet cobblestones. It looked like it could've been serious, but some people laughed—and that drove him into a frenzy.

"Are you laughing at me?" he shouted, stumbling back up the stairs. "Are. You. Laughing. At. Me?"

There was something very Travis Bickle about him. He was one bad decision away from doing something violent.

"I was out all night, but my friends left me—they were weak!" His voice cracked out of sorrow. "They... were weak."

One of the tour leaders tried a different approach. He picked up a water bottle and handed it to the drunk man.

"That was so kind," he said, his mood shifting instantly. "So kind. Thank you."

He began to stagger away, safely down the stairs this time, and out into the street. He picked up the guidebook he'd thrown, which seemed to remind him of his grievance. He walked a few meters and turned.

"Fuck you!" he screamed at no one in particular.

Soon, but not soon enough, he was gone.

All this rain and drama had distracted me from the reason CJ and I were here today: the Colosseum, Forum, and Palatine Hill Tour.

This moment had been a long time coming.

As a pre-pubescent history nerd, Ancient Rome was one of my ever-cycling top two civilizations: Rome and Egypt. Egypt and Rome. It depended on what book I was reading at the time. And nothing captured the imagination of a boy more than the Colosseum. It was the ultimate symbol of Roman glory—gladiators fighting to the death in front of roaring crowds, the monumental scale of its architecture, and the idea of a society so different from, yet so connected to, our own.

As I grew older, my fascination began to shift. The Forum Romanum took on greater significance. This wasn't just a place for grand spectacles—it was the center of Roman life. Here, the Senate convened, and later, the Caesars consolidated their power. It wasn't just a collection of ruins; it was the heart of an empire, where decisions were made that shaped both the ancient and modern worlds.

Now, on the cusp of seeing it all in person, I felt a mix of anticipation and awe. These weren't just stones or relics—they were the foundations of history itself. Today, I'd finally get to walk the same paths as those who shaped the course of civilization.

Rain and crazy drunk guys were the furthest things from my mind.

I was ready to enter the arena.

But first, I had to get through the red tape.

Changed security arrangements at the Colosseum meant extra work for the tour companies. That was why we'd all been lined up outside when the drunk had abused us. Finally, CJ and I were assigned to a group and met our guide, Eugene.

"Pay attention," Eugene said. "We are going to walk from here to the Colosseum, where we'll have to join the correct line and stay together."

Eugene, wiry and bald, looked like he'd seen it all. His sharp-eyed stare dared you to break the rules. He wore a rain jacket over what looked like smart-casual clothes, as if prepared for both a storm and an aperitif.

"I know it's raining," Eugene said, "but you all have rain jackets, yes?"

We all nodded our agreement, except for one guy who adjusted his hoodie instead.

"Good. Let's go."

The Colosseum came into full view. It was just as grand and imposing as I'd imagined. History loomed ahead of us.

We joined a line, but the gates hadn't opened yet, so we had to wait.

"Pay attention," Eugene said again—it seemed to be his catchphrase. "The Colosseum was commissioned by Emperor Vespasian in 70 AD and was completed ten years later. As you can see, it is big—the largest ancient amphitheater ever built."

"It looked bigger in *Gladiator*," Hoodie Guy said.

"The filmmakers made that choice on purpose." Eugene had an answer ready. "We're so used to massive stadiums today, so they wanted the Colosseum to feel as impressive to us as it would have to the Romans. Call it artistic license."

"How come half of it is missing?" asked Hoodie Guy, pulling his hood tighter as the rain picked up.

"What can I say?" Eugene swept his hand toward the ruins, "Romans hate maintenance."

CJ and I laughed, but judging by the blank stares around us, Eugene's humor wasn't landing with everyone.

"Seriously," Eugene went on, "the Colosseum was damaged by earthquakes in the ninth and thirteenth centuries. Large sections of it collapsed. Who's been to St Peter's Basilica?"

Most of us raised our hands.

"Well, some of the stone from the Colosseum was reused there. And lots of other places too—in medieval times they used it like a quarry."

"What's it made out of?" someone asked.

"It's built of concrete and travertine," Eugene said.

"Concrete?" CJ sounded surprised.

"Yes, the Romans didn't even invent it." Eugene said. "They were just the first to use it on such a grand scale."

The line began to move.

"Pay attention!" Eugene barked. "I must now talk to the Colosseum staff. Please stay together and keep moving. I'll be back soon."

"Eugene might give Antonio a run for his money." CJ said.

"He's certainly a snappier dresser," I replied.

"That's a very low bar."

We followed Eugene through one of the many arches and into the Colosseum. A strange sense of familiarity washed over me, a kind of déjà vu.

"There's this idea in physics," I said to CJ as we walked. "Time isn't linear—every moment, past or future, is still out there, stacked together like pages in a book."

"And?"

"Maybe we're brushing past the 'ghosts' of people going to watch gladiators hack each other to pieces."

"Pay attention," Eugene interrupted. "We're heading to the arena floor. Please follow."

Eugene led us out of the dim corridors and onto the arena floor. I looked up at the towering remains of the seating area, imagining it packed with tens of thousands of Romans, cheering wildly. I pictured the sand beneath my feet, the raucous crowd baying for blood, and the Ima Cavea, where the Emperor, Senate, and Vestal Virgins once sat.

The feeling was different from Stonehenge or Pompeii. The Colosseum felt vivid, alive—maybe because I'd watched Gladiator right before the trip. Somehow, the CGI version from the movie had fused with the real thing in my mind.

I stood there, taking it all in. This definitely wasn't something I could've felt sitting at home, reading a book.

"Do you feel it, CJ?" I asked.

"If you mean how weird you're acting—then yes," he said.

The Colosseum floor was only partially reinstated, allowing us to see the underground workings of the arena.

"This is the hypogeum," said Eugene. "Chains rattled, pulleys groaned, and gladiators—or lions—rose up from the depths."

"What about Christians?" Hoodie Guy cut in.

Eugene raised an eyebrow. "What about them?"

"Weren't they fed to the lions here?"

Eugene shrugged. "Not really. That's a myth—something early Christian writers exaggerated to highlight their faith's endurance. Sure, Christians—and other criminals—were sometimes executed by wild animals, but it wasn't as common here as people think."

"So no Christians were martyred here?" another man asked.

"I didn't say that," Eugene replied. "Christians were executed in public arenas, but it was more common at places like the Circus Maximus. And when it did happen, it wasn't just some helpless, one-sided slaughter. Romans loved a good show. If Christians were executed here, it likely included some kind of dramatic buildup to entertain the crowd."

CJ leaned over to me and whispered, "Imagine the billing: Faith Meets Fury: Christians vs. Lions – The Ultimate Clash of Belief and Beast!"

I had to join in. "Devotion Meets Destruction: Christians vs. Lions – Be There!"

"Prayers or Predators: Only One Will Survive!" CJ added, grinning.

Apparently we weren't as surreptitious as we thought. Eugene raised an eyebrow at us. "Looks like you've missed your calling as Roman promoters."

As he started to move off, a question popped into my head.

"What about filling the Colosseum with water for naval battles—

did that happen?" I asked.

Eugene grinned. "Like in *Gladiator II*? Ancient sources claim it did. But modern experts say it's unlikely—logistically, it would've been a nightmare. So, did it happen? I'll hedge my bets and say... maybe."

After over an hour viewing the Colosseum from almost every conceivable angle—and discovering incredible amounts of Ancient Roman graffiti gouged into the bricks of the building—Eugene led us out of the Colosseum toward the Forum.

"I'll lead you into the Forum, then the tour's over—you can explore as long as you like," he said. "But as you walk, imagine this: Rome wasn't marble white. Statues, columns, even buildings were painted in vibrant colors. Michelangelo spent his life thinking they were all just plain marble."

Eugene led us past the Arch of Constantine, the remains of the Temple of Venus and Roma, and the Arch of Titus before we finally entered the Forum. He had one last thing to say.

"Pay attention. Look at the beauty here," he said, indicating the ruins all around. "And look at the destruction. It wasn't just barbarian hordes or the passage of time that left these ruins in pieces."

He turned to face us. "It was the Catholic Church."

A few people shifted uncomfortably, but Eugene carried on.

"Early popes looted the Forum for building materials—tons of marble, columns, and statues were stripped and hauled away. You'll find much of it in St. Peter's Basilica and other churches. Some pagan temples were converted into churches, but many were simply torn down."

He gestured around us. "Later popes kept up the tradition, raiding the ruins for artifacts to decorate the Vatican. Sure, neglect and natural disasters played their part, but the Catholic Church bears much of the blame for what's missing today."

A pause. Then, as abruptly as ever, he nodded.

"Goodbye."

And with that, Eugene took off at pace, striding back toward the Colosseum like he had somewhere far more important to be.

I turned to CJ. "I don't know about you, but I think Eugene harbors some bitterness toward the Catholic Church."

CJ snorted. "You think?"

But Eugene's rant stuck with me, and as I walked deeper into the Forum, I was overcome with a profound melancholy. Of course, I'd expected ruins, but—

"It looks like someone dropped a nuke," I said.

"Not a high-yield one," CJ said. "There are still things standing."

He wandered off for a bathroom break, leaving me alone with my thoughts. I took in the broken columns, the shattered marble, the vast emptiness where the heart of an empire once beat.

When CJ returned, I turned to him. "Do you want to stay?"

He hesitated. "I thought this was one of your highlights."

"It was," I admitted. "Before I saw what's left of it."

"True," he said. "But we're here now."

We started moving through the Forum again, still trying to reconstruct its former grandeur in our minds. Slowly, though, something shifted. My mood changed when we came across the remains of the Temple of the Divine Julius. In many ways, it was the most ruined of all the temples here—there's little left of the prostyle temple Augustus built in Caesar's honor.

And yet, this place, more than any other, felt alive with history.

Here, Julius Caesar's body was cremated after his assassination. Here, Mark Antony delivered his famous funeral speech—the one immortalized by Shakespeare: "Friends, Romans, countrymen"—that turned the people of Rome against the conspirators and set the wheels in motion for the Republic's downfall.

We wandered to the remains of Caesar's altar, where fresh flowers are still left daily. I found myself imagining that day: the anger and grief of the crowd, the conspirators' growing dread as the tide of public opinion turned against them. Octavian—who would become Augustus—was here. So were Antony, Brutus, Cassius, and probably Cicero, all gathered for what would prove to be one of the most pivotal moments in Roman history.

Standing there, I yet again reflected on the relative nature of time. The past, present, and future seemed to converge in this one spot. The Temple of the Divine Julius might be in ruins, but it certainly wasn't silent—it echoed with stories of glory and betrayal.

I felt a jumble of emotions I couldn't fully untangle, but one thing was certain: even in ruins, the Forum was unforgettable.

Emerging, soaked and exhausted, from what—for me—had been an intense emotional experience, I had one priority. CJ had already sensed it.

"Beer?" he asked.

"Many," I said.

A burger and a couple of Birra Morettis later, we were ready to resume our wanderings. We'd had an intense historical morning, but we still had some touristy boxes to tick.

"So, where next?" CJ asked, leaning back in his chair.

"We can't go to Rome and not see the Trevi Fountain or the Spanish Steps," I said, still nursing my second beer.

"Why?"

"I don't know," I admitted. "But we just can't."

"Do you even want to see them?"

"No. Not really."

"Then why do we have to?"

"Trust me," I said. "You'll get back to Melbourne, and people will ask if you've seen them. When you say no, they'll look at you like you're insane."

CJ rolled his eyes. "I'm still not convinced."

"Look," I said, pulling up Google Maps. "I definitely want to see the Pantheon. If we walk this way, we can hit the Trevi Fountain first, then the Spanish Steps, and finally the Pantheon. It's efficient."

"This was all so much easier when George was here to boss us around," CJ muttered, finishing his beer.

"Welcome to the brave new world we've fallen into," I said with mock seriousness. "We're untethered travelers now. We have to embrace spontaneity."

CJ sighed. "Fine. But if the Trevi Fountain's a letdown[1], I'm holding you personally responsible."

***

---

[1] The Trevi Fountain *was* a letdown.

Flayed Saxophonists Won't Teach Me Anything About Life

"Thanks for looking out for us," I said to James.

"Mum would've killed me if I hadn't," he grinned.

We hugged. I turned.

And stepped in front of a bus.

The bus' brakes screamed, its horn blaring—a cacophony that split the air. My head snapped toward the sound, chest tightening as I saw it: the hulking blue and white shape bearing down on me.

My feet refused to move, my brain struggling to catch up with what my body already knew—this was not good.

The driver's face was locked in a mask of panic, his hands gripping the wheel as if sheer willpower might stop the inevitable. Somewhere behind me, James yelled something—maybe my name, maybe a warning, or more likely "Fuck!"—then everything went strangely quiet.

One second, I was saying goodbye to my nephew. The next, I was next in line to become a tragic addition to Amsterdam's road toll.

To understand how I got here, we'll need to rewind a bit.

Two days before, CJ and I had woken up in the bright orange Vatican Airbnb, grabbed our bags, and slammed the massive door behind us.

The entire building shuddered.

We'd hopped an Uber to the airport, then flown ITA to Amsterdam.

To be clear, Amsterdam wasn't on my 'must see' list of historical locations. The reasons for going there were twofold. One, my nephew James—who I hadn't seen in twenty years—lived there with his girlfriend Jen. And secondly, CJ wanted to go to Amsterdam's famed Red Light District.

The flight was mercifully quick, and I'd managed to mask my fear of flying from CJ, who would've taken the piss out of me relentlessly. No sympathy there.

We grabbed our luggage in no time.

"We have to catch a train, then switch to a tram. Then walk," CJ said, sounding like he had everything under control.

"I'm happy to pay for a taxi," I said.

"Nope. We can do this."

The train ride was quick, and we got off at the correct station. But that's where my relationship with Amsterdam's public transport system began to unravel. Somehow—neither of us could explain how—we exited the train, passed through an automatic door into a small vestibule... and got trapped.

We could see the exit just ahead, tantalizingly close, but it wouldn't open. Nor could we go back onto the train platform. We were stuck. Completely alone—except for the people we could see strolling past on the street beyond the glass door.

"Someone will come," CJ said confidently.

No one came.

"We might starve," I said.

"Relax, there's a vending machine."

Then, I spotted an unmanned kiosk with a button labeled 'Hulp nodig?'—which I guessed meant "Help" or "Assistance," though for all I knew, it could've said "Self Destruct."

I pressed it.

Nothing happened.

I pressed it again.

"Kan ik u helpen?" came a put-upon male voice.

"I'm sorry," I said. "My friend and I are stuck—we can't get out."

"How did you manage that?" The disembodied voice switched to English with a heavy note of sarcasm.

"We're in the—"

"I can *see* you," said the voice. I could almost hear his eyes rolling.

"Could you help us... please?" At this point, I was wishing it had been a 'Self Destruct' button.

"This is highly irregular," said the voice. Then, a resigned: "There, it is open."

We looked around and saw no change.

"Where?"

"Behind you. Now do not do this again."

"Thank you."

And with that, we were out and into the street.

As with *Arnold* the Houseboat and the Orange Airbnb, CJ had been in charge of booking the accommodation in Amsterdam. The Hotel Titus was, by all accounts, well-located, even though we'd had to drag our bags an interminable distance from the tram stop.

"Are you sure this is the way?" I moaned.

"We're nearly there," CJ snapped over his shoulder.

When we finally rounded the corner and saw it, I was impressed. From the outside, it looked straight off an Amsterdam postcard—a slender, gabled building with tall windows and a timeless, crooked charm. Across the road, a canal flowed lazily past. And as if on cue, an attractive young blonde woman in a sundress cycled by.

"Okay," I said. "You're three-for-three. Well done."

"You sound surprised."

We opened the door and the first thing I saw was the steepest, narrowest staircase I'd ever seen. Interesting, but I put it down as part of the Amsterdam charm. We dragged our bags upstairs with some difficulty and found our room.

This was where the charm ended and the nightmare began.

For one person, this room would've been a drab, airless mausoleum. For two people it was a tiny coffin. I imagined lying in that cramped space, and wondered if it would be like rehearsing for the inevitable.

There were two beds—each hard against opposite walls of the room—separated by a single bedside table. There was an infinitesimally small wardrobe, and no floor space other than that which separated the beds.

The bathroom was clean but comically small.

Swinging a cat was out of the question.

"Er—we won't be spending much time here anyway," said a clearly horrified CJ.

"A hobbit wouldn't be spending much time here either."

It was then I noticed the large window hidden behind a curtain next to my bed. I opened it and it looked out onto an alleyway.

"Not so airless, at least," I said.

"Let's get out of here."

We wandered aimlessly, soaking in the ambience and getting our bearings. Amsterdam was both quaint and beautiful, the long rows of tall, skinny homes, the picturesque canals that crisscrossed the city, and the infamous 'coffee shops' that sold weed and shrooms. Every now and then—in an echo of Venice—a waft of sewerage smells drifted up from the canals, adding an unexpected note to the otherwise idyllic scene.

We stumbled across a couple of bars to drown our sorrows. The second of these, the *Beer Temple*, was exactly what CJ needed: a craft beer haven with more taps than seemed physically possible to mount on a single wall.

"I better let James know we've arrived," I said. I thumbed out a WhatsApp message.

James is my nephew, the son of Maggie and Eric. I hadn't seen him since my ill-fated second wedding in 2004, when nineteen-year-old

James got spectacularly drunk at the free bar and entertained himself by mimicking the Australian accents of several guests—to their faces.

My phone buzzed.

"Meet you guys at Mikkellar tomorrow at 3," I read.

"Excellent," said CJ. "That's the craft beer place I'd been planning to go to anyway."

"Hey, I noticed they have that *Body Worlds* exhibit here," I said.

"What's that again?"

"It's where they preserve dead bodies with plastic or something, then peel off the skin and pose them doing weird stuff."

"And you want to *see* this horror show?"

"Absolutely."

"I can't talk you out of this?" asked CJ. "What about Anne Frank's house instead?"

"Ah, the happiest place on earth. No, I'm doing *Body Worlds*."

"How about you do that in the morning, and I'll go to the bar?"

"Sure."

We spent the rest of the night drinking and/or walking without a goal, united in a silent pact to stay as far away from Hotel Titus as possible—until sheer exhaustion forced us to return to our crypt.

The next morning saw me striking out alone to *Body Worlds*. I'm an early riser and even though the exhibition didn't open till ten, I was out walking the streets in the cool morning air by 7:00 am. It felt good to be out of the claustrophobic confines of the Hotel Titus and alone for the first time in two weeks.

CJ and I are great friends, but we hadn't spent this much time together for forty years. Tensions were beginning to show. I was pretty confident that his refusal to come today was as much about his need for space as it was revulsion at the subject matter.

And it's reasonable to be revolted at the idea of looking at dead bodies posed like eviscerated Barbie dolls. Similar exhibitions have caused controversy all over the world.

Nevertheless, since I'd turned 60 I'd become somewhat obsessed with death. The recent death of an old school friend had left me fixated on my own mortality. Not that I expected death to come soon—unless I was hit by the proverbial bus. But, truth be told, the idea of coming face-to-face with death at *Body Worlds* was something I hoped might snap me out of this phase.

Death: the Final Frontier.

I had two-and-a-half hours to kill, so I took my time over breakfast, having a second cup of Americano and chatting to the waitress.

"You're going to see the dead bodies?" she said when I told her where I was going next.

"You're not interested?"

"Death's everywhere," she said with a shrug. "Why pay to see it?"

She had a point.

But, I thought, as I walked around killing time before ten, maybe I wasn't paying to see death, but to stare it down—to show it I wasn't afraid.

Even so, wasn't wanting to see dead bodies the trait of a serial killer? Sure, I wasn't exactly keeping body parts in a fridge, but still.

By the time the doors opened, I was conflicted. And embarrassed to be first in line.

Body Worlds wasn't a museum—it was *Ripley's Believe It or Not*, with corpses.

I won't go into exhaustive detail describing the horrors within, but I will mention the plasticized woman, 'seductively' posed with her legs akimbo on a child's swing, her skin removed and her stomach unzipped to reveal her internal organs. Then there was the plasticized man, also stripped of his skin, playing the saxophone with his wedding tackle swinging freely.

These people had once been as alive as I was now, never knowing their future was to become glorified side-show attractions. But as I looked into their plasticized faces, I saw no sign of that humanity.

They were just meat marionettes.

I messaged CJ a selection of some of the more lurid photos—including a couple having skinless sex—and his reaction was not what I expected.

"Please don't send any more of these," he texted, "people in the bar are looking. It's getting weird."

It was weird I guess, and if I was being honest, I was revolted by my lack of revulsion.

I walked out knowing two things: One, flayed saxophonists wouldn't teach me anything about life. And two, my morbid phase wasn't going anywhere.

Around 1 pm, CJ and I regrouped at the bar he'd been haunting and briefly popped back into the Hotel Titus to shower and change for the evening.

"Were the dead bodies everything you hoped they would be?" CJ asked.

"Let's just say I've had my fill of body-horror," I answered truthfully. "There'll be no need to revisit."

"Seriously, was it good?"

"I can't answer that question yet." It felt like something I'd have to sit with for a while.

At three, we strolled a few hundred meters to the Mikkellar at Morebeer, the bar where we were to meet James. I'd seen photos of him over the years, but I still wasn't sure if I'd recognize him in person. I walked in expecting to awkwardly scan the bar like a lost tourist. But it wasn't a problem: we recognized each other immediately—his red hair and beard did a lot to ease that process.

"Hi mate, great to see you," James said, smiling as he walked up.

"Great to see you too," I said. We gave each other a quick, perfunctory hug—how do uncles and nephews greet each other after twenty years?

"Is this weird?" James asked.

"A little," I said, smiling. "The last time I saw you, you were hammered at my wedding. The time before that, you were a little kid."

"Yeah, I didn't cover myself in glory that day."

"CJ, James. James, CJ."

Introductions out of the way, we grabbed beers and sat down to talk. After catching James up on our trip so far, the conversation shifted to our plans for the evening.

"We're meeting Jen at the Argentinian steakhouse around six," James said.

"Sounds great," I replied, though I wasn't entirely sure what made a steakhouse Argentinian. Was the cow flown in from Buenos Aires, or just the chef? Either way, I wasn't going to argue with steak.

"And you guys really want to go to the Red Light District?" James' face twisted slightly, like he was trying to hide his distaste. "You sure I can't talk you out of that?"

"I'm not that invested," I said.

"I figure while we're here," CJ said, "we should see what the fuss is about."

"Jen'll be into it," James said reluctantly. "I'm not really a fan."

I raised an eyebrow at that. My assessment of James so far was that he was a little out there and up for just about anything. He had this easy, confident energy—the kind of guy who could strike up a conversation with anyone at a bar or jump into a plan without overthinking it. His distaste for the Red Light District surprised me. Maybe it was just too cliché Amsterdam for him, like when visitors want me to take them to a koala park back home.

Maybe it was something else.

"Your mum tells me you're writing," I said, changing the subject.

"Yeah, I write for computer games. Narrative, cut scenes, that sort of thing."

"That's pretty cool," I said. "Sounds like a dream job. Anything I would've heard of?"

"Unlikely," CJ butted in, punctuating the sentence by draining his glass. "Name one video game."

"Er—*Fortnite*?" I said with hesitation, "*Call of Duty*?"

"Better than I expected." CJ laughed. "Seriously, James, what have you worked on?"

"Smaller things so far. It's difficult to break into."

"That's writing for you," I said, raising my beer.

CJ leaned forward. "What kind of games do you want to write? Like RPGs or shooters?"

"More story-driven stuff," James said.

From there, the conversation plunged into a world of jargon and acronyms I couldn't follow. NPCs, cut scenes, and something about loot boxes—they may as well have been speaking Dutch.

Gamers have a way of finding their own, so let them have at it, while I went to the bar for another round.

Just before six, we wandered off to *Salmuera*, the Argentinian steakhouse. The place was all chunky wooden furniture, exposed beams, checkerboard floors, South American murals, and antique portraits of Mary and Jesus. Clearly, this was no cheap and cheerful restaurant. This was going to be an experience.

Jen was running late, but we boys got started with shots. It was from this point things started to get blurry, and I'm blaming the many shots of mezcal.

"In Tijuana back in '84, after you took a tequila shot, the waiter covered your mouth with a dish-towel to make sure it went down," CJ recalled.

"This is infinitely better quality stuff than that," I said.

"What was the name of that place?" asked CJ.

"*Tijuana Tilly's* as I recall," I said.

On my way to the bathroom, I passed a mural that sent a chill through me. It was the face of a beautiful woman, one half alive and vibrant, the other half a skull with flowers in her hair. I stopped, staring.

"It is life and death," a waiter said, noticing me. "Amazing, isn't it?"

"Definitely." The hollowed-out eye socket seemed to follow me as I walked away. After the bathroom, I was going to need another mezcal.

Any maudlin thoughts were banished when Jen arrived. It was easy to see why my sister—and clearly my nephew—loved her so much. She was attractive, vivacious, and sharp, with a quick wit that instantly put everyone at ease. James had done well for himself— she fit in like she'd been drinking with us all afternoon.

"So, are you boys up for the Red Light District?" Jen seemed genuinely excited at the prospect.

"Do we really have to?" James looked pained, his usual easygoing vibe replaced with something I couldn't quite place—discomfort, maybe, or embarrassment.

"Absolutely," CJ said.

We had what seemed like course after course of amazing steak, and with each course, a guy would come and advise the perfect mezcal pairing.

"Can you actually tell the difference between these mezcals?" I whispered to CJ.

"Um—I'm going to say no," he said. "But I'm loving them anyway."

This was the kind of meal you had to have at least once in your life. Incredible food and wonderful company. I was amazed at how easily James and I got on, even after all the years. What could've been quite awkward had gone smoothly. I guess that's family for you—that, and the incredible amount of alcohol we'd all consumed.

I knew it was going to be expensive, and I had fully intended to pick up the bill. But when it arrived and I saw the total—let's just say, I was relieved when James suggested we split it fifty-fifty. Otherwise I'd have needed another couple of shots to recover.

"Okay, off to the Red Light District," Jen was hyped, but James still looked pained at the idea. It was still hard to square his usual vibe with this reluctance—but maybe Jen's enthusiasm would win him over.

And so, with the mezcal warming our veins, we spilled out into the night.

The first thing that struck me about Amsterdam's much vaunted Red Light District is how very tame it was. We meandered in around 9:30 pm, about the time I'd expect it to be starting to come to life, and it was full of gawking tourists—like myself—and not much else.

Most of the windows were empty, and the girls who were there looked bored, scrolling on their phones or chatting like coworkers at the water cooler. It could've been the least sexy thing I'd ever seen. There was more life in *Body Worlds*—at least the plasticized corpses didn't look like they'd rather be elsewhere.

"Can't we just go somewhere, anywhere else?" James pleaded.

"Come on," Jen urged. "Let's go to a strip club!"

Jen dragged James off to look for one, which proved to be far more difficult than I would've expected.

While I waited, I googled the Amsterdam Red Light District.

"Apparently this area is known to the locals as 'De Wallen'—which translates as The Wall." I read aloud. "It's been a den of ill-repute since 1385."

"Fascinating," CJ yawned.

"Fun fact," I said, "In the fifteenth century, being a prostitute was legal but visiting a prostitute was not."

"Well, that kinda defeats the purpose," CJ said. "It's like making it legal to be a plumber but illegal to fix anyone's pipes."

After some searching, Jen and James finally found a place: the *Brasil Music Bar*. It was appropriately seedy, with a €10 cover charge. Inside, three topless women danced lethargically on the bar, occasionally making eye contact with potential lap dance clients and beckoning them over.

CJ came back from the bar with two Coronas and a Heineken, looking like a man who'd been violated.

"That just cost €50," he said, shaking his head. "They're not going to get me drunk enough for a lap dance at those prices."

Just when the vibe in the bar was going from minimal to nonexistent, a guy was dragged up from the crowd and set upon by the strippers. Two of them tore off his clothes while the third slapped him with the belt from his jeans, leaving red welts. It was part lame sex act, part physical assault.

"This has to be a set-up," CJ said as the—quite repugnant—display continued.

"Nothing like going to a strip club with your uncle," James muttered, awkwardly looking away.

"It's not great this end, either," I laughed.

We left the *Brasil Bar* and staggered back out onto the street, where things hadn't gotten any better. If anything, the crowds of gawkers had almost doubled.

"You guys really aren't going to get into this, are you," said Jen. It must have become clear that no amount of her unbridled enthusiasm could revive the night.

James and Jen had a quiet chat, and then:

"We might go, guys," James said. "I'll message you tomorrow and we'll catch up."

"Cool." I said. "It was really great to meet you Jen."

"Thanks for trying," CJ said.

As we walked away from the bright lights and empty windows where ladies of the night should be, I couldn't help but think: for a place so notorious, it felt like a caricature of itself. Maybe that's the danger of fame: it inflates expectations and can turn even the wildest thing into something ordinary.

We walked off back in the direction of the Hotel Titus, which—at 11:30pm—was as damning a review of the Red Light District as I can give.

Our last day in Amsterdam dawned, and we packed our bags for the last time in Europe. Packing in the tiny room was like choreographing a fight scene in a phone booth, but eventually, it was done. Getting the bags downstairs was easier, with gravity doing most of the work. All we had to do was stop them from smashing through the front door of the Hotel Titus.

After leaving our bags at reception, CJ struck out in a random direction. "Breakfast?"

"Absolutely."

Thirty minutes later, after wandering aimlessly and muttering about Europe's lack of cafés, we finally stumbled into one. Coffee, toast, and we were back on our way. Soon, we found ourselves outside the Anne Frank House, greeted by a sign that read: Sorry, we zijn uitverkocht—Sold out for today, sorry.

It felt wrong not to pay tribute to the girl who had hidden here for two years, only to lose her life in Bergen-Belsen. The sight of the building stirred a quiet reverence, a reminder of the horrors she and her family endured. It put my own fleeting anxieties into perspective.

And then, as if to pull me back into the present, my phone buzzed with a message from James: "Meet you at the *Ton Ton Club* at 1:00 pm."

We looked it up on the map. It was a thirty minute walk, which left us more than enough time.

When we arrived at the *Ton Ton Club*, we found James alone in the outdoor eating area vaping.

"Sorry, guys—it's my dirty little habit," he said, deliberately blowing a cloud of white vapor as far away from us as possible.

"No problem," I said. I was pretty much against smoking, and I knew vaping wasn't really any better for a person's health, but it wasn't my place to lecture.

Besides, it kind of suited his vibe.

"This place is cool," James said. "It's a bar, it's an Asian bistro, and it's got old school pinball machines and arcade games upstairs."

"Sounds perfect," CJ said. "What are you drinking?"

Today's James was a more subdued and thoughtful character than yesterday's hi-octane version. But then, I guess, so was I.

"Sorry Jen couldn't make it," James said, "she had some work to do."

"No worries," I said. "She's great, by the way."

"Yeah, I know," James said with a smile. "When do you guys fly out?"

"Eight-thirty tonight."

"When do you go back to Oz?"

"I fly out of London in a couple of days," CJ said.

"I'm in London for another week-and-a-half," I said.

"With Mum and Dad?" James asked.

"Yep. I'm going to see West Ham versus Luton at London Stadium with your dad, and some other stuff. Then we're all off to Oxford for a couple of days."

We went upstairs and played pinball—I'd never been good, but CJ it seemed, had had a misspent youth. James and I raced each other at *Mario Kart*, and because of my experience racing both my daughters over a long period, I managed to hold my own.

When it was time to leave, I'd decided I'd had enough walking and decided to catch a cab.

CJ, who'd probably walk to Australia if it were an option, waved me off with a grin. "Great meeting you, James." They shook hands, then he said to me: "See you back at the hotel."

He strode off, leaving James to escort me to where I could catch a taxi.

"Thanks so much for looking out for us while we were here," I said to James.

"Mum would've killed me if I hadn't looked after her little brother," James replied with a grin. We hugged briefly, then I turned to cross the road.

Now, in my defense, in Australia, when you cross a busy, four-lane road at traffic lights, they stop traffic in both directions and you can cross all the way to the other side. Unfortunately, this is not the case in Amsterdam. The lights stop the traffic in one direction; you cross to an island in the center, then it's the same process on the other side.

I saw the lights turn green on the far side and stepped forward—

into the path of an oncoming bus. Time slowed. In a split second I saw the looming blue-and-white shape, heard the blaring horn and screech of brakes, and saw the driver's panicked face.

Somehow, I had the presence of mind to step backward.

The bus missed me by centimeters.

"What the fuck?" I said, strangely more angry than shaken. "But the light was green!"

"Fuckin' hell! Are you okay?" James asked, his face white.

"Yeah, I'm fine," I said, though my hands were starting to tremble. "Mum would never have forgiven me."

"I'm not sure that's the biggest take away here."

We said our goodbyes again. I crossed the street without further incident—still fuming about Dutch road rules.

But in that moment, I could tell something had shifted.

***

Unearthed

Let's Just Say, I Had an Epiphany

Nearly being hit by a bus had done what no flayed saxophonist ever could. As far as I can tell, it was the closest I've come to death. And yet I didn't feel dread. Or even relief. I was rattled, but not undone.

I couldn't put words to it until we were on the flight to London.

"That was you?" CJ's eyes widened.

"Yep."

"I heard the screech and the horn from down the road."

"I would've been an ex-parrot!" I laughed, the near-finality of it all settling over me like an unexpected calm.

"Ladies and gentlemen, as we start our descent, please make sure your tray tables are stowed and your seat backs are in their upright position. Make sure your seat belt is securely fastened—"

"You seem amazingly together," CJ said.

"Let's just say, I had an epiphany."

CJ raised an eyebrow. "Oh yeah?"

I shrugged. "You never know when your time's up. I guess I should stop overthinking things."

"That sounds like something an overthinker would say. Did you come up with that before or after nearly becoming roadkill?"

"During," I said.

*

"Where to?" said the cabbie at Heathrow.

"The Novotel London West," I told him sheepishly.

"The Novotel London West?" repeated an incredulous CJ. "You kept that under your hat."

"I booked it before we left home."

"Why?"

"I thought it would be familiar because we would've already stayed here," I said. "How could I know what would happen?"

"You could've canceled and booked somewhere else."

"I didn't think about it until a couple of days ago. By then it was too late."

"You realize you can never complain about my accommodation choices again?" CJ said, shaking his head, half-serious.

But our fears were baseless. We checked in without issue.

No spandex-clad children. No obstructive employees. No single room.

This time, the Novotel actually felt like an upgrade.

Then again, after the shoebox at the Hotel Titus, it might as well have been the Taj Mahal.

Maybe history doesn't repeat itself after all.

It was late, and I was exhausted. As I collapsed onto the bed, I let myself appreciate the small miracle of a better room—and the fact that I'd quite literally survived another day.

To my surprise and relief, there was no PTSD-like reliving of the moment earlier. No flashbacks, no lingering panic. Just gratitude.

Europe had been everything I'd hoped for—and more. The fun, the frustrations, the moments of genuine awe—all of it had left its mark. But that chapter was over.

Now I was back in London, with even more to experience. Tomorrow promised new adventures, more chaos, and, hopefully, fewer brushes with death.

"I've gotta say," CJ said through a mouthful of pancake, "for all the trash-talking of British cuisine, a full English breakfast beats a Continental one hands down."

"Totally agreed," I said. "Give me bacon and eggs over stale croissants any day."

"So, Mr. Tour Guide, remind me—what's on the agenda today?"

"First up, British Museum," I said. "Self-guided."

"Controversial choice," CJ said.

"The imperialism, the theft, or the 'self-guided' bit?"

"A little from Column A, a little from Column B," CJ said. "And definitely some from Column C."

"From there," I continued, ignoring the jab, "we have to get to the Tower of London by 2:30 pm."

"We better get cracking then—right after my second cup of coffee."

It was a quick Tube ride from Hammersmith to Russell Square, followed by a short walk to the British Museum. Its grand Ionic columns and imposing façade loomed ahead, just as I remembered. It looked every bit the vault of the world's greatest treasures—even if, let's say, some acquisitions were questionable at best.

CJ flipped through the visitor map. "The Parthenon Marbles—aren't they always in the news?"

"Definitely," I said. "But these days, half the collection is controversial. Egypt wants its artifacts. Nigeria wants the Benin Bronzes. It's a bit of a mess."

"So basically, half this museum is stolen?"

"Pretty much."

Walking through the entrance, I felt the same awe that had hit me forty years ago. As an eighteen-year-old history nerd, I'd been floored by the sheer scale of it—Egyptian, Greek, and Roman antiquities all in one place. Back then, it had seemed obvious: why not safeguard humanity's cultural inheritance in one central museum?

Let's Just Say, I Had an Epiphany

"Naive," CJ said as I explained my younger self's perspective.

"Naive and paternalistic," I agreed. "But that's what I thought back then. Now, I can see the problem."

CJ raised an eyebrow. "Imperialism?"

"Among other things," I said. "But here's the thing—this might be our last chance to see some of this stuff before it gets handed back."

"That's a diplomatic way of saying, 'I like it even if it's wrong,'" CJ said.

"Fine, you got me," I said. "But let's see how you feel when you're standing in front of the Rosetta Stone."

CJ drained the last of his coffee. "Challenge accepted."

For a while, we drifted through the exhibits.

"This is interesting, but we should probably focus on the highlights," said CJ.

"Agreed. If we're going to see the big ticket items and still get to the Tower in time, we need to get organized."

It was around then that our wanderings led us into an enormous open space with a cylindrical building in the center and covered with a massive torus-like roof.

"Well, that definitely wasn't here forty years ago," I said, open-mouthed.

CJ again referred to the map.

"This is the Great Court," he announced, "it's two-acres in size, making it—and I quote—'the largest covered public square in Europe.'"

"Impressive. What's the thing in the center?"

"That thing," CJ said, clearly relishing the fact that he was the one providing information, "is—I quote again—'the World Famous Reading Room.'"

It was in the Great Hall that CJ and I sat and made our plan. First stop: Egypt and, of course, the Rosetta Stone.

As we approached the famous artifact, CJ studied the stone, tilting his head with a smirk. "What's the big deal? It's just a rock with a lot of scribbles."

"Three kinds of scribbles," I said, rolling my eyes. "Greek, Demotic, and hieroglyphics. It's how scholars figured out how to read hieroglyphics."

CJ nodded sagely. "Sort of like an early Google Translate."

"Exactly," I said. "Except working it out took decades, not seconds."

"So we could now tell what 'eye, eye, snake, ankh, bird' meant?"

"Exactly" I said. "Look at it—How many languages can you see?"

"You said three. And it looks like three," CJ said. "So I'm going with—three."

"That's what I would've said too," I said, "but I was reading something the other day that said there were four. See?"

I pointed to the side of the Rosetta Stone, and there in faint stenciling—but as conspicuous as a fingerprint at a crime scene—were the English words CAPTURED BY THE BRITISH ARMY IN 1801; PRESENTED BY KING GEORGE III.

"Nothing like desecration to make grand larceny seem less serious," CJ muttered.

"Apparently, when Britain defeated France in Egypt, they nicked the Rosetta Stone, which Napoleon's archaeologists had only just found."

"So if they hadn't beaten Napoleon, we would've seen it two weeks ago in the Louvre," CJ said.

"Probably."

We worked our way through the building and eventually ended up at the most contested of all the contested items in the museum: the Parthenon Marbles.

A large room in the museum had been set aside for the frieze from the Parthenon. The marble bas-relief sculptures were mounted on the walls at eye level, looking decidedly worse for wear.

"These don't look so great for being 2,400 years old," said CJ.

"It's amazing they're still here at all. They've been hacked at, burned, and even blown up."

CJ turned to me, eyebrows raised. "Blown up?"

"The Turks were using the Parthenon as a munitions dump. The Venetians shelled it in 1687, and—boom."

"And then the British swooped in and swiped the leftovers?"

"Pretty much."

"And now the Greeks want them back?"

"Looks like they might actually pull it off this time."

"I'll believe that when I see it," CJ said.

We wandered around the museum for another hour, knowing that it would be impossible to even scratch the surface of its vast holdings in our limited time. We saw the Easter Island moai statue, the Benin Bronzes, the Assyrian Lion Hunt Reliefs, and the Japanese samurai armor.

As we left I glanced back at its imposing facade. The British Museum is an undeniable marvel—a testament to human achievement and arrogance in equal measure. It's a place where history is preserved, but also where wounds remain exposed. It speaks of power, conquest, and the legacy of empire.

CJ looked at his watch: "So, Tower of London?"

"Yep," I said. "And it's a monument to man's inhumanity to man. You're going to love it."

We set off on what was essentially a self-guided walking tour, weaving through Trafalgar Square, down Whitehall, and past the heavy security outside Number 10 Downing Street.

CJ gave the security detail a once-over. "Looks like someone's expecting trouble."

"The British are always having trouble with their Prime Ministers."

CJ snorted. "It's not exactly the White House, is it?"

"Nope. It's subtle and understated. But I'd bet they've reinforced everything—and I wouldn't be surprised if there are bunkers and secret escape tunnels."

"Secret escape tunnels?" CJ said. "You've watched too many Bond movies."

We crossed into Parliament Square Garden, where the iconic landmarks of Westminster came into view. CJ pointed toward the Elizabeth Tower.

"So, that's Big Ben, huh?"

"Not exactly," I said. "Big Ben is the name of the bell inside the tower, not the tower itself."

CJ shot me a look. "Why does everyone call it Big Ben, then?"

"Because it's catchier than 'Elizabeth Tower.'"

"It's the alliteration that does it," he said. "But now that I know the truth, I feel obligated to correct everyone back home."

"You'll be as popular at parties as I am."

Finally, we reached the *Statue of Abraham Lincoln*, where we met our guide, Marko, a cheerful man in his late thirties wearing a green jacket with a patch that read 'Official Tower Guide,' who was—it turned out—a Croatian immigrant. After signing in, we joined the rest of our Tower of London tour group and Marko led us to Westminster Pier to board our cruise down the Thames.

The ferry moved past the London Eye, its massive circular frame reflecting in the river. Then cruised under the Waterloo and Blackfriars Bridge, the city unfolding around us. As we approached the Millennium Bridge, CJ leaned over the rail.

"I've seen that before..." he said.

"It's the Harry Potter bridge—the one the Death Eaters destroyed," I said.

CJ raised an eyebrow. "Never watched those movies... I must have seen it on a TV show. Maybe *Sherlock*?"

To our left, the dome of St. Paul's Cathedral rose above the skyline.

"Now that's impressive," CJ said.

On the other side of the river, we passed Shakespeare's Globe.

"Is that the real Globe?" CJ asked.

"Nah," I said. "The original burned down."

CJ tilted his head. "So Shakespeare never worked there?"

"No," I admitted.

"To be or not to be authentic," CJ quipped.

A building familiar to any fan of the later Bond movies then glowered to our right: The headquarters of MI6, Britain's foreign intelligence agency.

"I'm glad to see that it's still in one piece," I said. "Blofeld blew it up in Skyfall."

We passed under a succession of bridges, the city's layers of history reflected in their design. When we reached the 'new' London Bridge, CJ raised an eyebrow.

"Wait... isn't this the one that's always falling down?"

"Congratulations," I said. "You're the billionth person to make that joke. Your prize is my silent judgment."

CJ sighed. "That's it? No plaque? No dramatic lighting? Not even a slow clap? What a letdown."

Ahead of us, Tower Bridge loomed over the river.

"After the beer tour debacle, I'd be happy never to see that bridge again," CJ said.

"Agreed."

Finally, the Tower of London came into view on the left, its ancient walls standing in stark contrast to the modern city around it. The ferry berthed at Tower Pier, across the Thames from HMS *Belfast*, and we filed off with the rest of the tour group.

"That was a pleasant break," CJ said as we stepped onto solid ground.

"Glad you enjoyed it," I said. "It's all beheadings and torture from here on in."

The group shuffled along the cobbled path, a mix of tourists, although judging by the voices, mostly from North America. Marko halted us just outside the imposing White Tower. He spun on his heels with theatrical flair.

"Welcome to the Tower of London!" Marko said, gesturing dramatically. "Founded in 1066-ish. Built to keep the Normans in charge and everyone else terrified."

"Worked like a charm, I bet," CJ muttered.

"Oh yes. The locals believed it was a symbol of oppression," Marko grinned. "William the Conqueror really knew how to win friends and influence people."

Marko led us into the shadow of the White Tower, and on an impossibly green lawn were a number of large black birds. "According to folklore," he said, "if the ravens ever leave the Tower, the kingdom will fall. To prevent this, at least six ravens are kept at the Tower at all times, under the care of a dedicated Ravenmaster."

"Now there's a job," CJ said. "'Hello, I'm Ravenmaster at the Tower of London.'"

Marko continued: "The Tower's been many things over the years: a royal palace, an armoury, a treasury, and even a menagerie—yes, folks, a zoo. Lions, leopards, and even a polar bear who was allowed to swim in the Thames on a leash."

"Okay, now I'm impressed." CJ perked up. "Imagine having a polar bear in your moat?"

"I can't even imagine having a moat."

"What the Tower is most famous for, though, is being a prison." Marko said. "Between 1100 and 1952, it held some of the most infamous prisoners in history. The phrase 'sent to the Tower' wasn't just a metaphor—it was a real, terrifying fate."

He paused for effect, then added, "Elizabeth I herself was imprisoned here before becoming queen. And Sir Walter Raleigh spent thirteen years locked up in the Bloody Tower—though, to be fair, he did have a writing desk and access to his books."

"Wow," CJ whispered, "Raleigh was locked down and working from home before it was a thing."

"Quick question:" Marko said to the group. "In which century do you think most people were executed in the Tower of London?"

"Fifteenth?" someone called out.

"Sixteenth?" came another voice.

"Not even close," Marko said. "The twentieth century."

"What?" came a few scattered voices.

"During the First and Second World Wars, the Tower was used as a prison for spies, and twelve men were executed for espionage—before then, only seven people had been executed in the Tower grounds. Most executions took place on Tower Hill, just outside the walls."

Marko then pointed to a round, glass memorial on the green, his tone growing somber. "This site is where Anne Boleyn, Queen Catherine Howard, and Lady Jane Grey were executed, among others."

The group fell silent.

Anne Boleyn—once queen of England—escorted to the scaffold. The expert swordsman from France. The thud of a single stroke. The crowd's stunned silence.

It was another moment where history cut through the banality of tourism.

Then Marko brightened, breaking the group reverie. "But it's not all doom and gloom, the Tower also houses the Crown Jewels, which have been kept here since the seventeenth century. And speaking of which, I'll meet you guys over at the entrance to the Crown Jewels in an hour. Until then, please feel free to explore on your own."

CJ and I decided to use this time to check out the White Tower. As we climbed the external stairs, we paused at a sign marking the spot where two children's remains were discovered—bodies that some believe belonged to the infamous Princes in the Tower.

CJ frowned at the plaque. "Not ringing any bells."

"Oh, this is a good one," I said. "When Edward IV died, his son Edward V and his little brother were sent here by their uncle Richard—supposedly for their protection, before Edward's coronation."

"Yeah... that never actually means protection, does it?"

"Nope. Turns out, Uncle Dick had other ideas. He declared the boys illegitimate and made himself king as Richard III. Then, at some point... they just vanished."

"And centuries later, the skeletons of two children turn up in the walls?"

"Yep."

CJ exhaled. "Yeah, okay. That's a lot darker than I expected."

We carried on into the Royal Armouries, a shiny and impressive display of armor and weapons. It was, for the most part, your standard museum fare—interesting, but nothing too thrilling.

That was until CJ stopped in front of a glass case and squinted. "Wait... is that what I think it is?"

I grinned. "Henry VIII's armor. Impressive, huh?"

"Impressive isn't the word I'd use," CJ said. "That codpiece has its own gravitational field."

And that set us off—we spent some time brainstorming Henry VIII dick jokes, because, honestly, how could you not?

"'I wouldst challenge thee to a duel, my king, but thy lance appears far too mighty.'"

"'Why only six wives, sire? With that codpiece thou couldst handle a dozen!'"

"'Is that a blunderbuss in thy pants, my liege, or art thou pleased to see me?'"

I couldn't help wondering how the teachers chaperoning a class of ten-year-olds on a school excursion explained that particular detail.

Soon we were back with Marko for our session with the Crown Jewels.

I'm no royalist and this extravagant display of wealth, even though it technically doesn't belong to the monarch, didn't sit well with me.

In particular, the dazzling yet controversial Koh-i-Noor diamond. Once held by Mughal, Persian, and Sikh rulers, it was looted by the British East India Company and gifted to Queen Victoria.

The Koh-i-Noor's ownership is murky—India, Pakistan, Iran, and Afghanistan all claim it—but its legacy of Imperialism is no less troubling. The fact that it supposedly carries a curse adds to its allure. It is said that no male should ever wear it.

"All that for a glorified hat?" CJ yawned as we re-entered the light of day. I couldn't help but agree.

Once we emerged from the Crown Jewels, the tour was officially over and as we were leaving, we walked past the Traitors' Gate, the ominous water entrance beneath St. Thomas's Tower.

"Traitors' Gate would be a great name for a heavy metal band." CJ made devil's horns with both hands.

"True," I laughed, "but this was, reputedly, where prisoners were brought by boat to the Tower. Anne Boleyn, Sir Walter Raleigh, and even Guy Fawkes came through here."

After leaving the Tower, we walked past a curious church which had a stone arched gateway topped with a bas relief of three skulls. It was the famed St Olave's.

"Traitor's Gate could use those skulls as a logo," CJ said. "This is my kind of church."

"Look," I said, pointing to a sign on St Olave's wall. "This was Samuel Pepys' kind of church too."

"Um, let's pretend I don't know who Samuel Pepys is."

"Samuel Pepys lived through the Great Fire of London and the Great Plague and wrote a famous diary about it all."

"Oh, okay," CJ said.

I continued to read the sign: "Apparently, Charles Dickens called this 'the churchyard of St Ghastly Grim.'"

"Really? I can't see why."

By the time we got back to the hotel bar, it was beginning to hit us: This time tomorrow night, CJ would be on a flight back to Melbourne.

For him, this journey was over.

"It's been a great trip," he said.

"It has, hasn't it?"

"Okay," he said, downing his scotch. "Now I have to tell you an uncomfortable truth. And please remember, I'm telling you this as a friend."

I was taken aback. For once, CJ had a serious look on his face.

"Pappy is not working," he said. "You've been snoring a lot."

"When?"

"Usually after we've been drinking."

"You're going to have to be more specific."

"I'm just saying that the CPAP's not working properly," he said.

"I knew that, but I thought it was passable." I said, mortified. "Have you been able to sleep?"

"You've driven me fucking crazy some nights."

"Oh God... I'm so sorry," I said.

"Not my problem after tonight," he said. "But you better look into it."

The next day dawned bright and clear, with only a few streaky clouds overhead. It was CJ's last day, but my mind was elsewhere.

Did Pappy work okay last night?

Before bed, I'd given my CPAP machine a thorough once-over—changing filters, checking connections, and hoping the unpredictable UK power supply wouldn't betray me. It must have been doing something right, since I was sleeping better than those horror nights in Seoul. But the fact that I could still snore loud enough to bother CJ? That was concerning.

CJ caught my expression and grinned. "I slept fine," he said. "Had to boot your bed at one point, but you stopped."

We had checked out early, since our tour would overlap with the actual checkout time. After my nightmare experience with the Novotel's *Forget Me Not* baggage storage, I wasn't thrilled about leaving my bags with them a second time. But we didn't have much choice. It made the plan simple: we'd do the tour, return in the afternoon, grab our bags, and we'd go our separate ways. CJ to the airport, and I'd go back to Maggie and Eric's place.

"So my last tour is Burnings, Butchery & Black Death," CJ said. "Sounds like a hoot. You're not going to get all maudlin on me again, are you?"

"No," I said, "I told you, I'm a changed man."

Another full English breakfast and a couple of Americanos later, we walked to Hammersmith Station, from where it was a quick trip from the Barbican, where we'd meet Tom, our guide. From there, we'd walk through Smithfield, the site of medieval executions, a mass grave, German bombings, and the notorious slum featured in Dickens' Oliver Twist.

Tom was easy to spot—he was the guy standing outside Barbican station in a T-shirt and antique-looking flat cap. The clipboard and the crowd gathering around him were the dead giveaway.

"Welcome gentlemen," he said, ticking off his list as we approached, "You're our last two. Let's go."

It was a short walk to the Charterhouse, a beautiful old stone and brick building nestled behind a lush green park.

"This," Tom indicated the park behind him, "looks like a peaceful, verdant place, doesn't it? Well, it's actually the site of a fourteenth century plague pit. It's believed over ten thousand plague victims are buried here."

CJ raised an eyebrow. "I love a good mass grave to start the morning."

"And the building behind me," Tom said, "is the Charterhouse. This was initially built in the fourteenth century as a monastery, and stayed that way until Henry VIII's Great Matter—his divorce from Catherine of Aragon."

"I think his oversized codpiece had something to do with it too," I muttered to CJ.

"When the Prior of the Charterhouse opposed Henry VIII's claim as Head of the Church, he was executed, and the other monks fared no better—most starved to death in prison."

"Perhaps a *slight* over-reaction," CJ said.

"Henry then handed the Charterhouse to nobleman John Dudley," Tom said. "Over the years it changed hands, until eventually, Thomas Sutton transformed it into a charitable foundation, establishing a school for poor boys and a home for impoverished old gentlemen."

From the grim history of the Charterhouse, Tom led us through winding streets to St. John's Gate, pausing before the imposing stone archway. It was the entrance of Clerkenwell Priory, the English headquarters of the Knights of the Order of St John. Otherwise known as the Knights Hospitaller, they were a Catholic military order founded by Crusaders in the eleventh century to look after the sick and injured. It would, eventually, become the modern St. John Ambulance.

"So... Crusaders with first-aid kits?" CJ muttered.

I had to stifle a laugh.

"After the dissolution of the monasteries," Tom said, "it served many purposes. William Hogarth spent time here as a child at his father's coffee house. Later, it became the printing-house for The Gentleman's Magazine, where Dr. Samuel Johnson worked—he's the guy who created the Dictionary of the English Language."

From there, we walked into Smithfield Markets, once a livestock market for over eight hundred years, but now being transformed into the new Museum of London.

However, its history goes way beyond that:

"Smithfield was a prime spot for executions," Tom said cheerfully. "William Wallace—yes, the Braveheart guy—was hanged, drawn, and quartered right here. Supposedly shouting 'Freedom!' the whole time."

"More likely, 'Aaaaarrghhh!'" said CJ.

"Less heroic," I said. "But probably more accurate."

"Later, Bloody Mary had over two hundred Protestants burned at the stake here," Tom added.

Not for the first time, I reflected on the sites of misery and death I'd encountered on this tour—the Colosseum, Pompeii, probably Stonehenge, and now the brutal executions at Smithfield. Maybe it was just my imagination, but these places felt like the veil between past and present was at its thinnest.

People really were bastards.

Our next stop was the Priory Church of St Bartholomew the Great. Tom ushered us inside the historic Norman building.

"St. Bartholomew the Great is one of the oldest surviving churches in the city," Tom said. "It was founded in 1123 and named for St. Bartholomew, one of Jesus' Apostles. St. Bart took the gospel to Armenia, where he was flayed alive for his trouble."

"I think I've met him in Amsterdam," I said. "Was he playing the sax?"

Tom went on, ignoring my idiocy. "The church is renowned for its stunning Norman architecture. It's still an active Anglican parish, and a popular filming location—it's appeared in *Four Weddings and a Funeral* and *Shakespeare in Love*, among others."

Tom led us to the Lady Chapel, explaining how it was cut off from the church during the Reformation and repurposed for commercial use. At one point, it even housed a printshop, where Benjamin Franklin worked for a year as a printer.

The tour moved on to a memorial marking the 1381 Peasants' Revolt, when Wat Tyler led an uprising against the young King Richard II. It was here that Tyler met with the king to negotiate, but after a scuffle and a brief chase, he was captured and executed—along with several other leaders of the rebellion.

We walked past Pye Corner, where the Great Fire of London was finally extinguished. The spot is marked—for no good reason as far as I could tell—with a sculpture of a naked boy, carved in wood but covered with gold.

At the entrance to a small street, prosaically named Cock Lane, Tom launched into the tale of 'Scratching Fanny of Cock Lane.'

"In 1762, London was gripped by the story of a ghost, said to be the spirit of Fanny Lynes, who had died under mysterious circumstances," Tom said. "The 'spirit' communicated through knocks and scratches, drawing huge crowds—until it was exposed as a hoax by the landlord, who was trying to settle a financial dispute."

"And I thought it was about a pox-ridden prostitute," CJ said. "How wrong can you be?"

After the tour wrapped up, CJ and I walked with Tom toward the Barbican.

"So, how long have you been doing this?" I asked.

"Oh, guiding? About six years now."

"Cool tour," CJ said.

"Thanks," Tom replied. "I run a few different ones, but this is my favorite. London's medieval history is everywhere—if you know where to look."

As CJ and I made our way back to the hotel, I found myself thinking about the weight of history we'd walked through in the past couple of weeks—human triumphs, tragedies, and everything in between.

Tom's tour had been gruesome and fascinating, but also oddly beautiful in its honesty. These were places where you could almost hear the whispers—or scratchings—of those who came before.

CJ interrupted my thoughts. "I'm going to miss these cheerful little outings."

He wasn't wrong—this was an ending.

It had been forty years since CJ and I last traveled together on our Contiki tour across the USA. Would we ever do something like this again?

We certainly couldn't wait another forty years.

As this part of my journey came to a close, I realized it wasn't just the places or the history I'd remember most—it was sharing them. It was the camaraderie that made even the darkest stories feel lighter.

And then I smiled, imagining exactly what CJ would make of that thought.

In a shocking turn of events, the Novotel staff retrieved our bags with speed and efficiency. As we wheeled them out of the foyer, we passed the Cosmic Tour desk, where a new group of travelers had gathered—a ghostly echo of tours past.

An elderly man in a stained polo rearranged bags, looking vaguely bewildered. Nearby, a loud, disembodied sniff echoed. And then, we overheard a woman—who looked like she'd sucked on about ten lemons—speaking to Doris at the desk.

"Look, I'm not one to complain, but—" she began.

I nudged CJ. "Is it just me or—"

"No, I see it too."

"I guess every busload of European travelers comes with a recurring set of archetypes."

As if on cue, two middle-aged men stumbled into the group. They looked like they were still recovering from the night before, but they managed to smile as they exchanged bemused glances with their busmates.

"That's just eerie," CJ said.

Then, his Uber arrived. It was time to say goodbye.

"No tears, okay?" CJ said as the driver tossed his bags in the trunk. "I know saying goodbye to me is traumatic."

"I'll try to hold it together," I said, rolling my eyes. "Don't crash or anything."

"And fix your bloody CPAP machine," he added. "I'm serious. Next time, I'm bringing earplugs."

I raised an eyebrow. "Next time?"

CJ grinned. "What, you think I'm letting you do Europe without me again? You'd get hit by a bus."

"You weren't even there to save me the first time."

"True. But you wouldn't have survived the Cosmic tour without me."

"Fair point."

"Thanks for inviting me."

"You invited yourself."

CJ smirked. "That doesn't sound like me."

We hugged briefly. Then, he was gone.

CJ didn't need a heartfelt goodbye or a dramatic send-off. That wasn't his style.

And maybe that was the point. Some people leave with a bang. CJ had left with a smirk—and somehow, that felt just right.

***

Churchill's Chamber Pot

Churchill's Chamber Pot

"You almost got arrested in the Louvre?" Maggie raised an eyebrow.

"More like an unwitting extra in a French farce."

I'd gotten back to Maggie and Eric's place around nine last night and had almost immediately crashed. After nineteen days of dodging guards, eccentric tour characters, and too much drinking—not to mention an existential crisis and a near-death experience—I needed a break.

Today was the only day of rest I allowed myself before plunging back into chaos. Seven days left. Seven more days before real life came knocking.

"And James said you nearly got run over by a bus!" Maggie said, her voice hovering somewhere between sisterly concern and amusement at my expense.

"Yeah, that happened," I said, embarrassed that this incident had already filtered back from Amsterdam.

"You scared the shit out of him," Eric laughed.

"Believe me, I know," I pressed my index fingers into the bridge of my nose.

"Well, get your rest," Maggie said. "Peter, Jo, and the kids are coming over this afternoon."

Peter was Maggie's eldest son, and like James, I hadn't seen him in over twenty years. The thought of reconnecting with him and meeting his young family was something I'd been looking forward to, but after the whirlwind of the past nineteen days, I wasn't sure I had the energy to face small children and their boundless enthusiasm.

As it turned out, the afternoon went surprisingly well. Peter and Jo were lovely—warm, welcoming, and fully consumed with the Herculean task of keeping up with their kids. Miles, their eldest, was a bundle of energy and curiosity, keen to test my dinosaur knowledge.

"What's your favorite dinosaur?" Miles' gaze was that of a seasoned interrogator.

"Er—I dunno. T-Rex?"

"Oh." Disappointment was evident. Clearly, Maggie had oversold me as the 'king of the dinosaurs.' It seemed clear that, as far as Miles was concerned, I did not live up to the hype. Baby Louise, meanwhile, was sweet, funny, and blissfully uninterested in grilling me about the Jurassic period.

"Let's not leave it twenty years this time," Peter said, cradling armfuls of toys and child-related paraphernalia, while Jo corralled the kids.

"I'll see what I can arrange."

"And don't get run over, okay?" Peter quipped as they headed out.

"No guarantees," I called after him.

Maybe a day of rest had been exactly what I needed.

Later, I glanced at my phone and saw a message from CJ: "Just arrived in Abu Dhabi. Only 16 hours to go." His message was a few hours old, so by now, he'd likely be back in the air again. Poor bastard. That twenty-four-hour flight home was grueling, and my turn was less than a week away.

Yesterday, CJ's departure had felt like the natural ending—like a full stop after weeks of chaos, camaraderie, and unforgettable moments. But after a day surrounded by family and looking ahead to the Churchill War Rooms, Westminster Abbey, Duxford Air Museum, Greenwich Observatory, and Oxford, I realized how much more there was to see and do. The story wasn't over yet.

I wasn't ready for the adventure to end.

Maggie, Eric, and I emerged from the Westminster Tube station into light rain and an establishing shot from every movie ever made in London. The Elizabeth Tower and Houses of Parliament filled my field of vision to the left, and magnificent gothic architecture of Westminster Abbey dominated my right. Across the road there was the famous statue of Winston Churchill, the man to whom this morning would be devoted.

We were in Westminster for two experiences I'd been looking forward to: exploring the Churchill War Rooms in the morning and delving into the history of Westminster Abbey in the afternoon. I took a moment to savor the quintessential London-ness of it all, but Eric was already on the move, quickly pulling five meters ahead of Maggie and me.

"He always does this," Maggie shook her head.

"At least he knows where he's going," I said.

Eric stopped, exasperated, when he saw how far behind we were. "Hurry up, woman."

I hoped he was speaking to Maggie.

Eric had all of CJ's impatient confidence—only with actual local knowledge—and soon, we were outside the entrance of the War Rooms. The rain was steadier now and umbrellas bloomed. It was a relief when we were ushered inside.

Located beneath Westminster, between the Foreign Office and the Treasury, the War Rooms served as Britain's nerve center during World War II. In these underground chambers, Winston Churchill—widely regarded as the greatest Prime Minister and arguably the greatest Briton of all time—huddled with his cabinet and military advisers, while the Luftwaffe rained bombs down on London.

From here, they planned England's defense under the constant threat of German invasion.

"Have you guys ever been down there?" I asked.

"Nope," said Maggie. "First time for both of us."

The cramped foyer—it was underground after all—was already

soaked with the moisture tracked in by many visitors.

On this self-guided tour, our first stop was the Cabinet War Room.

It was a small room reinforced with two heavy red metal beams, and was home to a square arrangement of tables and chairs, and a round-backed wooden chair for the Prime Minister—its arms famously scarred by Churchill's restless fingers.

Behind the PM's chair hung a map of the world that wouldn't have been out of place in a 1970s classroom. The only concessions to comfort were a couple of fans bolted to the wall.

"Imagine it," Maggie said, "this tiny room filled with Churchill's cigar smoke."

"Worse. Everyone smoked in those days," I replied.

We came to Churchill's secret telephone room, where he would speak directly to President Roosevelt. It was a tiny room, no bigger than a closet, with a mannequin of Churchill, cigar in hand, hunched over the phone.

"It says here," said Eric, reading the information card, "that all the staff thought this was Churchill's private loo."

"Look, there's even an occupied/vacant lock on the door," Maggie said.

"Maybe 'Excuse me, I'm just going to take a shit' was code for calling FDR?" I said.

Crude jokes aside, this felt deeply consequential. In so many of the places I'd visited, the passage of time had blurred the certainty of history. I *might* have stood near the spot where Caesar was cremated or where William Wallace was executed, but I could never be sure of the exact location.

Here, there was no ambiguity. Churchill had spoken to Franklin Roosevelt in this very room.

It made history feel immediate, tangible and alive.

We filed past the Map Room, the Switchboard Room, and the suite of rooms reserved for Churchill's family and personal staff. All of them were starkly utilitarian, as befitted wartime necessities.

Churchill's personal room even had a chamber pot tucked beneath the bed—a reminder that not even the Prime Minister lived in luxury during the Blitz.

"Even the great man had to rough it," Eric said, peering inside.

"Well, relatively speaking," I added. "He still had a proper bed, which is more than most Londoners had during an air raid."

And yet, for the three meter thick layer of concrete added to protect it, the War Rooms were still vulnerable to a direct hit from a 500-pound bomb. Their true safety lay in secrecy, as the location of Churchill's bunker remained unknown to the enemy throughout the war.

After the War Rooms, we entered the Churchill Museum. Compared to the stark intensity of the underground bunkers, this felt polished—even sanitized. Still, seeing an actual Enigma Machine, a silent witness to the cryptographic genius that helped turn the tide of war, made it worth the visit.

The Churchill War Rooms drive home the enormity of Britain's finest hour. It wasn't just Churchill—it was everyone who toiled here. Together, they embodied the resilience and determination of a nation confronting an existential threat.

Emerging from the subterranean command center, we decided to grab lunch before our Westminster Abbey booking. Eric, naturally assuming the role of leader, powered ahead.

"He really needs to slow down," Maggie said, shaking her head. "His legs have been bothering him lately."

"Doesn't look like he got the memo," I said.

He led us to the *Westminster Arms*, one of six pubs equipped with a 'division bell'—a signal for members of Parliament to down their pints and return for a vote. Over the years, it has hosted numerous politicians and luminaries, including Bill Clinton, Angelina Jolie, and Bishop Desmond Tutu—though I assume not all at the same time.

They weren't here now, of course, but the restaurant was busy.

"Hey Scott," Eric said in his characteristically sardonic fashion, "black pudding's on the menu."

Talk about a callback.

"That was forty-five years ago," I said.

"And yet still funny."

The story goes like this: The last time I was in the UK, Maggie and Eric took me on a driving tour of the Lakes District, Edinburgh, and York. One morning at a B&B, I ordered a full English breakfast, which included black pudding.

"What's this?" I'd asked, prodding it with my fork in obvious disgust.

"Black pudding," Eric replied. "Try it—it's good."

I cut off the tiniest piece imaginable, popped it in my mouth, chewed, and immediately reached for my water glass.

"Ew—that tastes like dried blood," I said.

It was one of those offhand comments destined to haunt me forever. For the uninitiated, black pudding is essentially a sausage made of pig's blood, fat, and oatmeal. For me, it was exactly as bad as it sounds.

"'Tastes like dried blood,'" Eric echoed, still chuckling to himself—forty-five years later.

A good meal—mercifully free of black pudding—and a couple of pints later, we were back on track for Westminster Abbey.

It was a short walk to the Abbey, taking us back past the Churchill statue, which now carried an extra significance after our visit to the War Rooms. Rain continued steadily, umbrellas bobbing above the heads of the crowd.

As Westminster Abbey's soaring Gothic spires came into view—every inch as grand and imposing as I'd imagined—I couldn't help but reflect that this was more than just a building. It was a monument to centuries of history, a silent witness to the coronations, weddings, and funerals of kings, queens, and national heroes. And beyond that, it was a mausoleum, housing some of the greatest figures in British history.

If I'm being honest, it was purely the historical significance of the Abbey that drew me most. Much like St. Peter's Basilica, the religious significance of the structure mattered little, except in how it provided the backdrop for some of the most pivotal moments in history.

Since William the Conqueror was crowned here in 1066, almost every English and British monarch has followed suit—save for two. Edward V, the boy king who was likely murdered in the Tower on Richard III's orders before he could ascend the throne, and Edward VIII, who abdicated before a coronation could take place.

"Think about it," I said to Maggie, "all the Henrys, the three Charleses, both the Elizabeths, and Victoria—every one of them stood here, right at this spot."

"Mind blowing," she said, looking around as if she could see them all.

"It's strange to think about—like maybe time isn't what we think it is."

"What do you mean?" Maggie asked.

"Ever heard of the 'block universe' theory?"

"No."

"I was reading about it recently—probably because of the déjà vu I've been getting at all these historical sites," I said. "The idea is that time isn't really a straight line from past to future. Instead, every moment—past, present, and future—already exists, like frames on a film reel. We're just experiencing them one at a time."

"So right now, every king and queen is here with us—we just can't see them?"

"Maybe. But in a place this steeped in history, you can almost feel it."

We entered through the Great North Door and were immediately greeted by a somewhat haphazard assortment of statues—historical figures, clergy, and other notable Britons. They stood in an awkward cluster, as if the Abbey's management committee had once debated their placement but lost interest halfway through:

"We've got all these statues—what'll we do with them?"

"Oh, just stick them by the doorway for now. We'll sort it out later."

It was a chaotic introduction to a space designed to inspire order and reverence, though the statues themselves were undeniably impressive.

Once past this minor distraction, my eyes, as with any good cathedral, were drawn skyward. The Gothic arches soared overhead, their intricate ribs converging in a vaulted ceiling that seemed to hover, weightless, above the space. Light streamed through stained glass windows in fragmented hues, their colors deepened by the glow of long-hanging chandeliers.

I stood, awestruck, my gaze still fixed upward—until a man in a wet raincoat bumped into me, equally mesmerized by the spectacle above.

The spell was broken. As my eyes dropped to ground level, the Abbey's grandeur was immediately tempered by the sheer number of people inside. Bodies shuffled in seemingly random patterns, their low murmur filling the space. Though not as jarring as the noise in the Sistine Chapel, it still undercut the sense of reverence I might have otherwise felt.

By my estimate, the Abbey held as many people as St. Peter's Basilica had when I visited a few days ago. But in St. Peter's—its cavernous interior eight times the size—the crowd was swallowed by the sheer scale, leaving the atmosphere intact. Here, however, the press of people was inescapable, a constant reminder that the Abbey was both a place of worship and a bucket-list attraction.

And, as a card-carrying atheist, I was here for the latter.

At first, Maggie, Eric, and I tried to stay together, but it quickly became clear that was a lost cause. Eric voted with his feet, striding ahead.

"I think we're better off doing our own thing," Maggie said.

"Agreed."

And at that point, I did something I'm not particularly proud of. I couldn't resist the pull of certain names—the thought of standing near the mortal remains of Sir Isaac Newton, Charles Darwin, or Stephen Hawking was too tempting to pass up. So I took off on my own, collecting burial sites like Pokémon.

I just had to catch 'em all.

Poet's Corner made for an easy start to my mental checklist: Dickens—check. Chaucer—check. Kipling—check. Lewis Carroll—check. Add to that the memorials to Shakespeare, Shelley, Jane Austen, and Byron—check, check, check, and check.

So many people were walking over James Watt's stone that I had to wait for a clear shot to get a photo. It felt irreverent, but given its placement in a high-traffic area, there wasn't much choice.

Occasionally, I'd cross paths with Maggie or Eric as we made our way through the Abbey. One such moment was in St. George's Chapel, where the Coronation Chair stood behind glass.

"Look at all the carvings on it," Maggie said.

"How'd they let that happen?" I wondered.

The answer, I later learned, was that it hadn't always been so well protected. In the eighteenth and nineteenth centuries, visitors had carved graffiti into it, including the infamous inscription: "P. Abbott slept in this chair 5–6 July 1800."

Then, in 1914, a bomb—believed to have been planted by militant suffragettes—caused minor damage. Finally, in 1950, Scottish nationalists broke the wooden panels to remove the Stone of Scone, though it was later recovered.

As we were leaving, I paused at Winston Churchill's stone near the main entrance. He'd been a recurring theme today—a man who soared to prominence, crashed after the failure of the Dardanelles campaign, and yet clawed his way back in his sixties to become the greatest wartime leader in history.

What a legacy.

A museum, a graveyard, a cultural icon, a place of worship—what exactly is Westminster Abbey? The truth is, it's all of these at once, and perhaps that's what makes it so extraordinary. The Abbey doesn't just hold history—it is history, in all its imperfection, grandeur, and humanity.

For a history nerd, this wasn't just a visit.

It was a pilgrimage.

The next morning, the three of us piled into Eric's car for the forty-five-minute drive north to Duxford Airfield. As we set off, I couldn't help but think back to another road trip—forty-five years ago. That was when Eric first introduced me to Peter Green's Fleetwood Mac.

"That's great, but this isn't Fleetwood Mac," I'd said after hearing *Green Manalishi* for the first time. "Fleetwood Mac play West Coast pop-rock—real middle-of-the-road stuff."

"They were a great blues band long before that," Eric had replied, pressing play on *Oh Well*. "The band you know came later. Mick Fleetwood and John McVie are the only ones left from the original line-up."

In the early 1980s, that revelation had blown my mind. Today's drive, by contrast, offered no such epiphanies—just a pleasant ride through the countryside, which, to my surprise, was a shorter trip from London than I'd imagined.

Before long, we arrived in Duxford.

Duxford Airfield was established during the First World War as a training station for the Royal Flying Corps, the RAF's predecessor. Later, it became an active RAF base and played a crucial role in the Battle of Britain, serving as home to No. 19 Squadron—the first to be equipped with Spitfires. The airfield hosted other Allied squadrons and, in 1943, was transferred to the United States Army Air Forces, becoming a base for P-47 Thunderbolts and P-51 Mustangs.

Today, Duxford is home to the Imperial War Museum Duxford, where its sprawling airfield is lined with massive hangars housing an eclectic collection of aircraft. Spitfires, Cold War jets, and even a Concorde sit side by side—each a testament to human ingenuity, courage, and, at times, folly.

As we pulled into the car park, a Spitfire sat parked on the tarmac.

"Do you think it still flies?" I asked.

"I'm sure some still do," Eric said. "Don't know about that one."

"If it didn't, I guess it'd be in a hangar," I mused.

"Maybe."

I'd already checked out Duxford online before leaving Australia, so I had a few must-see exhibits. I had to see the Concorde—the first supersonic airliner—the de Havilland Comet, the first jet airliner, and any planes that had played an active role in the Battle of Britain. After that, I'd just explore whatever caught my eye.

When we entered the main hangar, we agreed to go our separate ways—just as we had at Westminster Abbey. Which was just as well.

Maggie and Eric took their time, reading every information card and being exemplary museum visitors. Meanwhile, I reverted to my Hampton Court approach—demented gerbil mode—racing through everything as quickly as possible before doubling back to the most interesting exhibits.

Duxford's Concorde never flew commercially, but for a child of the 1960s, it still held a certain romance. I was nine when I watched Concorde do a flypast over Sydney in 1972—something that seemed impossibly futuristic at the time.

No commercial aircraft has ever matched Concorde's style and grace—unless you count the Tu-144, the Soviet knockoff—and I didn't.

Back in 1972, if someone had told me I'd visit Europe in the 2020s, I'd have assumed I'd get there in a supersonic jet—a space-age iteration of the Concorde—not endure a 24-hour slog in a glorified bus.

Even now, the prototype's exterior looked impossibly sleek—decades ahead of its time. But inside, it was a different story. The cabin was just a shell—no passenger seating, just exposed wiring, a linoleum floor, and barely any headroom. Compared to today's widebody jets, it felt claustrophobic.

"Seriously, how would a tall person even fit?" I asked, marveling at the tight quarters.

"No chance if a shortarse like you is struggling," Eric said. Of average height himself, he only had a couple of centimeters to spare.

But if Concorde's exterior still looked cutting-edge, the same couldn't be said for the flight deck. Stripped-down and packed with analog dials, it had more in common with a Spitfire than an A380—a stark reminder of how far aviation technology had come.

Next to the Concorde sat the de Havilland Comet—the aircraft that truly ushered in the jet age. Its revolutionary pressurized cabin and jet engines allowed it to fly higher, where the air was thinner and more efficient. However two early Comets broke apart mid-air due to structural weaknesses, grounding the fleet and forcing a major redesign.

The Comet 4 on display at Duxford was the improved model that finally got commercial jet travel right. In 1958, this very aircraft made history with the first scheduled transatlantic jet flight. Unlike the Concorde, which remained an outlier, the Comet's design laid the foundation for every modern airliner.

As we left the first hangar, my question about the Spitfire on the tarmac was swiftly answered. The unmistakable roar of its engine filled the air as it taxied toward the runway, kicking up dust. Moments later, we were treated to what might be routine at Duxford but felt extraordinary to me—a Spitfire taking off from a Battle of Britain airfield, climbing into the sky.

"Those guys must've had balls just to fly that thing," I said, "let alone dogfight a Me109."

I was reminded of yesterday's star, Winston Churchill: "Never in the field of human conflict was so much owed by so many to so few."

Watching it soaring into the distance, those words felt more alive than ever.

Later, in the Battle of Britain exhibition, we saw the Spitfire's great nemesis, the Messerschmitt Bf 109E-3. The Me109 in question had crash-landed in Sussex, and its propellers were bent accordingly.

Another hangar housed the American Air Museum, which had a Liberator bomber, a B-29 Superfortress, and the only aircraft ever to come close to matching Concorde's sleek beauty, a jet black Lockheed SR-71A Blackbird.

But perhaps the most unexpected exhibit wasn't an aircraft. It was a section of twisted steel from the World Trade Center. Like anyone alive at the time, I had watched in horror as the Towers were struck by planes and then collapsed.

Two thousand seven hundred and fifty-three people died in the World Trade Center that day. Running my fingers over the rusted, warped metal—once part of the building's exterior, near one of the impact zones—felt surreal.

It was profoundly moving, a tangible fragment of a moment that changed the world—and is still shaping it today.

"You seen enough?" Maggie asked.

"Yes," I replied, taking one last look around. "It was more intense than I expected. The planes, the history—even that steelwork. It all hit harder than I thought it would."

I was glad I'd visited Duxford after my brush with death and my re-evaluation of mortality. Standing among relics of war and sacrifice, I didn't leave with a sense of dread. Instead, I left with gratitude—for those who had given their lives, not just for their sacrifice, but for their courage and resilience in the face of unimaginable odds. It was a reminder that while death is inevitable, what truly matters is the legacy you leave behind.

The pint at the *Plough Inn* in Duxford was just what the doctor ordered—a moment to let it all sink in, from the roar of the Spitfire to the haunting silence of that rusted steel.

"I'm forever blowing bubbles, pretty bubbles in the air," sang the full-throated West Ham crowd at the London Stadium. The sound reverberated around the packed arena, sending a ripple of goosebumps down my spine. Scarves waved, hands clapped, and the stadium seemed to pulse with the energy of tens of thousands of voices.

The only people not singing were Eric, me, and the small, defiant pocket of Luton fans, huddled together in their designated corner 100 meters away.

The only people not standing were that same pocket of Luton supporters—and Eric.

I stood to get a better view. Everyone around us was on their feet, shouting, cheering, and proudly wearing claret and blue. Eric, however, remained seated, arms crossed. For an Arsenal fan like him, standing during *I'm Forever Blowing Bubbles* was out of the question.

As for me, I didn't care much for West Ham or Luton. In fact, I didn't really have a team. I was just here for the experience—to witness a Premier League game in all its glory. Eric, ever the good brother-in-law, was indulging my tourist bucket list.

Ideally, we would've gone to an Arsenal game, but with the team flying high at the top of the league, tickets to their final matches were outrageously expensive. So instead, we found ourselves at the London Stadium for West Ham's last home game of another disappointing season.

The match meant nothing to the Hammers, and Luton had already been relegated, marking one of their last appearances in the Premier League before dropping back down to the Championship.

"Why the hell do they sing *I'm Forever Blowing Bubbles* of all songs?" I asked Eric.

"No idea," he replied. "But they've been singing it for over a hundred years."

"Doesn't seem to have done them much good."

Still, it was theirs—a weirdly whimsical anthem passed down through generations. Maybe it didn't matter that it wasn't often a victory song.

Maybe that was the point.

We could've gone to another game today. There was one just across town. But I hadn't dared ask Eric to take me to a Tottenham Hotspur match. Spurs were Arsenal's mortal enemies, and the North London Derby was one of the most contentious fixtures on the calendar.

The chances of Eric setting foot in Tottenham Hotspur Stadium were about as likely as him walking on the moon.

On my last visit to the UK, forty-five years ago, I'd accidentally committed Arsenal heresy by buying a Spurs shirt—not because I liked them, but simply as a souvenir. I had no idea of the enmity between Spurs and Arsenal, so I was utterly unprepared for Eric's reaction.

"Are you taking the piss?" he'd asked, genuinely angry.

"What—er—I don't know—" I'd spluttered, blindsided by his vehemence.

It was Maggie who had to explain the depth of the rivalry I'd unknowingly waded into. Even now, I don't fully understand it—we have team rivalries in Australia too, but they don't seem to come with quite the same rabid intensity.

Eric and I had taken the Tube to today's game—along with nearly all of the other 62,000 attendees. Yet, despite the sheer volume of people filing out of Stratford Underground Station toward the London Stadium, the crowd was remarkably orderly.

The last time I'd been in London, football hooliganism was at its height. Back then, attending a match meant navigating a volatile mix of team pride and tribal fury. But time, tighter security, and exorbitant ticket prices seem to have tamed the worst of it.

In 1981, a ticket to a West Ham game cost less than £2 (about £11 today). Now, the cheapest seat goes for around £30. No thug would bother paying that for a fight when they could have one for free at the pub.

Modern, all-seater stadiums have also played a role in controlling supporter behavior. The London Stadium—originally built for the 2012 Olympics—features an athletic track around the pitch, creating a buffer between fans and players. While this aids crowd control, it comes at a cost: it dulls the atmosphere. In fact, London Stadium regularly tops lists of the worst Premier League venues, largely due to its lack of vibe.

Of course, atmosphere isn't just about the stadium—it takes an exciting game and meaningful stakes to create one. This match had neither.

I'd played soccer in my youth and had a decent appreciation for the game, but even I had to admit this was dull. The final score was West Ham 3 - Luton Town 1, yet not even three home goals could stir the crowd in any meaningful way. It felt like the energy had peaked during the pre-game rendition of *I'm Forever Blowing Bubbles*—nothing on the pitch came close to matching that moment.

After the game, Eric and I stopped at a pub before heading home. It was there that, for the first time in my life, I drank a Foster's—supposedly 'Australia's Beer.' In reality, no self-respecting Aussie drinks it, and it's damn near impossible to even buy back home.

"This is shit," I said to Eric.

For my second pint, I ordered something drinkable.

The tree-lined street leading through the green, park-like grounds toward the Royal Observatory at Greenwich was blocked by a fleet of film crew vans, though not a single crew member was in sight.

"I wonder if they're filming at the Observatory or the Maritime Museum?" I mused.

"Maybe," Maggie replied. "Hard to say."

That morning, I'd woken up to a WhatsApp message—no words, just a selfie of an exhausted CJ in front of a sign reading Melbourne. He was home. And soon enough, I'd be back in Sydney too. After nearly five weeks away—the longest I'd ever been from home—I missed my kids. But even so, I wasn't ready to leave.

Without a doubt, though, the manic pace of the trip was winding down.

Today marked my last full day of excursions in London. Tomorrow,

Maggie, Eric, and I would head to Oxford for two days. The day after that, I'd be gone. And yet, to my surprise, I wasn't flagging. That single day of 'rest' with Peter and his family had done the trick, recharging my batteries for one final push—a last assault on England.

The Greenwich site had two main museums: the Royal Observatory and the National Maritime Museum. On my first visit in 1978, I'd come with my family to the Maritime Museum and had been fascinated. But I remember feeling like I hadn't gotten the most out of it—simply because I didn't know enough at the time.

If we'd visited the Observatory as well, it must not have made much of an impression on fifteen-year-old me, because I had no recollection of it. Which is a shame—because it's an amazing place.

The Royal Observatory at Greenwich honors legendary astronomers like Edmund Halley and William Herschel. Halley—best known today for predicting the return of the comet that now bears his name—was instrumental in advancing navigation and celestial mapping. Herschel, meanwhile, cemented the observatory's legacy in astronomical innovation with his discovery of Uranus.

If CJ had been here, I'm sure we'd have spent a good five minutes on Uranus jokes.

Juvenile humor aside, the Observatory houses a fascinating collection of astronomical instruments, clocks, and historical artifacts. One of its most significant contributions was pioneering the measurement of longitude—a breakthrough that changed navigation forever.

A quick refresher on latitude and longitude for anyone feeling a bit fuzzy on the concept: they form a grid of imaginary lines used to pinpoint any location on Earth. Latitude lines run horizontally, measuring distance north or south of the Equator. Longitude lines run vertically, measuring distance east or west of the Prime Meridian.

And of course, the Prime Meridian is defined at Greenwich.

Like countless visitors before me, I stood astride the metallic Prime Meridian Line, one foot in the Western Hemisphere, the other in the Eastern. From that line, one could measure longitude, but without an accurate clock, sailors had no reliable way to calculate their position. Even a tiny error—just four seconds—could throw a ship's location off by a mile. That's why the Royal Navy needed John Harrison's marine chronometers.

The advent of these accurate, seagoing clocks revolutionized navigation. I was looking at one of Harrison's clocks when I was approached by a museum guide, a tall spindly man with kind, deep-set eyes.

"You know, every time Neil Armstrong came to London, he'd come here to look at Harrison's clocks," said the guide.

He had my full attention now. Neil Armstrong—one of my personal heroes—had stood in this very spot, looking at these same clocks?

Mind blown.

"Yes," the guide continued. "Armstrong believed that without Harrison's breakthrough in navigation, space travel wouldn't have been possible. He thought if we couldn't master navigation across the oceans, how could we ever hope to navigate across space?"

Leaving the Observatory, we then walked down the hill to the National Maritime Museum which is nestled on the banks of the Thames. By this point, Maggie and Eric, who'd seen this all before more than once, decided to sit things out.

This allowed me to demented gerbil all through the place.

As fascinating as the whole museum was, there was one exhibit I was desperate to see: the display on Horatio Nelson—yet another of my personal heroes—in the south wing.

And he's not just *my* hero.

Nelson is England's greatest naval commander, renowned for his fearless leadership that secured victory over the French and Spanish fleets at the Battle of Trafalgar in 1805. His death in the heat of battle cemented his status as a national icon.

Nelson's career reads like a *Boy's Own* adventure—rising through the ranks, losing an eye in Corsica and an arm in Tenerife, yet outmaneuvering the French at the Nile and Copenhagen. By the time of Trafalgar, he was Britain's greatest naval hero. His affair with Emma Hamilton scandalized society, but his place in history was untouchable.

The Nelson exhibit did not disappoint. It was a masterclass in storytelling—both triumphant and tragic. There were letters in his own hand, a model of the HMS *Victory*, and various artifacts from his storied career.

But the centerpiece of the collection was the very uniform Nelson wore when a French sniper's bullet struck him down on the deck of HMS *Victory*. The fatal bullet hole is still visible.

He was a slight man—not physically imposing in the least. And yet, what a colossus.

I lingered for a moment longer, taking it all in. Nelson had sacrificed so much for his country—his eye, his arm, and ultimately, his life—but in death, he became immortal.

Satisfied, I decided not to push my luck by dragging Maggie and Eric to the *Cutty Sark*. I'd been on board the clipper ship forty-five years ago, and after Nelson, nothing else could measure up.

As we trudged back up the hill toward the car, the weight of the last few days settled over me. From Churchill's War Rooms, where leadership was forged under unimaginable pressure, to the heroism of the Battle of Britain airmen, to Harrison's clocks—whose breakthroughs in navigation helped unlock the path to the Moon—it was clear that history's greatest figures shared one thing: the drive to go beyond what seemed possible.

And then there was Nelson's uniform—a relic of triumph and sacrifice, a reminder that greatness often comes at a cost.

But not all heroes stride across the world stage. Some just open their homes, guide you through their cities, and make sure you're fed and rested for the journey ahead.

Tomorrow, I'd set off with two of those heroes for Oxford—a city of scholars and dreamers. It felt like the perfect place to end this journey—one last chance to immerse myself in the history, ideas, and connections that had made it so unforgettable.

***

A Demented Gerbil on Speed

The Lakes District, 1981
"Pull over," Maggie said, tapping Eric on the shoulder. Her voice had the kind of urgency usually reserved for UFO sightings or imminent car sickness.

"What? Why?" From the driver's seat, Eric shot her a glance.

I sat in the backseat, watching the scenery blur past while Fleetwood Mac's *Albatross* played on the tape deck. The dreamy melody was the perfect soundtrack to the ethereal views outside.

Her insistence snapped me out of my trance.

"Just—look!" she said, pointing toward the rolling hills that stretched endlessly in every direction. "You have to pull over."

A beat passed before Eric seemed to register what she meant. With a sigh that suggested he was still skeptical, he eased the car onto the narrow shoulder of the road. Gravel crackled under the tires as we came to a stop, and when he turned off the engine, the music cut out abruptly. We stepped out in silence, cool air rushing in to replace the car's stuffy warmth.

The hills—I'd never seen anything so green—were straight out of the fantasy worlds I devoured in books. Australia's rugged landscape had nothing that compared to this.

The air was sharp and clean, carrying the faint, earthy scent of damp grass. This wasn't just a landscape—it commanded attention, breathtaking in its sheer, impossible beauty.

"Wow," Maggie finally said, breaking the silence.

"Yeah," I agreed, and even though I was a shallow eighteen-year-old, it still felt like an inadequate word.

Even Eric, usually masked in amused indifference, was now just as awed as Maggie and me.

We stood there in near silence for fifteen minutes. The only sound was the soft whistle of the breeze through the trees, as if the world itself had hushed to let us take it all in.

Even the occasional passing car couldn't break the spell.

"You don't see that every day, do you?" Maggie said.

"No," Eric agreed, "but we better keep moving."

I said nothing. This was special—something I'd carry with me forever.

Oxford, Present Day

As we drove through the green fields toward Oxford, that moment in the Lakes District came back to me, still vivid. Of course, this wasn't that perfect moment—though the countryside was pretty enough—but sitting in the backseat with the same company stirred something familiar.

"Fucking GPS," Eric muttered under his breath.

We stopped—not to admire the view, but so Eric could fiddle with Google Maps.

Somehow, we'd ended up in a small village, its winding lanes lined with quaint cottages and the occasional newer building. It was charming, but clearly not the main road into a city of over one hundred and fifty thousand people.

Eric soon had us heading back in the right direction—toward Oxford.

"Is this another 'all Australians are convicts' joke?" I asked as we pulled up to the Malmaison Hotel.

"We just thought it was cool," Eric chuckled.

The Malmaison Hotel was, unmistakably, a former stone prison—

now a luxury hotel.

"It's just... well, it wouldn't be the first time," I said, recalling nearly fifty years of convict-related jabs.

"No," Maggie chimed in. "I promise."

Not that I ever minded convict comparisons. Ever since my eldest sister had discovered a convict in our family tree, I'd worn it like a badge of honor. Having an ancestor on the First Fleet is Australia's version of boasting a Mayflower connection—though, in my case, my forebear, David Kilpack, was a convicted chicken thief who arrived at Sydney Cove in chains.

Malmaison was a cut above.

After weeks of middling-to-shite accommodations on the Cosmic Tour and in Amsterdam, stepping into the lobby felt like luxury—though deprivation may have exaggerated the effect.

"I know my standards have lowered recently," I admitted, taking in the surroundings, "but this place looks amazing."

I grabbed a brochure from the desk and flipped through it. "This wasn't just any old jail. It says here this is Oxford Castle. It's a thousand years old. That's awesome."

"We thought you might like it," Maggie said.

I grinned. "I unreservedly retract my earlier comment. It is very, very cool. Thank you."

After check-in, we stepped out of the lobby and into an elevator, which opened onto what can only be described as a surreal fusion of prison and boutique hotel.

A long central atrium stretched before us, lined with narrow former cell doors—now, I assumed, leading to modern rooms. Overhead, metal walkways crisscrossed the space, their railings a stark reminder of the building's grim origins. Above it all, an arched ceiling bathed in soft pink and purple lighting gave the scene a surreal, almost playful vibe.

The transformation was as bizarre as it was brilliant.

"How cool is this?" I said.

"Told you," Eric said.

Unfortunately, we had to pass through this section into another, less atmospheric building. But any disappointment vanished when I saw my room—it was clean, modern and fully four times the size of the one I'd shared with CJ in the Hotel Titus.

"We'll get settled in and meet out here in half an hour, yeah?" Maggie said.

"We'll grab some lunch and take a walk around before the Christ Church College tour," Eric added.

"Sounds good," I said.

Oxford was exactly as I'd imagined—yet somehow entirely different.

I'd known the colleges were scattered throughout the town, but seeing them in person still caught me off guard. At the universities I'd attended, everything was neatly confined within a single campus. Here, the colleges weren't separate from the city—they *were* the city, woven into its very fabric.

We grabbed sandwiches and strolled down High Street, passing some of Oxford's most iconic colleges. Queen's College stood with its elegant classical facade, while University College—the oldest at Oxford—was surprisingly understated. Between these historic institutions, cafés and souvenir shops nestled into quaint old buildings, a reminder that this ancient setting was still very much alive.

We veered slightly off the main street to admire the grandeur of the Bodleian Library, but access was limited to students and guided tours, leaving its secrets tantalizingly out of reach. The Radcliffe Camera, an iconic domed masterpiece from the eighteenth century, proved just as elusive—its treasures hidden behind closed doors.

Eric checked his watch. 'We'd better get to Christ Church.'

"I'll see you guys back at the hotel," Maggie said.

The entrance to Christ Church exuded timeless academic charm. The Gothic-style building, with its pointed arches, intricate stonework, and ivy creeping across the facade, felt like something out of a classic novel.

After checking in and picking up our 'multi-media guides' and headphones at the gift shop, we set off on our self-guided tour.

I fumbled with my touchscreen guide, skipping the introduction three times before finally pressing play. Eric, less patient, jabbed at his "bloody piece of shit."

Eventually, we both figured it out—and to my surprise, the guides were actually quite good.

True to their name, the guides didn't just provide audio narration—they also displayed images of artifacts and locations, adding an extra layer of context to the experience.

Originally conceived by Cardinal Wolsey in 1525, Christ Church's construction was abandoned after his fall from grace. It wasn't until twenty years later that Henry VIII refounded it. During the English Civil War, Charles I even held sittings of Parliament in the Great Hall.

"Apparently, Lewis Carroll wrote Alice in Wonderland while living here," I said, parroting the multimedia guide.

"Slimy old pervert," Eric said with disgust.

"Yeah, 'artistic' photographs of children?" I said, punctuating *artistic* with air quotes. "Let's just say that nowadays, he'd be canceled—at the very least."

It was hard to miss the Harry Potter connection, especially with a few visitors wrapped in Gryffindor scarves. It wasn't long before we stepped into full-blown Potterworld: the Hall Staircase and the Great Hall.

The Hall Staircase, with its grand stone steps and vaulted ceilings, appeared in several Harry Potter scenes, often during the arrival of new students at Hogwarts.

The multimedia guide informed me that the Great Hall did not actually appear in the movies, rather that it served as inspiration for the scenes in the Hogwarts dining hall.

And it's easy to see why.

It is stunning, with its high vaulted ceiling, rich woodwork, and portrait-lined walls featuring well-known alumni, including the 'slimy old pervert' Charles Dodgson—aka Lewis Carroll.

Light streamed through a series of stained glass windows, making the room surprisingly bright. The largest of these, the 'Alice Window' *celebrates* the connection between Dodgson and Alice Liddell, the daughter of the Dean of Christ Church.

It really was a strange time.

Aside from authors with questionable pastimes, Christ Church has produced thirteen British prime ministers, including Sir Robert Peel, founder of the modern police force—and the reason British police officers are called 'bobbies.'

After leaving the Great Hall, we descended the Hall Stairs and came across a piece of history tied to Peel: the infamous 'No Peel' door. According to our multimedia guide, during his tenure as prime minister, Peel supported Catholic emancipation in Ireland—a stance that outraged the staunchly Protestant members of Christ Church. In protest, they nailed the words 'No Peel' to this very door, leaving a lasting reminder of the era's political and religious tensions.

Eric and I stepped into the vast expanse of Tom Quad, dominated on one side by the imposing Tom Tower, a masterpiece of Christopher Wren's design. A young woman sat alone on the edge of the stone path, feet dangling just above the grass, engrossed in her laptop.

The scene struck a familiar chord, reminding me of the woman in Venice who had so deeply affected CJ. Like her, this figure seemed to bridge the centuries, a quiet juxtaposition of modern life against the timelessness of the setting.

Finally, we entered Christ Church Cathedral, a Gothic masterpiece of rib-vaulted ceilings and soaring arches. It was undeniably beautiful, but after weeks of cathedrals, abbeys, and churches, my sense of awe was wearing thin.

It was time to leave.

After the tour, Eric went to meet up with Maggie while I decided to make the most of the time I had left. It was nearly 4:30 pm, and if I moved quickly, I could just make it to the Ashmolean Museum before it closed at 5:00 pm.

Founded in 1683, the Ashmolean is less a museum and more a treasure hunt—Egyptian relics, Renaissance art, even teapots. There was no time for careful exploration.

This would be the demented gerbil on speed.

By the time I got inside, it was already 4:45 pm, so I rushed past countless displays I wished I could linger over. Roman, Egyptian, and Sumerian artifacts blurred past my vision. It felt like sacrilege, but I had little choice. Occasionally, I'd stop when something caught my eye, snap a picture, and move on.

One exhibit, however, made me pause. Among a collection of hominid skulls, something looked oddly familiar—I'd seen this skull before.

Wait.

I *had* seen this skull before.

In my own home.

I was pretty sure it was the original of the 3D-printed Neanderthal skull I kept in my display case. I stopped to confirm, and after a few moments, I was certain.

This was *my* Neanderthal skull.

It felt like unexpectedly running into an old friend—if that friend happened to be 40,000 years old.

The clock had ticked over to 5:00 pm, and patrons were being herded out—my time was up. As I stepped outside, I wondered how much I must have missed. No. Time to reframe. I could've skipped the Ashmolean entirely and missed even this fraction of its wonders.

This was a win.

On the way back to the hotel, I ducked into the *Chequers*, an old pub with thick wooden furniture and leather-upholstered chairs studded with brass.

I sat back with a pint of Hells Lager and finally relaxed.

For dinner that night, we settled on Thai—far less common in the UK than in Australia. Naturally, this meant more walking. So much walking, in fact, that it felt like Maggie and Eric were channeling CJ.

On the way, we passed clusters of student share houses, many occupied by international students. They looked incredibly cool, and for a brief moment, the idea of being an international student in Oxford seemed very appealing. Too bad I was a few decades too late for that.

The Thai food was good, though noticeably different from home—either adapted for British palates or made with slightly different ingredients. Still, it was enjoyable.

Back at the Malmaison, we grabbed drinks and sat outside the bar. The day had been long and full—just one more in a series of long, incredible days. From our seat, the tower of Oxford Castle rose above us, lit from below in warm orange light. It looked incredible.

"How am I supposed to readjust to real life?" I asked Maggie and Eric.

"It's like any vacation," Maggie said. "Soon, it'll feel like you were never away."

As the sky deepened to a rich blue and the tower glowed against it, I found myself doubting her. No, I thought. This wasn't just any vacation.

Reentering real life might be harder than she realized.

We'd decided to leave Oxford after checking out of the Malmaison. Sure, there was plenty more to see, but I got the impression Maggie and Eric had had their fill—and to be honest, so had I. My lukewarm reaction to the undeniably magnificent Christ Church Cathedral was a warning sign: I was teetering on the edge of tourist overload.

I'm an early riser. By 6:30 am, my bags were packed, and I was off for one last walk around Oxford. The air was crisp, and the town was just beginning to stir. The streets carried that quiet hum of early morning life.

By this point, I'd abandoned any notion of structured sightseeing. Instead, I wandered the way CJ had taught me—letting the rhythm of the town guide me.

There's no doubt that walking is the best way to truly connect with a place. Throughout this trip, I'd walked through London, Bath, Paris, Lucerne, Rome, and Amsterdam. And every time I'd done so, I'd learned something—some good, some not so good.

Oxford, though, was definitely one of the good.

Back at Malmaison, it was breakfast time.

I sat alone—most normal humans on vacation weren't awake this early—in the restaurant, housed in the old part of the prison. My table was flanked by heavy cell doors, silent reminders of the misery once endured here. This place had been designed for hardship.

And yet, here I was, taking an Instagram-worthy shot of my coffee, bacon, poached eggs, hash browns, and baked beans. It felt almost obscene.

Maybe that contrast made breakfast taste even better.

I crossed paths with Maggie and Eric as they arrived for breakfast just as I was leaving. We agreed to meet and quickly check out the Oxford Castle tourist site before we set off back to London.

As with any poorly thought-out plan, the tour of Oxford Castle struck a hitch. The guided tour had only just left, and the next one wouldn't be for an hour.

"Do you want to wait for it?" Maggie asked.

I looked at her and then at Eric. They'd have done it, for sure, but their hearts didn't seem in it. And for that matter, neither was mine. I felt tired. Apparently, there are only so many human-made piles of stones a person can look at in a five-week period.

And I'd reached mine.

"Maybe not," I said.

"You can visit the Mound," the man at the desk said. "That's self-guided."

And so in a rare act of mercy, Maggie and I left Eric behind and climbed the spiraling path to the top. According to the guidebook, the Mound, built in 1071, had served as a strategic defensive position.

We braced ourselves for the majesty of this grand historic landmark.

It was a big hill with a single tree on top.

To be fair, there were some interesting stone structures hidden within, but they were off-limits to tourists.

We trudged back down and found Eric sitting, engrossed in the guidebook.

I envied him.

He glanced up at our faces. "That good, huh?"

As a final act in Oxford, I'd hoped to have a pint at the *Eagle and Child*, and Eric had agreed to swing by on our way out of town. This legendary pub was where J.R.R. Tolkien and C.S. Lewis regularly gathered with their literary group, the Inklings. Over pints in the snug back room, they critiqued each other's work, including drafts of *The Lord of the Rings* and *The Chronicles of Narnia*. But when we arrived, it might as well have been in Mordor—it was closed for renovations.

If that wasn't a sign to leave Oxford, I didn't know what was.

I'd seen castles, colleges, and cathedrals; wandered streets steeped in history; raced through a famous museum—pausing just long enough to visit an old Neanderthal friend. I even tried to squeeze in a pint at Tolkien's old haunt.

Maggie and Eric had been wonderful travel companions, but I could tell they were ready to return to the quiet rhythm of their everyday lives.

One that didn't involve babysitting a needy tourist.

As the car rolled past Oxford's spires and into the countryside, I thought about how much this place had embodied the themes of my journey—discovery, history, and the connections we make, both with the past and with each other. Oxford had been the perfect place to wind down, its timeless atmosphere a quiet reminder that all journeys, no matter how extraordinary, must eventually come to an end.

There would still be time for reflection in London. But as Oxford disappeared behind us, the trip had already begun to shift—from vivid reality to memory.

Hopefully, one as enduring as those fifteen minutes in the Lakes District.

***

Keep Your Hands Off Our Barmaids

The *Victoria Tavern* was the perfect place for a final meal in the UK. It was more than a pub—it was England in miniature. Welcoming, quaint, and, sure, it had seen better days. But it had a sense of history and the quiet comfort of tradition.

The brass sign behind the bar still read, "Keep your hands off our barmaids"—it was equal parts old-school charm, casual misogyny, and pointed warning.

Sitting at the same table and inhaling the same aromas as I had weeks ago, I felt a comforting sense of symmetry, but also a reminder of how much had changed since that first meal.

When it came to ordering food, I didn't have to look at the menu.

"I'll have the salt beef and mustard sandwich."

"You're such a creature of habit," Maggie said.

"Maybe not as much of one as I used to be."

"He can change," Eric said, setting a pint of London Pride in front of me, "he's got better taste in beer now."

"Looking forward to getting home?" Maggie asked.

"Yes and no. I miss the kids, of course," I said.

"What about work?"

"Not so much," I said, thinking about the class of misfits waiting for me—almost a mini-Cosmic tour of their own.

"When are you coming back?" Maggie asked.

I laughed, not because the idea was ridiculous, but because I'd recently been kicking it around in my head.

"Honestly, I don't know," I said. "This was supposed to be a one-and-done, but now I'm not so sure."

The thought of returning had been lingering in my mind ever since the Notre-Dame debacle. There was still so much I hadn't seen, so much left to unearth. For years, I'd put travel on the back burner. Now, I wasn't sure I wanted to stop.

"Well, you're always welcome back, kiddo," Maggie said.

"Just don't make me go to another West Ham game," Eric dragged his index finger across his throat.

"I promise," I said. "Anyway, thanks for everything."

"Our pleasure," Maggie said.

Eric quietly raised his pint.

"You guys are saints," I said, reflecting on what a poor host I might have been. "I wouldn't blame you if you never want another suitcase in your house again."

As I stepped out of the car at Stratford Underground Station, the three of us lingered for a moment, the usual goodbyes hanging in the air. Eric gave me a brief hug, while Maggie wrapped me in a squeeze that took me back to my childhood.

"Don't be a stranger," she said.

"Not a chance," I replied.

As I walked through the turnstiles, I turned back and saw both of them waving—like Jethro and Elly May in *The Beverly Hillbillies*. It was such a silly moment, but somehow, it also felt very real.

Two weeks later, I was back home, and CJ and I were gearing up to record our first *What's My Age Again?* podcast in ages. We used an app called Riverside—CJ in Melbourne, me in Sydney—essentially Zoom with just enough polish to let us pretend we were professional podcasters.

"Let's have another podcast featuring two middle-aged white men with opinions," said no one ever.

But we did it anyway.

It wasn't really about the audience. That was almost non-existent.

It was about sharing stories, making stupid jokes, and staying connected—no matter the slings and arrows of outrageous fortune.

Waiting for CJ to log into Riverside, I again thought about how much this trip had shaken me up.

For years, I'd pieced together history from books and photos.

Now, I'd stood where Caesar had been cremated.

Wandered the streets of Pompeii.

Watched the sun set through stones that had kept silent vigil for millennia.

I'd originally planned this trip like a shopping list of places I needed to visit to feel legitimate.

But now I understood how they rewired my perspective. I'd been truly moved and changed by the things I'd seen, the people I'd met, and the unpredictable magic of it all.

I didn't make it to Notre-Dame or Versailles, and Florence had been, in many ways, a missed opportunity—but that was okay. If this trip had taught me anything, it was that travel wasn't about ticking every box. It was about letting go of perfection and finding joy in what I did see.

For years, I'd been too afraid to step out of my carefully controlled world. Now, I wasn't sure I ever wanted to stop.

Just then, CJ's photo popped up in Riverside.

Other than the occasional WhatsApp message, we hadn't talked since London over three weeks ago. As always, we had some catching up to do before pressing record.

"So, how was the last week in England?" he asked.

"Amazing. You'd have loved the Churchill War Rooms—and the jail-hotel in Oxford."

"The what?"

"A prison turned luxury hotel."

"Cool—And the air museum?"

"Duxford was amazing too," I said. "Definitely one to see if you go back."

"Would you?"

"Go back? If the planets align, sure," I said. "This'll sound pretentious, but I feel like Europe opened something up for me."

"You're right, it does sound pretentious," he said.

Then, more seriously, "You actually think it changed you?"

"I don't know if it was the travel, the history, the near-death experience, or all of the above—but yeah, I do."

"Near-death experiences, plural," he corrected. "Don't forget how close I came to murdering you in your sleep."

"Pappy's working properly again, by the way."

"Too little, too late," he said.

"I really am sorry about that."

"So, what's next?" he asked. "Another 'tour' with George, Cruella, and Mole Man?"

"God, no. I'm never setting foot on a Cosmic bus again."

"Wise move."

"But here's something freaky," I said. "Facebook suggested Cruella as 'someone I may know.'"

"You have to add her!" CJ nearly jumped through the screen. "It would be hilarious."

"Not a chance."

"Coward."

I shook my head. After weeks of dodging petulant complaints, snotty nasal expectorations, and deranged breakfast-table conspiracy theories, I thought I'd escaped Cosmic Tours. But apparently, they weren't done with me yet. Maybe they never would be.

I glanced at the clock. We needed to get cracking.

"Shall we record?" I asked.

"Do I have a choice?"

I clicked the record button. Riverside counted us in—and we swung into our usual intro.

Later, as the podcast wrapped up, I realized this, too, was something I'd unearthed: the importance of connection—whether with family, old friends, new ones, or even with myself.

Through all our adventures, CJ kept me grounded—mocking me just enough to stop me from taking myself too seriously and walking me far enough to see what I'd otherwise be missing.

Yes, we drove each other a little crazy, but spending nearly three weeks together, 24/7, was a test many friendships wouldn't survive. The fact that we could still chat freely and take the piss out of each other?

That was proof of something.

Podcast over and with a pleasant beer buzz, my mind drifted back to that chaotic moment in the Louvre—sweating, jostling, and somehow nearly coming to blows over a selfie with the Mona Lisa.

At the time, it felt like everything had gone wrong: the crush of the crowd, the guard's irrational anger, the sinking realization that I hadn't even enjoyed the moment.

But now, I see it differently.

Her smile wasn't mocking me—it was teaching me. It was never about the perfect photo or the flawless experience.

It was the connection with history I'd always longed to feel.

My sources weren't secondary any more.

They were primary.

I went to Europe looking for something authentically ancient.

And I found it.

But I also unearthed something unexpected: a man finally open to a better life.

—The End—

Keep Your Hands Off Our Barmaids

Unearthed

I Raise a Glass...

This is my third time writing an acknowledgments page, and you'd think it would get easier—just grab the last one, plug in a few new names, say some nice things, and move on.

Simple.

But the truth is, it never gets easier—because a book is built on the generosity, support, and patience of many people. And this time, the challenge is even greater, for one good reason: unlike my previous books, this one includes real, living people who, for the most part, graciously allowed themselves to become characters in its pages. Occasionally, I've massaged the timeline or put words into their mouths for the sake of storytelling—but always with the spirit of the moment in mind.

It's even more difficult when the names are changed to protect the innocent—it makes heartfelt thanks difficult when you're thanking pseudonyms. And, CJ, Maggie, Eric, James, Jen, Peter, Jo, Miles, and Louise are ALL pseudonyms.

First and foremost, a massive thanks to CJ—friend of over forty years, intrepid travel companion, and undisputed king of the endless quest for the perfect craft beer. The real CJ is every bit as sardonic and sharp-witted as the version in these pages—but let's be clear: this is a comic-book adaptation, heightened for effect but always rooted in truth. Any embellishments or exaggerations are entirely mine—although, let's face it, he probably earned them. Thank you for putting up with my historical detours, tolerating my

CPAP/snoring, and not punching me in the nose when I slipped into tired toddler mode. Here's to more adventures (and misadventures) and—perhaps one day—the ultimate pint.

To Maggie and Eric: thank you for the Oxford, Duxford, and Westminster legs of the journey, and for your love and amazing patience. Your home was my sanctuary in the U.K., and I simply couldn't have done this trip without you. In truth, I spent a lot more time at your place than I acknowledged in the narrative, so I owe you a great debt. Also, thanks for the CPAP power cord, which made the journey bearable. I love you both.

To James and Jen: thank you for guiding CJ and me through the bars, Argentinian steakhouses, and—of course—the Red Light District of Amsterdam. Jen, it was wonderful to get to know you. James, it was great to catch up after all these years. And yes—I'm truly sorry I scared the hell out of you during the 'bus incident.'

Peter, Jo, Miles, and Louise—it was great to catch up with you all, too briefly. Hopefully next time, Miles will get the chance to complete his brutal interrogation.

To George, Cruella, Sad Sack, Mole Man, Mr. Sniffy, and all the Cosmic crew: thank you for sharing this journey. Let's be frank—CJ and I would've had a far more fulfilling European trip without you. We'd have spent more time in places that mattered—like Florence—and far less time being frustrated. But would it have been as funny? Unlikely. I apologize for all the ribbing—but, for the most part, you deserved it. And yes, Cruella, you did make it into the book… just be careful what you wish for.

I owe a debt of gratitude to my trusted editor, Jim Bessey, for his keen eye, insightful feedback, and support in shaping this book into something worth reading.

To my early readers—Lisa Li, Brian Wilkie, Colin Howe, Mika Paananen, Charlie C., Dawn Brodey, and CJ himself—your feedback was invaluable.

Thanks also to the passionate guides who made history unforgettable—especially Michael, doyen of Beatles tour guides; Tom, whose gleeful enthusiasm for the Black Plague was, ahem, infectious; and Antonio, the 'Professor of Pompeian Graffiti,' who proved that looking homeless is no obstacle to historical expertise.

To the Mona Lisa, and the Louvre guard who nearly flattened me: thank you for reminding me that travel is best experienced where beauty and chaos collide.

To readers, both new and returning: thank you for taking this journey with me. Writing about history is one thing; bringing it to life through travel is another. Turns out, getting lost in strange places is a pretty good way to find yourself. I'm grateful I could share these stories with you.

To my family—my kids, Sarah, Sebastian, and Cate; and my sisters, whose travel exploits I can only hope to match: thank you for always encouraging, and inspiring, my love of history and adventure.

Magdalena the kitten was my constant companion during the writing of this book. She wasn't always helpful, but she kept me company during my early morning writing stints.

Finally, to my wonderful partner, Lisa: your love and encouragement made writing this book not just possible, but joyful. For any reader wondering where Lisa was during this European trip—wonder no longer. I hadn't met her yet. But within weeks of returning, we met, and life has been amazing ever since. This book simply couldn't have happened without you, my love.

With that, I raise a glass to all of you. Here's to the next journey—wilder, less predictable, and as full of history as ever.

Next stop: Asia.

Let's see what I unearth next.

***

The Nerd Behind the Oversized Codpiece
(AKA: *About the Author*)

SCOTT EDWIN WILLIAMS is a writer, educator, and card-carrying history nerd who explores the past the only sensible way: with a plane ticket, a pint, and just enough questionable judgment to keep things interesting.

He's the author of *Lightbulb Moments in Human History*, a series that unpacks the pivotal ideas and events that shaped our world—with curiosity, humor, and absolutely no patience for historical snobbery.

After years spent hiding behind a desk, Scott finally decided to step out and stumble over history in real life—plague pits, ruins, oversized codpieces, and all. These days, he travels in search of the places where history actually happened—and where it still echoes through alleyways, whispers in cathedral corners, or hides in plain sight—waiting to be noticed.

Whether being chased by a Louvre guard, getting lost in ancient stone circles, or pondering the absurdity of it all over a pint, Scott is always on the lookout for the strange, revealing, and often ridiculous places where history and travel collide—then writing about them (when Magdalena, the Russian Blue kitten, isn't jumping on the keyboard to edit).

This book is the result. Magdalena has notes.

***

Because Apparently, Facts Matter

"30 Things You Might Not Know about Stonehenge." *English Heritage*, 18 Nov. 2016, www.english-heritage.org.uk/visit/inspire-me/blog/blog-posts/30-things-you-might-not-know-about-stonehenge/.

Allen, Graham. *Mary Shelley*. Basingstoke, Palgrave Macmillan, 2008.

Allen, Moira. "The Roman Baths of Bath." *Www.timetravel-Britain.com*, www.timetravel-britain.com/articles/stones/romanbaths.shtml.

Allison, Charlie. "Saint Mark, Corpse Theft and Lions." *Charlie Allison*, 31 Mar. 2021, www.charlie-allison.com/intermezzo-1-saint-mark-and-corpse-theft/. Accessed 4 Jan. 2025.

Bairner, Robin. ""I'm Forever Blowing Bubbles" - the Story behind Famous West Ham Chant." *Goal.com*, 20 Sept. 2019, www.goal.com/en-au/news/im-forever-blowing-bubbles---the-story-behind-famous-west-ham-chant/v2c0pje1uewx170vlhczghgxx. Accessed 26 Jan. 2025.

Beard, Mary, and Ferdinand Mount. *Pompeii: The Life of a Roman Town*. London, The Folio Society, 2013.

"Booking.com: The Largest Selection of Hotels, Homes, and Vacation Rentals." *Booking.com*, 2024, www.booking.com/.

"Cabinet War Rooms." *Imperial War Museums*, www.iwm.org.uk/events/cabinet-war-rooms.

Chik, Holly. "Was the Lion of Venice Made in China More than 1,000 Years Ago? Italian Scientists Have Evidence." *South China Morning Post*, 12 Oct. 2024, www.scmp.com/news/china/science/article/3281965/was-lion-venice-made-china-more-1000-years-ago-italian-scientists-have-evidence. Accessed 4 Jan. 2025.

Cowell, Alan. "Michelangelo's David Is Damaged." *The New York Times*, 15 Sept. 1991, www.nytimes.com/1991/09/15/world/michelangelo-s-david-is-damaged.html#.

Davenport, Caillan, and Shushma Malik. "Mythbusting Ancient Rome – Throwing Christians to the Lions." *The Conversation*, 19 Sept. 2018, theconversation.com/mythbusting-ancient-rome-throwing-christians-to-the-lions-67365.

"Explore the 9/11 Story at IWM." *Imperial War Museums*, 2020, www.iwm.org.uk/history/explore-the-911-story-at-iwm. Accessed 26 Jan. 2025.

Folkenflik, Robert. "Samuel Johnson - the Gentleman's Magazine and Early Publications." *Encyclopedia Britannica*, www.britannica.com/biography/Samuel-Johnson/The-Gentlemans-Magazine-and-early-publications.

"Fosters Is so Not Australian for Beer, Says Australians." *Craft Brewing Business*, 16 June 2017, www.craftbrewingbusiness.com/news/fosters-not-australian-beer-says-australians/.

Frank, Anne. *Anne Frank: The Diary of a Young Girl*. Paramus, N.J., Globe Fearon Educational Pub, 1995.

"Great Court." *The British Museum*, British Museum, 2019, www.britishmuseum.org/about-us/british-museum-story/architecture/great-court.

Because Apparently, Facts Matter

Heaphy, Linda. "The Bawdy Graffiti of Pompeii and Herculaneum." *Kashgar*, 19 Apr. 2017, kashgar.com.au/blogs/history/the-bawdy-graffiti-of-pompeii-and-herculaneu?srsltid=AfmBOop6XsKsLfqPNnvVzKdbSVqwZnK4e19zZJIe2LTBjRylv_QG3fx. Accessed 12 Jan. 2025.

Historic London Tours. "Historic London Tours." *Historic London Tours*, 2025, historiclondontours.com/tales-of-london. Accessed 22 Jan. 2025.

Historic Royal Palaces. "Henry VIII." *Historic Royal Palaces*, Historic Royal Palaces, 2019, www.hrp.org.uk/hampton-court-palace/history-and-stories/henry-viii/.

https://www.facebook.com/sarahcascone. "Sistine Chapel Tourist Hordes Set to Triple - Artnet News." *Artnet News*, 2 July 2014, news.artnet.com/art-world/sistine-chapel-tourist-hordes-set-to-triple-53467. Accessed 15 Jan. 2025.

Jashemski, Wilhelmina. "Pompeii | Facts, Map, & Ruins." *Encyclopædia Britannica*, 29 Oct. 2018, www.britannica.com/place/Pompeii.

Jay, Tom. "Westminster Abbey: A Beautiful Confusion." *Crisis Magazine*, 24 Feb. 2017, crisismagazine.com/opinion/a-beautiful-confusion. Accessed 25 Jan. 2025.

Kieran Press-Reynolds. "Malmaison Oxford: British Hotel That Was Once a Prison Faces Backlash." *Business Insider*, 23 Sept. 2021, www.businessinsider.com/malmaison-oxford-hotel-former-prison-twitter-2021-9. Accessed 27 Jan. 2025.

Klein, Christopher. "The Man Who Bought Stonehenge." HISTORY, 21 Sept. 2015, www.history.com/news/the-man-who-bought-stonehenge.

Koenig, Chris. "How a Prime Minister Fell out with the Christ Church Canons." *Oxford Mail*, 21 Jan. 2009, www.oxfordmail.co.uk/news/4065255.prime-minister-fell-christ-church-canons/. Accessed 26 Jan. 2025.

Kuiper, Kathleen. "Mary Wollstonecraft Shelley." *Encyclopædia Britannica*, 28 Jan. 2019, www.britannica.com/biography/Mary-Wollstonecraft-Shelley.

Kwan, Jacklin. "Scientists May Have Found Magic Ingredient behind Ancient Rome's Self-Healing Concrete." *Www.science.org*, 6 Jan. 2023, www.science.org/content/article/scientists-may-have-found-magic-ingredient-behind-ancient-romes-self-healing-concrete.

"Leaning Tower of Pisa - Useful Information – Florence Museums." *Www.florence-Museum.com*, www.florence-museum.com/leaning-tower-of-pisa.php.

Lynch, Jack. *Jane Austen*. Pasadena, Calif., Salem Press, 2010.

Mao, Frances. ""Real Bodies" Exhibition Causes Controversy in Australia." *BBC News*, 26 Apr. 2018, www.bbc.com/news/world-australia-43902524.

Martin, Sean. "Time Is NOT Real: Physicists Show Everything Happens at the Same Time." *Express.co.uk*, 4 July 2021, www.express.co.uk/news/science/738387/Time-NOT-real-EVERYTHING-happens-same-time-einstein.

"Michelangelo and the Cathedral of Florence: From David to the Pietà to the Dome." *Duomo.firenze.it*, duomo.firenze.it/en/opera-magazine/post/5145/michelangelo-and-the-cathedral-of-florence-from-david-to-the-pieta-to-the-dome.

"Michelangelo's Statue of David Is Unveiled to the Public - HISTORY." *Www.history.com*, www.history.com/this-day-in-history/michelangelo-statue-of-david-unveiled-to-public.

"Mikkeller at Morebeer." *Mikkeller.com*, 2025, www.mikkeller.com/locations/mikkeller-at-morebeer. Accessed 18 Jan. 2025.

Morrill, John S, and Geoffrey R Elton. "Henry VIII | Biography, Wives, & Facts." *Encyclopædia Britannica*, 17 Aug. 2018, www.britannica.com/biography/Henry-VIII-king-of-England.

Moss, Candida. "Why Is This Tub One of the Vatican's Most Valuable Pieces of Art?" *The Daily Beast*, 27 Nov. 2022, www.thedailybeast.com/why-is-this-tub-one-of-the-vaticans-most-valuable-pieces-of-art/. Accessed 15 Jan. 2025.

Muñoz-Alonso, Lorena. "Was Lewis Carroll a Pedophile? His Photographs Suggest So." *Artnet News*, 30 Jan. 2015, news.artnet.com/art-world/was-lewis-carroll-a-pedophile-his-photographs-suggest-so-237222.

Mussio, Gina. "7 Things You Didn't Know about the Incredible Florence Duomo - Walks of Italy." *Walks of Italy*, 6 Dec. 2016, www.walksofitaly.com/blog/art-culture/7-things-didnt-know-incredible-florence-duomo.

"Our History, Heritage & Museum - What We Do." *Https://Www.sja.org.uk*, 2020, www.sja.org.uk/what-we-do/our-history-heritage-and-museum/.

Percival, Jack. "From the Archives 1972: Whoosh! Concorde's First Sydney Landing." *The Sydney Morning Herald*, 16 June 2022, www.smh.com.au/national/nsw/from-the-archives-1972-whoosh-concorde-s-first-sydney-landing-20220519-p5amr4.html.

"Perfectly Preserved Popes in St Peter's." *Eternally Rome*, 13 Apr. 2012, eternallyrome.wordpress.com/2012/04/13/incorruptible-corpses-popes-st-peters/.

"Piazza Della Signoria." *Wikipedia*, 2 Oct. 2020, en.wikipedia.org/wiki/Piazza_della_Signoria.

Poe. "Poe." *Poe.com*, 2024, poe.com/.

"Red Light District Amsterdam." *Www.redlightsecrets.com*, www.redlightsecrets.com/history/.

"Restaurant Salmuera." *Restaurant Salmuera*, 2016, www.sal-amsterdam.nl/. Accessed 18 Jan. 2025.

Rinke, Mario. "Construction History, Kapellbrücke Luzern." *Issuu*, 11 June 2016, issuu.com/akselstave/docs/ervik_aksel_stave_costruction_histo. Accessed 31 Dec. 2024.

Roller, Sarah. "Christ Church, Oxford." *History Hit*, 2021, www.historyhit.com/locations/christ-church-oxford/. Accessed 27 Jan. 2025.

Royal Collection Trust. "Visit Buckingham Palace." *Www.rct.uk*, 2024, www.rct.uk/visit/buckingham-palace.

Royal Museums Greenwich. "What Is the Prime Meridian and Why Is It in Greenwich?" *Www.rmg.co.uk*, www.rmg.co.uk/stories/topics/what-prime-meridian-why-it-greenwich.

Seddon, Sean. "Elgin Marbles: UK-Greece Deal on Parthenon Sculptures "Close."" *BBC*, 3 Dec. 2024, www.bbc.com/news/articles/cy8y97x8xm0o.

"Shakespeare Insult Generator." *Literarygenius.info*, 2025, www.literarygenius.info/a2-shakespeare-insult-generator.htm. Accessed 2 Jan. 2025.

Southam, Brian. "Jane Austen | Biography & Novels." *Encyclopædia Britannica*, 8 Feb. 2019, www.britannica.com/biography/Jane-Austen.

Stone, Iwan. "How World's Oldest Meat Market Smithfield's Will Be Transformed into £250million London Museum When..." *Mail Online, Daily Mail*, 27 Nov. 2024, www.dailymail.co.uk/news/article-14133225/Smithfield-Market-Architect-future-historic-meat-market-London-Museum.html. Accessed 23 Jan. 2025.

Swift, Adrian. "From the Archives, 1985: Concorde's Record-Breaking Flight to Sydney." *The Sydney Morning Herald*, 13 Feb. 2020, www.smh.com.au/national/nsw/from-the-archives-1985-concorde-s-record-breaking-flight-to-sydney-20200131-p53wlf.html.

"Ten Hidden Details at the Churchill War Rooms - Living London History." *Living London History*, 24 July 2024, livinglondonhistory.com/ten-hidden-details-at-the-churchill-war-rooms/. Accessed 24 Jan. 2025.

"The Best Tour Experience. Europe without the Crowds!" *Theromanguy.com*, theromanguy.com.

"The Casts." *Pompeii Sites*, pompeiisites.org/en/pompeii-map/analysis/the-casts/.

"The Cutty Sark Fire." *Www.rmg.co.uk*, www.rmg.co.uk/cutty-sark/history/fire.

The Editors of Encyclopedia Britannica. "Rialto Bridge | Bridge, Venice, Italy." *Encyclopedia Britannica*, www.britannica.com/topic/Rialto-Bridge.

"The History of Smithfield Market." *London Museum*, 2024, www.londonmuseum.org.uk/collections/london-stories/history-smithfield-market/.

"The Tabard (Talbot) Inn in Southwark, London." *Historic UK*, www.historic-uk.com/HistoryMagazine/DestinationsUK/The-Tabard-Inn-Southwark/.

Because Apparently, Facts Matter

Tikkanen, Amy. "Coronation Chair | England, Gilt Lions, Stone of Scone, & Fascinating Facts | Britannica." *Www.britannica.com*, www.britannica.com/topic/Coronation-Chair.

Viator. "Book Things to Do, Tickets, Tours & Attractions | 2019 | Viator." *Viator.com*, 2019, www.viator.com.

Wang, Ione. "The Story behind Juliet's Balcony in Verona." *Culture Trip*, 31 July 2017, theculturetrip.com/europe/italy/articles/the-story-behind-juliets-balcony-in-verona.

"Why Is the British Museum Always in Trouble?" *The Economist*, www.economist.com/britain/2023/11/30/why-is-the-british-museum-always-in-trouble.

Wikipedia Contributors. "Jet Set." *Wikipedia*, Wikimedia Foundation, 9 Oct. 2024, en.wikipedia.org/wiki/Jet_set.

---. "Laocoön and His Sons." *Wikipedia*, Wikimedia Foundation, 28 Mar. 2019, en.wikipedia.org/wiki/Laoco%C3%B6n_and_His_Sons.

---. "London Marathon." *Wikipedia*, 1 May 2023, en.wikipedia.org/wiki/London_Marathon.

Williams, Scott Edwin. *Lightbulb Moments in Human History (Book II)*. John Hunt Publishing, 29 Mar. 2024.

---. *Lightbulb Moments in Human History - from Cave to Colosseum*. S.L., John Hunt Publishing, 2023.

Willsher, Kim. "Eiffel Tower Riddled with Rust and in Need of Repair, Leaked Reports Say." *Theguardian.com*, 4 July 2022, www.theguardian.com/world/2022/jul/04/eiffel-tower-riddled-with-rust-and-in-need-of-repair-leaked-reports-say.

Wilson, Sean. "10 Worst Stadium Atmospheres in British Football [Ranked]." *GiveMeSport*, 27 Sept. 2024, www.givemesport.com/worst-stadium-atmospheres-in-british-football-ranked/. Accessed 26 Jan. 2025.

The Roman Baths, 2021, www.romanbaths.co.uk/.

***

ALSO BY SCOTT EDWIN WILLIAMS

LIGHTBULB MOMENTS IN HUMAN HISTORY
FROM CAVE TO COLOSSEUM

Big Ideas. Bad Decisions. Brilliant Mistakes.

From the first flint tools to the roar of the Colosseum, humanity has stumbled forward—powered by big ideas and even bigger consequences.

In this smart, irreverent, and unexpectedly hopeful tour of the ancient world, Scott Edwin Williams traces the sparks that lit the fuse of civilization.

This is NOT a textbook.

It's a guided wander through the best (and worst) ideas our species ever had—from storytelling and bureaucracy to religion, war, and philosophy.

Some ideas changed the world. Others exploded mid-launch. Most managed to do both.

Welcome to the history of progress, pratfalls, and lightbulb moments.

BUCKLE IN. LIGHT THE FUSE. LET'S GO.

www.ingramcontent.com/pod-product-compliance
Lightning Source LLC
Chambersburg PA
CBHW071233070526
44583CB00017B/2166